W9-CUA-728

THE AUTHOR TRAINING MANUAL

- *DEVELOP MARKETABLE IDEAS*
- *CRAFT BOOKS THAT SELL*
- *BECOME THE AUTHOR PUBLISHERS WANT*
- *SELF-PUBLISH EFFECTIVELY*

WRITER'S DIGEST BOOKS

WritersDigest.com
Cincinnati, Ohio

NINA AMIR

Foreword by JAMES SCOTT BELL

For more resources for writers, visit www.writersdigest.com/books.

To receive a free weekly e-mail newsletter delivering tips and updates about writing and about Writer's Digest products, register directly at http://newsletters.fwpublications.com.

18 17 16 15 14 5 4 3 2 1

Distributed in Canada by Fraser Direct
100 Armstrong Avenue
Georgetown, Ontario, Canada L7G 5S4
Tel: (905) 877-4411

Distributed in the U.K. and Europe by F&W Media International
Brunel House, Newton Abbot, Devon, TQ12 4PU, England
Tel: (+44) 1626-323200, Fax: (+44) 1626-323319
E-mail: postmaster@davidandcharles.co.uk

Distributed in Australia by Capricorn Link
P.O. Box 704, Windsor, NSW 2756 Australia
Tel: (02) 4577-3555

Edited by James Duncan
Cover Designed by Elyse Schwanke
Interior Designed by Rachael Ward
Production coordinated by Debbie Thomas

Nina Amir, the Inspiration to Creation Coach, inspires people to combine their purpose and passion so they **Achieve More Inspired Results**. She transforms writers into authors and motivates people from all walks of life to create books that positively impact readers, to develop careers as authors, and to fulfill their potential.

Amir is the author of the best-selling *How to Blog a Book: How to Write, Publish, and Promote Your Work One Post at a Time* (Writer's Digest Books). She is a nonfiction developmental editor, proposal consultant, author and book coach, blog and blog-to-book coach, and results coach with more than 35 years of experience in the publishing field. Amir writes five blogs, including Write Nonfiction NOW!, How to Blog a Book, and As the Spirit Moves Me, and is the founder of National Nonfiction Writing Month, a.k.a. the Write Nonfiction in November Challenge.

Amir holds a BA in magazine journalism with a concentration in psychology and lives in the Santa Cruz Mountains above Los Gatos, CA.

DEDICATION

To every aspiring and published author who wants to turn a vision of writing and publishing successful books into a reality.

PRAISE FOR *THE AUTHOR TRAINING MANUAL*

"*The Author Training Manual* is a must-read for writers who aspire to publish and for published authors who want to publish more successfully. Successful publishing requires more than great writing. It requires a mindset backed by smart strategy and execution. Nina Amir's *The Author Training Manual* delivers the secrets to successful authorship."
> — Mark Coker, founder of Smashwords

"Nina Amir's ideas on Author Attitudes are exactly what all authors need to know and what authors who yearn for greater success need to hear."
> — Carolyn Howard-Johnson, author of the multi award-winning HowToDoItFrugally series

"*The Author Training Manual* lifts the fog of confusion around getting published and illuminates the need for every nonfiction and fiction writer to create a plan, keep on track, navigate all publishing options, tackle promotion, open possibilities for sales and, plain and simple, succeed as an author. This is the book I've been waiting for to recommend to all editing clients and writers."
> — Elizabeth Lyon, author of *Nonfiction Book Proposals Anybody Can Write*

"Whether you are getting ready to break in—or almost ready to break out—this book is your essential manual for becoming the market-ready partner publishers seek. I am one of the agents who met this author when she herself was in author training; now we're all clamoring to be included in her books!"
> — Katharine Sands, literary agent and author of *Making the Perfect Pitch: How to Catch a Literary Agent's Eye*

"Nina Amir's *The Author Training Manual* will be of help to any writer, fiction or nonfiction. It's easy to follow and inspiring."
> — Elizabeth Pomada, literary agent, Larsen/Pomada Literary Agents

"One of the most important things authors can do for themselves is to prepare to become published and to succeed in this role, which takes more than just writing a good book. It takes a solid plan. If you want the tools to succeed no matter what or how you plan to publish, this is the book you want to read."
> — Penny C. Sansevieri, CEO of Author Marketing Experts, Inc., adjunct professor NYU, and author of *Red Hot Internet Publicity*

"Nina Amir's *The Author Training Manual* will save fiction and nonfiction writers decades of fumbling their way to publication. Her book is a sharp, supportive guide to give any writer all the tools to become a confident, savvy author in an ever-changing publishing landscape."
> — Jordan E. Roseneld, author of *Make a Scene, Write Free*, and *Forged in Grace*

"Nina Amir's *The Author Training Manual* is more than, well, a manual: Beyond telling you the ins and outs of writing and publishing a book, it helps you hone your Author Attitude to ensure success on all levels. Any serious author needs to have this book on her shelf."

> — Linda Formichelli, author of *Write Your Way Out of the Rat Race ... And Step Into a Career You Love*

"Finally a book that offers indie publishers a tool for becoming savvy business people. Fiction and nonfiction authors alike will benefit from *The Author Training Manual*, which shows them how to create a business plan for a book that can succeed in the marketplace. A good idea is great; a marketable one is better."

> — Jim Kukral, author of *Attention! This Book Will Make You Money* and founder of The Author Marketing Club

"From descriptive step-by-step instructions on how to write a book that will sell for almost any genre to the specifics of what's in a book proposal and why you need one even if you choose to self-publish, this book chunks down the writing process and the publishing industry into actionable steps any author will have no problem taking. ... So many authors jump into self-publishing not realizing all that goes into running a publishing company and marketing a book that sells. By following Nina's advice, authors will be well on their way to success and leaving their self-published competition in the dust. And I guarantee you'll never see the word, "WOOT!" quite the same way!"

> — Kristen Eckstein, publishing consultant and author of more than 35 books, including the Author's Quick Guide series

"In *The Author Training Manual*, Nina Amir distills the essence of what it means to be a successful author and delivers it with intelligence, grace, and tough love. Every author would do well to have a copy."

> — Peter Beren, literary agent and co-author of *The Writers Legal Companion*

"If you are serious about getting published, you will stand out from your competition by using all of the resources at your disposal to set yourself apart in the most positive way. Nina Amir's approach taps into your natural creativity and applies it to the important business considerations that will help get your book in the marketplace."

> — Sheree Bykofsky, Literary Agent and co-author of *The Complete Idiot's Guide to Getting Published, 5th Edition*

"Nina Amir is on the leading edge of book publishing, and in *The Author Training Manual* she provides authors with the tools—and even more important, the thinking behind them—that every author will need to be successful today. This up-to-date manual should be in every author's toolbox. Highly recommended."

> — Joel Friedlander, author of *A Self-Publisher's Companion*

ACKNOWLEDGMENTS

It took a village to raise this book, so I have many people to thank:

My Author Training 101 beta students, who not only read and used but also offered feedback on the first and, in some cases, the second draft of this book and also provided "aha moments": Rhonda Rae Baker, Dindy Yokel, Michelle Thompson, Penney Fox, Krystyna Bellamy, Amanda Socci, and Robert Medak.

Later readers: Victoria Hudson, who was one of the first writers to use the *How to Evaluate Your Book for Success* workbook, which has been integrated into this book. And my agent, Verna Dreisbach, for also having the idea to include business plan/book proposal reviews and for helping me find acquisitions editors to complete them.

Phil Sexton, my publisher, for helping me locate additional editors to do reviews and for being an approachable publishing pro who listens to his authors' concerns.

Those clients and students who contributed their work for review: Krystyna M. Bellamy, Rhonda Rae Baker, Amanda M. Socci, LaDonna Robinson, Dawn Raquel Jensen, Penney Fox, Deborah Cipolla, Meg Hill Fitz-Randolph, Haseena Patel, Shameema Patel, Charlene DeCesare, and Reba Cross Seals.

The acquisitions editors and agents who offered feedback on the business plans and proposals submitted by my students: Valerie Gray, Brooke Warner, Brendan O'Neill, Michelle Howry, Andy Ross, Verna Dreisbach, Katharine Sands, Sheree Bykofsky, Georgia Hughes, Janet Rosen, Rita Rosenkranz, Gordon Warnock, and Lori Perkins.

Eva Pohler, Francis Guenette, Kathleen Pooler, Fredric Meek, and Linda Joy Myers for their suggestions on how to map out a memoir. C.S. Lakin for letting me peek at her novel proposals. Kristen Eckstein for providing information on determining page counts.

James Scott Bell for his early feedback on my concept and fabulous foreword.

James Duncan, my editor, who pulled together two manuscripts and juggled a variety of additional pieces into a cohesive book—from one developmental editor to another, kudos! Also to Kim Catanzarite, Rachel Randall, Rachael Ward, and the entire *Writer's Digest* staff!

My husband, Ron, who continues to support my goal of becoming a successful author.

TABLE OF CONTENTS

SAMPLES

TRAINING EXERCISES

INDEX

FOREWORD

by James Scott Bell

Back there in the bad old days, when I was told you can't learn how to write (and I believed it), there wasn't much out there to guide the young writer on his perilous way. I was in college, you see, and they knew *everything*. And one of the things they made clear to me was that books on the craft of writing were a waste of paper. A scam. A way to separate rubes from their money. You cannot learn this stuff, they said. You either have it or you don't.

I wasted a lot of years believing that balderdash.

Then one day I knew I had to try, had to see if I could learn to write. Even if it turned out I was only pounding my head on the wall of stark failure, I wasn't going to go down without a fight.

Thus began my journey through what mythic structure mavens would call the "dark world." I needed light, so I subscribed to *Writer's Digest* and devoured many a WD book. And slowly—through trial, error, and my weekly quota of words—I made it through the woods and into a career.

I don't begrudge those years, nor the struggle. Still, I wish I'd had a Mentor, somebody who knew the path, the ins and outs, the obstacles to come, someone who could take me by my unsteady hand and say, "Okay, first you ought to do this. Got it? Now you need to do this."

You know what really would have been nice? Nina Amir's *The Author Training Manual*.

What I like about Nina's approach is that it is both practical and prioritized. It starts with the most important aspect, one that anxious new writers usually skip: mental preparation. Do you have what Nina calls "Author Attitude"? Do you really know what it takes to succeed in this game? Are you willing to practice, to pay the price? Miss this, and you might just be spinning your wheels—or should I say, clacking your keys? Nina would rather see your wheels get traction and your keys make words that will have a chance to connect.

You have a great book idea? How do you run that idea through a grinder that tells you whether it's worth pursuing? The steps laid out in this book will show you.

We all know we're in a new world of publishing options: Traditional, Self, or Blended. Nina lays out the details and tells you how to evaluate the choices.

There's just a lot in here of supreme value. Like the mythic Mentor who shows up when you need her, Nina is ready to hand you a lesson at the right time.

Success as a writer has always been a matter, in large part, of plain old hard work. But also smart work—knowing what to do and how. This latter aspect can't be emphasized enough. You can go out and hit a million golf balls, but if you've got a bad grip and you bend your elbows, all that effort won't help you break 90 anytime soon. Or maybe ever.

The same idea applies with this crazy business of writing as a profession. *The Author Training Manual* will help make it a little less crazy for you.

Start your journey.

MANUAL

INTRODUCTION

Never before has there been a "training manual" for writers. I'm not just talking about a book that teaches "how to write," but how to actually *be* a writer, an *author*, to train yourself to examine your ideas professionally, flesh them out, and turn them into publishable books. This realization came to me one day while on Twitter. Someone I follow tweeted, "Why is there no manual for authors?"

Such a manual, indeed, does exist.

To be more accurate, a *process* exists that helps train writers to become authors. Writers have been using this process for as long as anyone in the publishing industry can remember, and aspiring authors use it every time they compile the information they need to put together a book proposal for an agent or an acquisitions editor. Yet, it's a valuable—actually necessary—process whether you plan to self-publish or traditionally publish your book. It is this process that I will use to help you train yourself to become a publishable, successful author.

This is the only manual you will ever need to change your status from *aspiring* author to *published* author. Follow the steps. Train hard. Develop an Author Attitude, and you, too, can become a successful published author.

Nina Amir
May 2013

MANUAL

AUTHOR ATTITUDE:

The Essential Characteristic Necessary for Publishing Success

Millions of aspiring authors around the world dream of self-publishing or traditionally publishing a successful book. If you've picked up this book, you likely share that dream.

Today, almost any writer can change his or her status from *aspiring* to *published* author. More ways exist to self-publish a book than ever before, which means you have many options should you choose to go that route. You'll find it harder to change your status from *aspiring* to *published* author if you want to be traditionally published, but it's not impossible. You just need to convince a publishing company to produce your book for you by following the steps presented in this book.

No matter which path to publication you choose, the most difficult task before you involves creating a book that sells. According to *Publishers Weekly*, the average book sells three thousand copies *in its lifetime*—not per year. The publishing industry deems a book "successful" when it sells large numbers of copies—usually many more than three thousand copies per year. Bestsellers, for example, outsell other books in their categories.

Since you are reading this book, I'm going to assume from this point forward that you want to produce a book that sells an above-average number of copies per year or reaches bestseller status. That means you want to be a successful author by publishing industry standards, so keep the average books sales noted earlier mind as you work through this process.

Many aspiring authors think all they need to produce a successful book is an outstanding idea, a sound story structure, and a well-crafted manuscript. Indeed, these elements sometimes suffice, but more often creating a bestseller or a book with above-average sales involves much more.

In particular, it takes a certain type of attitude. I call this an Author Attitude.

The Cold, Hard Facts of the Publishing Industry

To develop Author Attitude, you must make yourself aware of the cold, hard facts about the publishing industry. These facts are meant to help you understand the difference between simply becoming an author and succeeding as an author.

While the number of books published each year increases—Bowker projected a staggering four thousand books per day were published in 2011—the number of people and publishers who buy them decreases annually. That means the marketplace has become increasingly competitive, making it harder to find readers and publishers. Yet, out of a U.S. population of 317,132,631 people (as of November 2013), 81 percent still want to write a book, according to *The New York Times*.

Many writers produce manuscripts or books only to discover later that their creations aren't viable. After spending months or years writing and honing their craft, these authors then suffer great heartbreak and disappointment when they discover traditional publishers don't want to publish their manuscripts or readers don't want to purchase their self-published books. Maybe the writing isn't up to par, or the book isn't unique or helpful to readers; the author might not have a "platform," promotion plan, or expertise in the subject area, among many other things. Platform is visibility, authority, and engagement with your book's target audience that gives you influences in that market.

Today, many readers simply cannot find most books. Bowker reported that in 2011, three million books were published in the United States. Marketing expert and best-selling author Seth Godin predicted that fifteen million ISBN numbers were purchased in 2012. If all of those ISBN numbers were used, it is possible that at least as many books were published that same year. That's a lot of books for readers to sift through when deciding to make a purchase. It's easy for yours to get lost among them all.

Not only that, if your book is traditionally published, it stands less than a one percent chance of being stocked in an actual brick-and-mortar bookstore, according to Berrett-Koehler Publishers. Self-published books almost never make it onto bookstore shelves. And if your book is not in brick-and-mortar bookstores, you miss another chance for readers to discover you or your book.

Even authors like Godin, with fourteen best-selling books, including *Permission Marketing* and *Tribes*, normally get only one or two copies of their books into each physical bookstore. In fact, Godin conducted a record-breaking Kickstarter campaign for his newest book, *The Icarus Deception*, primarily to prove to publishers that his books should be promoted inside bookstores. Even *his* publisher needed proof that booksellers should carry large quantities of his books and display them prominently. If a successful author like Godin has trouble getting books into a bookstore, you can imagine how hard this task proves for the average traditionally published author.

Once you get your book into either physical or online stores, you have to find ways to get it noticed. You have to ensure its cover makes readers feel they must not leave the store without it. The average nonfiction book sells 250 copies per year, reports *Publishers Weekly*—and nonfiction outsells fiction, so we can assume the average novel sells fewer copies per year. Taking into account the cost of editing and design, that's hardly enough for any traditional publisher or self-publisher to earn back the cost of producing and promoting a printed book, let alone make much money. (Average yearly e-book sales are about the same as print book sales, possibly just a tad higher. According to novelist Mike Cooper, the average Amazon e-book author earns under $300 per year.)

With these facts in mind, it's no wonder that along the way some writers discover they aren't cut out to produce successful books—ones that *do sell* to lots of readers and to publishers. They might discover this after they've self-published or traditionally published their books or maybe while they are trying to publish them (or even while exploring their options). Maybe they are unwilling to learn the necessary tasks, they can't or don't want to hire someone to help them do those tasks, or they simply don't want to compete in the industry or the marketplace. Maybe they have other commitments, like family or a "real" job. So these writers may decide they feel comfortable writing books that sell a below-average number of copies.

Others decide the path to publication is just too long and arduous. They leave their dreams of becoming authors behind and choose different paths. They give up.

Then there are the aspiring writers left wondering how—despite the above facts, their situations, and the often harsh and competitive publishing industry environment—they can change their status from *aspiring* to *successful published author*. They are not put off by the obstacles in the facts presented or by what life has thrown their way. Full of optimism, they cling to something else they have heard: "Now is the best time in history to become an author." They are willing to do whatever it takes to produce a salable book and to publish and promote it until it sells well. They are determined, persistent, and perseverant. In fact, they have the essential characteristic of successful authors: an Author Attitude.

I hope you have it, too.

If you aren't sure whether you have this attitude, no worries. This manual, and the training process it includes, will teach you how to develop an Author Attitude.

Of course, some writers have this attitude naturally; most, I believe, have worked at developing it. Jack Canfield and Mark Victor Hansen come to mind. They received over 140 rejections prior to getting *Chicken Soup for the Soul* accepted by Health Communications. The book has sold over 200 million copies due to the authors' commitment to promoting the book in every way possible—including sending free copies to the sequestered jurors serving on the nationally broadcast first O.J. Simpson murder trial. The jurors were then pictured on national television carrying the books! The authors promoted the book in five ways every single day after its release. Now *that* is Author Attitude.

Change Your Status From Aspiring to Successful Published Author

Let's take a closer look at the word *attitude*. As defined by Merriam-Webster's online dictionary, *attitude* is a position assumed for a specific purpose. It can be a mental position with regard to a fact or state of being. It also can be a state of readiness to respond in a characteristic way to a stimulus, such as to a concept or a situation. If you want to become a successful published author, you want to take a mental position—which means you adopt or *choose* that attitude—that helps you achieve a particular state of being, in this case successful authorship. You want to be ready to respond to your book idea and to all situations related to it with a successful author's mindset, or an Author Attitude.

Your attitude makes a huge difference in the results you achieve. Possession of this state of mental readiness will get you the specific result you desire: successful authorship.

Author Attitude consists of four primary characteristics: Willingness, Optimism, Objectivity, and Tenacity.

You may possess one or more of these characteristics, or you may not possess any of them at all. You may feel you display one characteristic more strongly than another or need to strengthen one even though you possess it.

I have created an acronym to help you remember the four characteristics of Author Attitude. The acronym spells a word that recently has come into common culture: *WOOT!*

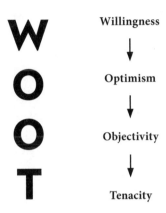

W — Willingness

↓

O — Optimism

↓

O — Objectivity

↓

T — Tenacity

"Woot" originated as a hacker term for *root* (or administrative) access to a computer. However, the term coincided with the gamer term, "w00t." According to the Urban Dictionary, "w00t" originally was a truncated expression for "Wow, loot!" common among players of *Dungeons & Dragons.* The term passed into Internet culture and then into common culture as a term of excitement. It works well for our purposes. As you will see, if you can access your own computer, your mind, you possess the key to successful authorship, which could result in loot—or at least a sense of abundance. That might cause you to exclaim, "WOOT!"

Let's look at each characteristic of WOOT. Know that—like attitude—each one reflects a choice you can make and you can learn each characteristic if you feel you don't possess it yet. Indeed, you can make the choice to learn it or adopt it into your way of being as you train to become an author. That's what the "Author Training Process" is meant to accomplish.

Willingness

To become a successful author you need a general willingness to change and grow. Your old attitudes, actions, behaviors, thoughts, decisions, beliefs, and habits have only gotten you this far. They helped you achieve your current results. If you want a new level of success as a writer, something has to change. For that to happen, first and foremost, you need to be willing to change. Every one of the following characteristics and each step in the Author Training Process requires that you have some degree of willingness to explore, do, learn, evaluate, try something that may be new or different, or do something you know how to do already but in a different way.

Additionally, you must be willing to change your book idea. The actual story, characters, subject, angle, theme, purpose, audience, or any number of other aspects of your project might need to be altered to make it viable in the marketplace. This may be difficult to swallow at first, but successful authorship relies on your ability to evaluate the marketability of your idea from every angle possible and make the tough calls. Only when you have discovered that you have created a salable idea can you turn to writing the book. When you have completed the manuscript, you must be willing to receive feedback on how your writing and manuscript can be improved to make it successful and to make those changes.

Additionally, you need the willingness to cycle through the Author Training Process more than once. The training asks you to return to several steps until you find the angle or focus that offers your book project the highest likelihood of success.

Optimism

Whether you call it faith, positive thinking, reverse pessimism, Positive Psychology, or learned optimism, to become a successful author you must be willing to see everything that happens to you as pushing you closer to your goal of successful authorship. This means a rejection from an agent presents an opportunity to improve your query letter or your book proposal. A negative review of your manuscript by a book doctor at a conference presents a chance to rethink your plot or your content—or even to hone your craft. A session with a proposal consultant who tells you your platform section needs strengthening offers the opportunity to rethink your pre-promotion activity level.

In case you think I am suggesting you become a Pollyanna, let me share some scientific data with you. In a report published in the *Journal of Personality and Social Psychology,* Michael F. Scheier, a psychologist at Carnegie Mellon University in Pittsburgh, wrote that optimists tend to respond to disappointments, such as being rejected by a literary agent, by formulating a plan of action and asking other people for help and advice. On the other hand, pessimists more often react to the same event by trying to ignore it or assuming they can do nothing to change their results.

In a similar study, Martin Seligman, a psychologist at the University of Pennsylvania, found that pessimists tend to construe bad events, such as low book sales or being told a manuscript doesn't fit a publisher's needs, as the result of personal deficits that will plague them forever in every aspect of their personal and professional lives. Optimists see the same events as caused by mistakes they can remedy by making changes, once they discover what changes are necessary.

You will have many reasons for optimism as you move through the Author Training Process and in your career as an author, and this optimistic attitude will help you achieve more positive results.

Objectivity

To become a successful author, you need to see yourself and your work objectively, from a different perspective than your own. Specifically, you need to see through the lens used by publishing professionals, such as literary agents and acquisitions editors. Both view your book idea not only as a creative project but also as a business proposition. They view you as a potential business partner. Even if you don't plan on seeking a traditional publisher for your book, you must learn to stand back and evaluate yourself and your work objectively from a publishing business perspective. Doing so becomes even more important if you plan to independently publish since you become the publisher of your own work.

The publishing industry is the book production and selling business; if you want to become an author, you must be willing to make this your business as well. You have to be willing to craft your work with an eye to the industry's needs and standards, which are, more often than not, focused primarily on marketability and sales.

You also must distance yourself from your idea. You must detach from it so you are willing to receive, hear, and act upon criticism—and so you can learn to evaluate your idea and offer constructive criticism of your own. And you must make the necessary changes without cringing as if you are cutting off fingers and toes. You must do this with *excitement* because you know you are making the end product more salable. In other words, you must act in your book's best interest—even when it feels hard.

Ultimately, you must see your project from the perspective of consumers as well. Only when you do this can you pinpoint why they might pick up your book, carry it to the register and purchase it, and then tell their friends they must read it, too. That's when you and your book become successful.

Tenacity

To become an author, you have to be willing to do whatever it takes for however long it takes to reach your goal. Determination, persistence, and perseverance carry you through to suc-

MANUAL

cessful authorship, whether you are rewriting your manuscript, building author platform, submitting to the one hundredth agent, contacting the one thousandth reviewer, or writing the fiftieth blog post or press release about your book. You must have passion for your project and feel a sense of purpose. Every day you must show up eager to move forward, even if it is only by one small step or in spite of the challenges that have presented themselves.

You must love what you do. You must be in love with writing, being an author (or the prospect of becoming one), and your book. For you, authorship must not be about making money or selling books; writing books or this particular book must feel like a passion, a calling, a vocation, or a "soul" purpose. This will keep you doing what must be done to succeed every day.

As I mentioned, you choose your attitude. According to Dr. Alan Zimmerman, author of *Pivot*, only a small percentage of the U.S. population chooses to have a positive attitude—but it can make the difference between success and failure. A study done by Harvard University proved that 85 percent of your success depends on your attitude and only 15 percent on your technical aptitude.

To a huge degree, your attitude is based upon your *beliefs*. Beliefs affect your decisions. Decisions then affect your actions, which affect your results.

As proven by Scheier's report, a pessimist rejected by a publisher might subsequently believe she is somehow personally deficient. Therefore, she may believe she doesn't have the ability to write and publish a book. Based on this belief, she then might make *decisions* that affect her *actions* and *results*. She might decide not to seek help so she can discover how to improve her current project, and she might never submit another proposal to an agent or publisher.

An optimist, on the other hand, might make a totally different decision and take totally different actions based on his beliefs. The same type of rejection might cause him to believe his book idea just needs tweaking—or that he, as a writer and aspiring author, needs tweaking. So he might reevaluate the angle of his book, the benefits it offers, and numerous other aspects of his project and then rewrite his proposal. He also might spend another six months building author platform, during which time he also might add several more items to the proposal's promotion plan. He then might begin submitting the book project to agents and publishers once again.

These examples demonstrate the importance of getting clear about your beliefs so you can achieve the results you desire.

Train Yourself to Have an Author Attitude

Despite this focus on Author Attitude, the need for a great idea and outstanding writing remains a factor in any book's success. These will take you far, especially if you write fiction. However, in all cases, to go the distance and become a successful author, you need the elements included in an Author Attitude—*WOOT!*

So how do you get this Author Attitude if you don't already have it?

If you've ever learned how to do something technical, you probably used a manual for assistance and you might even have entered a training program. There are manuals to teach you to use computers, televisions, clock radios, or video cameras. A manual is nothing more than a step-by-step guide on how to do or learn something—anything—from putting together a piece of furniture to producing an e-book to exercising with a Pilates ball.

Athletes train to build muscle, endurance, and facility in their chosen sport. Musicians and dancers train to achieve skill and artistry. Whether they use a personal trainer, coach, teacher, or manual to help them learn or refine their abilities, in the end, the result is the same: The time and hard work typically pay off for individuals who invest in training. They become accomplished at their chosen endeavor.

In the same way, you can train to become a successful published author. This book serves as your Author Training manual. It provides a time-tested Author Training Process—an evaluation tool. The nine unique steps outlined in the table of contents will help you move closer to your goal of successful authorship by teaching you to see yourself and your work from a publishing professional's perspective—both a creative and a business perspective. If you use them, you will develop muscle, skill, and proficiency. The process will give you successful author muscle in the form of Author Attitude.

Each step in this book requires that you evaluate a specific part of yourself and/or your book idea. In the process, you discover the necessary information, skills, activities, mindsets, and behaviors that help you and your book become more salable and publishable. Remember, evaluating yourself in this manner requires *WOOT!*—willingness, optimism, objectivity, and tenacity. By the time you have finished all nine steps, you will acquire the mindset and professional training needed to move from aspiring to successful published author.

You complete the Author Training Process by reading the chapters in this manual and completing the suggested exercises, which are included in the training exercises provided at the back of the manual. Later you will put all of these pieces together to create a complete business plan for your book. (These business plans often translate directly into book proposals.) This constant evaluation, along with the real examples of book proposals and business plans in the Samples section, which have been evaluated by agents and editors, will develop your ability to "see" your book project from an agent's or acquisitions editor's perspective.

One of my students—her name is Dindy—says the Author Training Process taught her how to determine if the book she planned to write, which profiled a group of artists, was worth pursuing. "That's wonderful to know before you spend years writing," she says. "Helping me view my germ of an idea through the eyes of an agent or publisher turned me 180 degrees in the right direction. It also gave me some new tools for looking at what makes certain books successful and others not so much."

Rhonda, another student working on a series of memoirs about adoption, says that seeing herself and her work objectively from a publishing business perspective provided "the turning point in my thinking about my ideas. Until I saw myself through this lens, I struggled with the message of my book. I struggled with the purpose of my writing and with finding my overall direction with this book and subsequent books. By learning how to have an Author Attitude, I have become a more focused writer," she says. "I am driven by a passion to share my story in such a way that my readers must buy a copy of my book."

Step by step, you, too, will discover what you need to do to produce a viable book project—one that sells to publishers and to many readers. You will train yourself to have an Author Attitude and become a successful author—one who produces salable books. *WOOT!*

HOW TO BEGIN:

Evaluate Yourself and Your Book for Success

If you want to ensure that you and your book succeed, you must behave like an "author-preneur" and create a business plan for your product—the book—before you introduce it into the marketplace. To do this you must spend the time evaluating yourself and your book idea to determine if you have what it takes to succeed as a businessperson—a published author—and if your idea has what it takes to compete in its bookstore category.

In the publishing industry, a business plan for a book is known as a book proposal, and we will use the standard book proposal as the foundation for your book's business plan. A proposal provides:

- the best free book conception and evaluation tool available
- the most effective resource for developing an impressive business plan for a highly salable book
- a practical way to produce an efficient writing guide that helps you keep both the creative and business aspects of your project in mind as you produce your manuscript
- the definitive training tool to develop the skills and mindset necessary for successful authorship

Whether you plan to seek a traditional publisher or to independently publish your book, and whether you write nonfiction or fiction, writing your book's business plan serves as an Author Training Process. That said, you must learn how to use the specific steps of the process, which are based on the nonfiction book proposal, if you want them to provide a successful Author Training Process.

The book proposal has been an industry requirement for traditional publication for years. Not only that, increasingly, self-publishing experts like best-selling novelist James Scott Bell are telling both fiction and nonfiction students that they need to read a book on how to write a book proposal and then actually write one if they want to produce a successful book. "Going through the hard work of creating a proposal forces you to think like a publisher, to find a market and focus, and to assess competition so you can bring something new to the table," says Bell. "It's an external discipline for creating a commercially viable book."

Almost all aspiring nonfiction authors go through the Author Training Process if they want to become traditionally published, but they often do so unwillingly and unwittingly. They complete the necessary steps because they know they must; they have to produce a book proposal to submit first to agents and then to publishers. They do so with one goal in mind: to become traditionally published authors. They *don't* do so with the intention of trying to objectively evaluate themselves or their idea. Thus, they often cut corners, do the minimal amount of work, and don't learn anything they can apply to the writing of the book (or to book idea generation) during the process. Nor at that point do they actually change or improve their project in any way to make it more marketable.

Most novelists don't think they need full proposals to land traditional publishing deals and so don't bother with the entire process explained in this book. They are told that all they need do is produce well-written books with sound and compelling plots to launch themselves and their books into successful publication. They study scene, plot, and character development, and they focus on craft. Many, if not all, ignore the fact that this process could help them move closer to success. While the traditional publishing industry more and more often asks aspiring fiction writers to behave like nonfiction writers and to focus on the business end of book publishing—even to provide fiction proposals that look a lot like nonfiction book proposals, other experts advise novelists to focus first on the pursuit of high-quality writing. Thus, many fiction writers, and even some memoir writers, continue to rely on their manuscripts to sell their books rather than any type of business plan.

Authors who choose to become independent publishers in order to self-publish their books also rarely use the Author Training Process. They know about book proposals, but they think they have no reason to bother with them since "selling the publisher" is the very step they want to bypass. They don't realize a book proposal serves as a business plan both for their book and publishing company. By bypassing this step, they fail to evaluate their ability to run a publishing company or help their books succeed. As a result, they sometimes find it difficult to attract readers to their books or get frustrated with their new jobs as "publishers."

For this reason, I would advise all authors—be it of fiction or nonfiction, traditional or nontraditional—to undergo the Author Training Process outlined in this book. It will provide you with the training you need to write and publish a book successfully. If you think this manual is just a thinly disguised book about how to write a book proposal, read on. I will tell you what the Author Training Process and this manual will and won't do for you before we examine each step.

This manual *will* show you how to use the Author Training Process in order to:

1. Conceptualize both the creative and business aspects of a self-published or traditionally published book. By putting in the time and effort to go through the Author Training Process at the conception stage, before you write your book, you avoid discovering too late that your manuscript has no market, too much competition, or in some other way will not achieve the sales (and success) you desire.
2. Give you an opportunity to assess the viability of a work you have completed in order to make it more salable. You then can decide how to alter or adjust your text to make it more marketable. If the creative side of your book appears sound, you then have the opportunity to consider the business side, such as market, platform, and promotion.
3. Evaluate how much or how little of the business end of authoring appeals to you and your nature. If looking at your book from a publishing business perspective and writing it with a publishing business mindset makes you balk, or if the tasks involved in producing a successful self-published book don't appeal to you, you might reconsider your goals.
4. Develop the attitude you need to get published and succeed as an author. You will develop a willingness to evaluate yourself and your work through the same lens that agents and acquisitions editors use. You will discover how you and your book idea can change to meet publishing industry standards and become more salable. You will make decisions and take actions to create the most high-quality and marketable book possible. Despite the fact that the process will require you to look critically at yourself, your idea, and your work, and though doing so may feel difficult or overwhelming at

times, you will become more willing, optimistic, objective, and committed to your project and your path. You will develop an Author Attitude.

5. Learn what is included in a nonfiction book proposal, compile the information necessary to write a proposal, and train to write one. You will put together the information necessary to complete all sections of a book proposal, and with just a bit more effort, you can turn it into a polished proposal ready for submission should you desire to submit it.

What this manual *won't* tell you is whether or not you should write your book. You must decide that based on the information you compile and your own evaluation of that information.

Why Do You Need a Business Plan For Yourself or Your Book?

The Author Training Process uses the nonfiction book proposal as its foundational tool because the varied sections provide numerous opportunities for evaluation and training. Also, it creates a more comprehensive business plan as the end product. A traditional fiction proposal contains fewer sections. As mentioned before, today increasingly more agents and publishers ask novelists to produce proposals that look like their nonfiction counterparts as well. The reason for this is simple: The additional sections provide a big-picture view of a book's market and competition and the author's ability to help sell a book. No matter how you publish, you want to create a business plan with this depth and scope.

If the necessity of a business plan for your book or yourself represents a new concept, let me explain the importance of having one. Every business needs a plan if the owner wants to succeed. As a writer with the idea for a book, I encourage you to see yourself as a business person. Better yet, see yourself as an entrepreneur, or an authorpreneur. You have an idea for a new business. You need a plan for how to get it off the ground and make it successful.

Anyone who becomes an author enters the publishing business. You are now in the business of creating books, which are products, and selling them. Each book needs its own business plan; if you write more than one book, you might need an overall publishing plan for all your books. You also need a plan for your career as an author.

If you self-publish your book, you start a publishing company of your own and back your own project with your own money. Before you invest your money, you want to be sure your new business venture is viable. A business plan helps you determine this.

If you traditionally publish, you seek a financial backer to fund your "start-up." A publisher becomes your venture capital partner; the publisher will want to see your business plan to make sure the investment is sound.

As you can see, a business plan helps you prove to yourself or to someone else that your business—your book—has all the necessary elements it needs to succeed. It also provides exactly what it says: *a plan* you can follow through all the stages of creating your business—writing, publishing, and promoting your book. In fact, a book proposal provides publishers with a business plan for your book as well. To a great extent, they rely on the information in this document as the initial—and sometimes the final—business plan for the book once they acquire it. You will rely on it—and use it—no matter how you publish as well.

What's in a Nonfiction Book Proposal Anyway?

Because the Author Training Process follows the identical structure used for a nonfiction book proposal, it's important to have a rudimentary understanding of what this type of proposal includes before we begin.

In my experience, the following list includes the vital sections of a book proposal. (I will describe each section in subsequent chapters.) In some writing manuals, you may find these sections listed in a different order, and not every proposal includes every section. Authors and agents sometimes choose to include additional sections (or fewer sections) or even attachments. However, most agents and publishers see a proposal that contains these sections as comprehensive.

1. Overview
2. Markets
3. Promotion
4. Competing Titles
5. Complementary Titles
6. Resources Needed to Complete the Book
7. About the Author
8. Author's Platform
9. Spinoffs
10. Mission Statement
11. List of Chapters
12. Chapter Summaries
13. Sample Chapters

Each step of the process asks you to evaluate your book idea or yourself through the lens of a publishing professional; that is, a literary agent or acquisitions editor. If you find your project lacking in any way after your evaluations at each step, you have ample opportunities to determine ways to improve your product and make it more viable. I call these opportunities "Precious Moments."

If you want to learn more about book proposals, great books on the topic include:

- *How to Write a Book Proposal* by Michael Larsen
- *Write the Perfect Book Proposal: 10 That Sold and Why* by Jeff Herman and Deborah Levine Herman
- *The Complete Idiot's Guide to Getting Published* by Sheree Bykofsky and Jennifer Basye Sander
- *The Great First Impression Book Proposal* by Carolyn Howard-Johnson

The Value of "Precious Moments"

Like many aspiring authors, I initially used the nonfiction book proposal out of necessity. I didn't really enjoy writing book proposals, but I did it anyway because I wanted to land a traditional publishing deal. Writing a nonfiction book proposal entails a lot of time and work. I joke that you could write a whole book in the time it takes to write a proposal. Despite the time commitment, the value you receive from these precious moments will be worth the time and effort because these moments show you exactly what your book is about. You know exactly what you want to say to your readers. You know you are the right person to write the book, and you know for sure *this* is the right time to write it. Plus, you know *this* is the time for a publisher to acquire the book or for you to self-publish. You can't wait to get started!

That moment is the most precious of all!

After I experienced that moment several times and enjoyed seeing my clients and students experience it, too, I realized the value of writing a proposal wasn't just in landing an agent or a publishing contract. It was in realizing that in the *process* of proposal writing I'd conceived the most marketable book possible. When I also learned that publishers actually use book proposals prepared by authors as *the* business plans for the books they acquire, this reinforced my belief in this document.

Then it dawned on me that I had *not* produced a proposal for my own self-published books, and I thought, "Why wouldn't I put the same forethought, market analysis, and promotional planning into my self-published projects as a publisher requires for a book I want them to publish for me?" I concluded that every self-publisher needs to have that very same document—a business plan—in hand prior to independently publishing the work.

I tested my premise when I ran into Dan Poynter, author of *Dan Poynter's Self-Publishing Manual* and more than 132 books, at a conference. He concurred: "Every self-published author needs to write a book proposal before they write a book. They need a business plan for their books!"

Yet, it's not just the end product, the proposal or plan, or that one "precious moment" you seek to achieve. It's the *many* precious moments you have along the way that move you closer and closer to successful published author status.

My student Rhonda says this about completing her business plan at the conclusion of the Author Training Process: "Now I have the confidence to write the book … the right book. And that's all I want to work on right now." Not only that, Rhonda claims, "I now have outlines for five memoirs, and the first is completely drafted less than thirty days since I finished the process."

How "Precious Moments" Turn Into "Successful Published Author" Status

I've seen many aspiring authors experience precious moments as they work with me on a book proposal or as they go through the Author Training Process. These are the moments when their attitude shifts, when they gain a new perspective, when they have an epiphany that makes their book more salable, or they realize they need to do something differently to help their book succeed.

For example, a client of mine experienced one of these precious moments when I handed him back his proposal and said, "Jim, this reads really well, and your book idea appears viable. I think a publisher might be interested in it." Then came that dreaded word: "But … I think you'll have to wait six to nine months before you approach a literary agent or a small publisher."

"Why?" Jim wondered.

"Because you have no author platform. It will take you at least that long to build one big enough to make you an interesting partner to a publisher. Until then, you won't be able to successfully self-publish your book either."

I discovered this "little" problem in the Author Platform section of his proposal, which was basically empty. Jim's book was already written. In fact, it was designed and ready for delivery to a POD company if he failed to find an agent and a publisher. He thought all systems were go when it came to transforming himself from aspiring to published author.

Not so fast.

Had Jim taken Step #8, *Weigh Whether You Are the Best Person to Write This Book…*Now, in the Author Training Process before he wrote his book and proposal he would have evaluated himself and realized he needed to begin building his platform. Instead, he had to choose between putting his project on hold while he built author platform or move forward now and face the reality of his self-publishing effort not achieving the results he desired. This is just one example of the many "precious moments" you will hopefully discover as you work through the Author Training Process.

Sandy was writing a novel and, like Jim, wanted to approach publishers before choosing self-publishing. She knew how hard it might be to break in as a first-time novelist. We went through the Author Training Process while midway through her manuscript. During Step #1, *Develop an "Author Attitude" and Plan Your Success,* Sandy discovered she had the willingness to wear a business hat. Later in the process, during Step #8, *Weigh Whether You Are the Best Person to Write This Book…*Now, she discovered, like Jim, she had little platform. Determined to find a way to promote herself and her work, she explored all aspects of her novel; she listed its benefits, ways to tie her themes into the news, and the topics people might search for on the Internet. With all of this research in hand, she started a blog and set out to create an author brand and platform revolving around these subjects. Additionally, Sandy revisited Step #7, *Discover Ways to Brand Yourself and Earn More Money*, and experienced a precious moment when she realized she could support her new brand with a series of novels revolving around the themes and topics she had isolated. She created five new book pitches! As she looked at how to better target her market with these new topics and themes (Step #3, *Analyze How Many People* Really *Might Buy Your Book*) she decided to add nonfiction to her array of published offerings (Step #7, *Discover Ways to Brand Yourself and Earn More Money*). She also went back and reworked her manuscript with all her new information in mind.

Dave, a therapist, had a reasonably large market for his book about single mothers. However, as we discussed his readers (Step #3, *Analyze How Many People* Really *Might Buy Your Book*), he had a precious moment. It turned out that many of them were not "classically single." Some of them had husbands absent from the parenting process. "Dave, I said, that means your market encompasses all types of mothers who feel they parent alone."

With this in mind, Dave re-angled his book to target a much broader market. He also changed the language he would use to write his book (Step #6, *Decide if Your Book's Content Matches Your Initial Vision*). Now he would write to a target market of divorced, unwed, or widowed mothers as well as to those with husbands who traveled extensively, worked long hours, or chose not to get involved in parenting duties.

How to Use This Manual

Even without going through every step in the Author Training Process, you can see that it provides you with many opportunities to evaluate what *you* need to do to go from aspiring to published author and how you can improve your book idea to make it more salable. While some of the steps help you conceptualize your book, others ask you to answer difficult questions about yourself and look at yourself critically. In all cases, the steps move you closer to successful authorship.

Now, let me explain how to use this manual. Each chapter elaborates on a step of the Author Training Process. After you complete the chapter, you can turn to the back of the manual where you will find corresponding training exercises and questions. The *real* training happens in these exercises as you compile the information for your business plan. Although the chapters tell you what to do in each training step, you actually complete the exercises in the back of this book.

You also will find samples of my students' and clients' work, which agents and acquisitions editors have reviewed, in the Samples section. These proposals closely mirror the business plans my students created using the process in this book. The reviews of these business plans/book proposals are not "typical" rejection or acceptance letters. I asked these industry professionals to offer feedback. This allows you to see how agents and editors evaluate real submissions—how they see you and your book idea. As you study their comments, you can train yourself to see yourself and your book idea through the same lens, through their eyes.

If you don't want to alternate between reading a chapter and then completing the training, you can read the whole manual first and complete the exercises later in one fell swoop. Review each chapter again as you go through the training exercises, if you feel the need to do so.

If you follow this manual and are *willing* to go through each step of the Author Training Process *optimistically*, looking at each evaluation *objectively* and then *tenaciously* moving toward your goal, you will produce a book with high potential to succeed in the crowded publishing marketplace. You will increase your likelihood of succeeding as a published author. Why? Because you will have developed an Author Attitude. *WOOT!*

Not only that, you will have produced a business plan for your book (or started on your book proposal), which will include a writing guide for a salable book. *WOOT! WOOT!*

Ready to start training?

MANUAL

STEP #1

Develop an "Author Attitude" and Plan Your Success

You say you want to become an author. You can. You can upload a document right now to Amazon's Kindle program and declare, "I'm an author." You can produce a twenty-page, saddle-stitched (stapled) booklet at your local commercial print shop with your name on the cover and announce, "I've been published." You can create a ten-page PDF and sell it as an e-book to your blog and e-mail subscribers, and this, too, changes your status from aspiring to published author.

If you have the ability to write and get a manuscript into print, you can become an author today. Right now. A multitude of ways exists to accomplish this goal, and some of them are not too difficult or expensive.

In general, you don't even need great writing skill to become a published author, although writers of literary fiction are (usually) the exception to this rule. For this reason, I rarely mention the need for good writing when I discuss what it takes to become an author. Great editors take the work of mediocre or lousy writers who have great ideas and produce adequate, even phenomenal, manuscripts. They also turn poorly constructed manuscripts into highly comprehensible, polished books with the potential to become bestsellers.

Some best-selling and well-known authors have their books ghostwritten, like Ellery Queen's *The Player on the Other Side* (ghosted by Theodore Sturgeon) and *The Madman Theory* (ghosted by Jack Vance) and Maurice McLoughlin's *Tennis as I Play It* (ghosted by Sinclair Lewis fifteen years before winning the Nobel Prize for Literature). Some books sell millions of copies despite questionable writing skills or story lines criticized by reviewers and readers alike, such as *Fifty Shades of Grey, Bared to You, Twilight,* and *The Da Vinci Code.* However, successful writers tend to have a strong Author Attitude. They have willingness, optimism, objectivity, and tenacity. *WOOT!*

Ready for your first evaluation in the Author Training Process? Step #1 asks you to assess if you have an Author Attitude. This requires brutal honesty. You might *believe* you want to become a successful published author, but have your past decisions, actions, and results proven this to be true? Are you cut out for the job? Let's find out.

Do You *Really* Want to Become a Successful Author?

This is the question you must ask before you even look at the Author Training steps that evaluate your idea. To conceive a successful book idea, you must know what you *want* and you must understand what it will take to get it. A clear lack of understanding about what achieving your goal entails—what actions you must take as well as how achieving your goal might positively or negatively change your life—can affect your ability to make progress toward your goal as well.

Look at this concept from the perspective of attitude. If you don't know what you *believe* about publishing success—what it looks like, entails, or means to you—you won't be able to:

- *decide* if it is something you really want to achieve, and then ...
- take concrete *actions* so you can ...
- achieve the *results* that move you closer to successful authorship.

At the very least, your lack of knowledge may breed fear, which may also make it harder to achieve what you want. Fear lies at the heart of writer's block, but when we gain knowledge, we often eliminate our fear and move forward quickly—and eagerly. We also may find ourselves in a position to perceive situations more objectively and to act more tenaciously.

Defining your goal removes uncertainty and helps you develop an action plan and achieve results. It helps you know when you've reached your goal. That explains why every goal achievement expert advises, "Quantify your goal!" This basically means that if your goal is successful authorship, you must first define what success means to you. This way you can plan how to go from here to there (*there* being, "successful publication or authorship"). Consider these concepts as Goal Setting 101 for Authors.

If you recall, in Lewis Carroll's *Alice's Adventures in Wonderland*, Alice and the cat have the following conversation.

> **Alice:** Would you tell me, please, which way I ought to go from here?
> **The Cat:** That depends a good deal on where you want to get to.
> **Alice:** I don't much care where.
> **The Cat:** Then it doesn't much matter which way you go.
> **Alice:** ... so long as I get somewhere.
> **The Cat:** Oh, you're sure to do that, if only you walk long enough.

Like Alice, if you "don't much care *where*" you and your book are going, "then it doesn't matter which way you go," and you will get *somewhere*—it just might take a long time, and you might not end up in the place you expected. You also may not realize you've arrived. If, however, you have a specific destination, or goal, you will set out down a specific path and arrive more quickly at your chosen destination. Right now, the path you *believe* you want to take leads you to successful authorship.

In his classic bestseller *Think and Grow Rich*, Napoleon Hill offers six steps for setting and reaching goals. They are:

1. Have a specific goal.
2. Have a specific time to achieve your goal.
3. Write down your goal.
4. Develop a plan to achieve your goal.
5. Decide what price you are willing to pay.
6. Think about your goal every day.

Now, let's go through these steps and see how they apply to your Author Training.

Define Your Success and Set Your Goals

Let's identify a few things.

- How do you define successful authorship? What does it mean to be a successful author or to have written a successfully published book?

- How is successful authorship quantified? Is it a place, thing, feeling, experience, or number?
- Is this really what you want? Do you have what it takes to achieve this goal? What are you willing to sacrifice to achieve this goal?

You have to "locate" successful authorship on your particular road map. Do this physically by writing your ideas in a journal. Think short term, long term, whatever you wish as long as you are specific. Write it out, and don't forget to answer the training exercise questions in the back of this book and perform the other activities found there. They will all help your goal to become more specific and quantifiable, which means more achievable.

Maybe you've always dreamed of having a best-selling book. Nothing less will do. You want to be the next Harold Robbins, Napoleon Hill, Stieg Larsson, C.S. Lewis, John Gray, or Lynne Truss. As part of your definition of success, you see yourself speaking before audiences, doing book tours, teaching workshops, writing more best-selling books, and having your book featured in book stores. Be as specific as you can, and write as much as you feel comfortable accomplishing.

Maybe success for you means writing and publishing a series of novels for Kindle. You don't feel the need to become a best-selling novelist but simply want to find a small group of fans who enjoy your work—and create a small income. This positive feedback on your work would give you enormous pleasure and fulfillment.

Or perhaps your book represents the first step in your business plan for an empire of information products. Success for you looks like e-books, reports, services, videos, webinars, and membership sites, all traced back to the success of your initial book.

Maybe success for you is a specific number of books sold. As you try to define successful authorship in book sales, consider what agent Sheree Bykofsky, co-author of *The Complete Idiot's Guide to Getting Published (5th Edition)*, says about associating specific numbers with a book's success: "I believe that the numbers will always be a function of the individual book's expectations. Each book will have its own expectations as determined in advance of an offer when a publisher prepares a profit and loss statement. They will figure on doing a print run that will allow them to earn back their investment, including any advance to the author. Most books do not make it to a second printing, but if a book does, that book is a success—whether the print run was two thousand copies or a million."

MANUAL

Once you have defined this in a quantifiable way, you can take the appropriate action to develop a route or get directions so you know how to arrive at your destination, thus achieving the end result you desired—successful authorship.

Create a Plan for Your Goals

So now you have an idea of what being a "successful author" means to you. It's your goal, and it's now quantifiable. Maybe it's having a novel released by a major publisher in New York. Maybe it's selling one hundred copies of your self-published family history. Maybe it's building a publishing empire like Stephen King or James Patterson. Whatever it may be, you know that you can't get there with an "Alice Attitude." And as with most trips, it's a good idea to know *when* you would like to arrive at your destination.

For example, your primary goal might be:

> Publish my first novel with a traditional imprint.

Put a time stamp on your goal. Perhaps:

> Publish my first novel with a traditional imprint by May 31, 2016.

You could break this goal down into "signposts" or "landmarks" along the way to your destination. For instance, you also might have these other goal time stamps.

> Finish my manuscript for [book title] by December 31, 2014.
> Find an agent for [book title] by April 15, 2015.
> Find a publisher for [book title] by December 15, 2015.
> Release my book, [book title], by June 1, 2016.
> Sell five thousand copies of [book title] between June 1, 2016 and May 31, 2017.

Look at these goals often. When you wake up and just before you go to sleep are good times. Put them on 3" × 5" cards, and carry them around, or stick them on your computer or on the bathroom mirror.

These are concrete goals, quantifiable, and you have specific dates for each. They are real now.

But they won't happen on their own. You must create a plan to help you reach your goal. To do this, break down each goal into actionable items. In other words, make decisions about how you will get to each destination. By identifying tasks and placing them on a to-do list, you create little signposts or landmarks to your final destination. For example:

Goal: Find an agent for [book title] by April 15, 2015.
Action Items:
Research agents.
Make a list of fifteen to twenty agents to contact.
Research how to write a query letter.
Write a query letter and/or book proposal.
Begin sending out letters to agents by February 1, 2014.

Or, if you plan to self-publish:

Goal: Self-publish e-book {Book Title} by August 30, 2015
Action Items:
Find an editor.
Determine method of e-book conversion.
Find cover designer and arrange for design by December 31, 2014.
Finish manuscript by December 31, 2014.

This becomes your plan, or map, to follow to success. For each step of the Author Training Process, you can either add to your overall plan or create an individual plan for that step. Train yourself to follow the map each day, moving from signpost to signpost. Determine how far you want to travel daily, weekly, monthly, and yearly. (You can create a general plan for developing your goals for successful authorship with the help of the training exercises.)

Create a Vision of Success

As you create these plans, also create a vision of your destination—your goal. Doing so will help you stay motivated and achieve it. Describe in detail what achieving success as an author will look like. Consider how this will affect all aspects of your life. You'll find these questions in the exercises in the back. Feel free to answer them in a journal.

- Will success allow you to build a business around your book or blog, travel more, become a speaker, or teach at a university? How so?
- How will successful authorship change your personal life and affect your relationships?
- Will success make it possible for you to spend more time with your spouse or children, pursue your hobbies, or write more books? How so?
- Will success make you feel as if you have fulfilled your purpose or potential? How so?

MANUAL

- How will success affect your income?
- How much money would you like to make from an advance and book sales?

You'll find great value in actually crafting this vision of success. This exercise is quite similar to the Best Positive Self (BPS) process often used in Positive Psychology. A BPS is defined as an "ideographic representation of goals" (Markus & Nurius, 1986). Studies have shown that those who visualize themselves on a regular basis—daily or weekly—achieving their goal or potential have improved ability to self-regulate their behavior, gain awareness and clarity about priorities and values, achieve positive attitude, gain insight into motives and emotions, and reduce goal conflict.

Numerous studies show that writing about your life goals and imagining your most favorable future helps you learn about yourself. This makes it easier to restructure behavior, priorities, goals, motivations, values, beliefs, and attitudes. Basically, doing so helps you achieve better results.

You can write a vision of successful authorship by imagining your BPS in the present tense. Your vision might sound like the following.

> "For me, book publishing success is receiving a book contract from a traditional publisher for [Book Title], receiving an advance large enough to make it possible for me to promote it well (at least $10,000), developing a speaking and coaching business around my book that brings in $60,000+ per month, book sales of 8,000+ per year, and monthly media coverage for myself and the book of five to ten radio shows, podcasts, blog posts, and magazine articles per month. This nicely supplements my family's income and affords me an opportunity to travel and meet new people as well as to enhance my professional life. It affords me the ability to pay a virtual assistant for eight hours per week of work to help me with a variety of tasks. I'd like my book to sell well over 150,000 copies in its lifetime."

A vision for self-publishing might sound quite similar but would begin:

> For me, book publishing success is self-publishing [Book Title] as a print-on-demand and e-book, developing ..."

Don't just guess at the figures you use. See if you can find sales figures for books similar to the one you want to write. The financial aspect of authorship can prove a shocking detail if you have never thought about it before. Advances vary greatly depending on fiction or non-fiction and from publisher to publisher. A traditional publishing contract typically stipulates that the author gets paid 15 percent royalties on copies up to a certain number based on the net amount received by the publisher on sales to retailers. Ouch. That's without the 15 to 20 percent you pay an agent on top of that.

If you have a self-published book, say on Amazon's CreateSpace or Kindle, or Smashwords.com, or at Bookbaby.com, you can earn 70 percent for each book you sell at the midrange level. On the other hand, if you choose to use Amazon's KDP Select program and offer free days or to discount your book in some way, you could earn much less.

It's important to think about how many copies of your book you want to sell as you write your vision and set your goals—as well as how you will be involved in selling them. Will you:

- spend time on social networks?
- hire a publicist or PR representative?
- pursue media attention?
- speak at conferences?
- teach workshops and webinars?
- simply write more books?

And will any of this cost you money or eat into your writing time? This is where a profit and loss statement comes into play. You might want to spend some time considering how many books you will need before you recoup your investment.

So try to be realistic when you write your vision. The publishing industry has seen advances trending downward but royalties trending upward as publishers try to encourage authors to take ownership for their books' success. That means you might only get an advance of $2,000 to $3,000 as a first-time author, should you be considering traditional publishing. Therefore, you might need that money for promotion and not get to use it for a vacation. Out of my two advances, I've used only a few hundred dollars for my own enjoyment. The rest has been reinvested in my book's success. This was part of my business plan and part of my vision.

You might choose to write your vision in the past tense, as if you have already achieved your goal. This method effectively turns your statement into an affirmation that this goal will be realized. In the past tense, the vision above would be written as follows.

My book, [Book Title], was picked up by a traditional publisher over a year ago, and I received an advance large enough to make it possible for me to promote it well ($10,000). I now enjoy a speaking and coaching business that revolves around my book and that brings in $60,000+ per month, book sales of 8,000+ per year, and monthly media coverage for myself and the book ranging from five to ten radio shows, podcasts, blog posts, and magazine articles per month. This nicely supplements my family's income and affords me a chance to travel and meet new people. It enhances my professional life and allows me to pay a virtual assistant for eight hours per week of work to help me with a variety of tasks. My publisher has asked me to write a second book in an effort to build a brand, and with this added push, I expect my first book to sell well over 150,000 copies in its lifetime.

You can even try writing your vision for more than one year at a time. Have a long-term vision for five years at a time. This will help you think beyond this one book and beyond the first year of sales or the book's release.

Read your vision as often as your goals—especially in the morning when you wake and at night prior to going to sleep.

With your goals and your vision written, you've created a good map to get you to your destination, and hopefully you've developed a greater understanding of where you are going and how to get there.

Are You Willing to Sacrifice to Become an Author?

It's easy enough to spend time visualizing your goal and feeling good as you imagine achieving it. Determining what "price" you are willing to pay to achieve that goal, as Hill asks us to consider, personally represents quite a different matter entirely. You can count on having to sacrifice or give up something you enjoy. For instance, a few hours of television, a vacation, some sleep, or time spent reading. You might also have to give up old ways of doing things or beliefs—all so you can achieve the goal you desire.

Rhonda told me that after writing her goals and vision, she realized she would have to make some changes if she wanted to succeed as an author. "I gave up reading three-and-a-half books a week, playing the piano every Saturday, and [spending] time in the morning to relax before work. I don't watch TV and seldom watch a movie with my husband unless I'm working on the laptop," she reported. "My lifestyle has completely changed to make room in my thinking as well as in my schedule to write."

Are you feeling a bit squeamish? Starting to squirm in your chair? Or are you feeling eager, willing, and excited to examine your habits and ideas with *change* in the forefront of your mind?

The writers who truly want to become successful published authors simply do whatever it takes to reach their goals, and sometimes this doesn't involve writing at all. It can involve a total lifestyle change. As you continue through the training, you will see that you need to take on many tasks in addition to writing to achieve your goal and realize your vision. You may not like or want to do all of them. Evaluate yourself again: Are you willing to take on these tasks if it means the difference between success and failure or a book with below-average, average, or above-average sales?

Dr. Wayne Dyer created a bestseller out of his first book, *The Erroneous Zone*, by purchasing copies himself and driving all over the United States to promote it. He would stop at every radio station and ask if they wanted to interview him. After the appearance and every chance he found, he would sell copies out of the trunk of his car. This certainly ate into his writing and personal life, but it helped him achieve his publishing goals. It was a major sacrifice, but it was worth it at the end.

Many writers I know balk at anything that takes them away from writing their books. I call them "purists." A few feel that anything related to marketing, promoting, and selling books somehow "dirties" them as creatives. Others think they should focus only on their craft. Still others just don't like anything to do with business-related publishing activities and therefore want nothing to do with them. Some maintain the outdated belief that publishers should handle all of the business-related stuff.

If you write to be read and to have your books purchased, the only way to let people know about your writing is to promote it and yourself as a writer. That means you have to start selling your book in one way or another, even before it's written. It also means you need to wear a lot of hats in addition to your writer's hat.

Learning this represented a turning point for Rhonda. She wasn't writing her memoir as just a healing journey for herself; she wanted to share the lessons she had learned and help and encourage others with similar experiences. "I realized that if I had no audience, then there was no reason to share my message. Also, if I'm not willing to reach out to my readers and sell books, then there is no reason to work and sacrifice this much to write my stories," she says.

So I ask again: Are you committed to writing your book? Are you committed to making your book and yourself as the author of that book successful? What does that commitment look like? If you do want to commit, *can* you commit? That is, do you have other obligations, such as children, a job, elderly parents whom you care for, or financial restraints that make it difficult for you to commit at the level you would like? Can you work around those obligations in some way, getting a college student to work with you for experience rather than pay, asking a retired parent to help you with some child-care tasks, or cutting back on hours at work while your spouse takes on more financial responsibility for the family? Take some time to think about this and to create another visualization, this time of an ideal yet typical day in your life as an author. For how many hours will you write, and for how many will you wear other hats?

Review the exercises in the back of this manual and write your answers in your journal.

Be realistic and honest with yourself because becoming a successful author is hard work. Publishers want projects from writers who will work hard to help sell books, which is why they look for those who have built author platform. Author platform is built with prepublication promotion specific to your book's target market. This creates an audience for you and your book. Having a platform shows your commitment to helping your book succeed and your desire to become a successful author. If you don't want to do what's necessary to build a platform, you can still go from aspiring author to published author. If you want to be a successful author by industry standards, however, this attitude won't cut it.

Every time I teach a workshop about how to become an author, a few hours into it someone typically sitting at the back of the room raises his or her hand. This frustrated writer always asks the same question: "Why can't I just write my book? I don't want to do any of that other stuff like promotion and platform building. I *just* want to write my book."

I always respond the same way—with the truth. "You can just write your book, but it may not sell a lot of copies and you won't attract a publisher—especially if you are writing nonfiction."

How to Develop Willingness

So you have now created a vision; you have seen the benefits clearly. You've examined how your life might change and the things you may need to sacrifice. But maybe you're still feeling uneasy about the changes and sacrifices you will have to make. Now is the time to ask yourself, "Why?" and to discover the reason for your resistance. There's a reason why you are unwilling to do what it takes to become an author or, more specifically, a successful author, and maybe that reason is as simple as fear.

Explore your resistance … your attitude. For a long time—three or four years—I didn't want to put in the effort to build platform. I piddled at it because I knew I "should," but I didn't put my heart into it. I had a fear of success and how it might change my life, and in particular my relationships. I believed that I wasn't a good salesperson—at least not of my own work—and that I wouldn't be able to sell books. And I wanted to just be a writer. I didn't even really want to write business plans or proposals. But when I decided I wanted to be an author more than I didn't want to do those business-related tasks, my attitude changed. I realized that I had to wear "many hats" in addition to my writer hat or I might never sell my books.

I put on a business hat. I put on a promotion hat. I put on a speaker hat. I wore a social-media hat. I wore these every day or as often as possible. I wore them more than my writing hat on most days. And I even grew to like wearing them. I got good at those tasks. And wearing those hats helped me become an author—a best-selling one.

Maybe you don't want to wear a business hat and do the tasks that go with it because you are shy and don't like to be out in front of people; possibly promotion makes you nervous. If you can develop a willingness to wear a business hat, you might discover you can promote yourself and build an author platform from the comfort of your home without anyone ever seeing you. If you have a fear of standing in front of your readers in public, utilize the power of social networking, podcasting, blogging, or radio appearances.

Or maybe if you plan to self-publish, you are afraid of having your new publishing company fail; fear of failure is a common reason people don't start projects. If you don't try, you won't ever know if you can succeed. The power of driving your book success lies primarily in you, the author, so the only way to assure your book has a shot is to overcome that fear and *try*.

Ask yourself: What's your "reward," or how might you "profit" if you choose to remain an *aspiring* compared to a *successful* published author? *What do you gain by keeping your current habits*? Consider the following questions, and respond to them in your journal. I will give you an example answer, but carefully consider each of these and add as many reasons for each as you can.

- What will I gain if I ignore the task of building a big enough platform to land a publisher and/or sell a lot of books? What will I lose? (Example: I gain more time to write, and people won't judge my blogging skills! But I lose a built-in audience once I'm done).
- How do I profit if I choose to ignore Twitter and Facebook? What do I lose? (Example: I don't have to worry about not becoming popular enough online! But I lose the chance to see how connected I can become in the writing community.)

MANUAL

- How do I improve my chances of successfully selling my book by not showing up in front of audiences? What do I lose? (Example: I don't have to deal with stage fright or a red face, or suffer from my fear of public speaking! I don't have to risk taking a hit to my self-image. I lose one of the most effective methods of connecting with my reader and selling my books and must rely on luck for the reader to find me.)
- What do I gain by leaving my business hat hanging on the wall? What do I lose? (Example: I can avoid the fact that I really don't believe I have a good business mind and will likely fail if I try my hand at becoming an authorpreneur. I lose the ability to achieve my dreams.)

Think about it: Do you have a payoff for remaining an unpublished or unsuccessful author? Or is the risk worth it?

Remember, your old thoughts and beliefs have only helped you achieve your current level of success. Henry Ford said, "If you always do what you've always done, you'll always get what you've always got." If you want to achieve a higher degree of success, rid yourself of the negative thoughts, beliefs, and behaviors that hold you back or keep you stuck where you are right now and create new ones. Then make new decisions and take new actions, even if these are baby steps, so you achieve different results. All of this goes back to attitude.

As I mentioned, one of the reasons I didn't succeed for so long was because I was afraid of success—yes, *afraid* of success. I thought success would draw me away from my husband and family; I thought it might harm my marriage. So I would procrastinate every day. I did a lot of talking about what I was going to do, but I didn't do it. The payoff: I didn't have to worry about the effect success would have on my family or my relationship with my husband. One day, I decided I wanted to become successful for myself as well as for my husband and family. The payoff: I could contribute financially to the family. I would be able to support myself. I would feel happier and more fulfilled. My family relationships—and my marriage—would benefit. I decided to work toward success as if my life, or my financial well-being, depended upon it.

Just as I did, you need to uncover your positive payoffs. If you become a successful author, how will you benefit? What reward will you receive? How will you profit? If you have difficulty with this exercise, go back to your vision and look for the positive payoffs you wrote about in different areas of your life.

Really, this comes down to making decisions that affect your attitude. In 2001, I decided I wanted to become an author. In 2009, I decided I would become published. Period. In 2011, I landed my first traditional publishing deal. I accomplished more in two years than I did in eight. How? I changed my attitude.

One day, when I thought I might have to go back to work full-time rather than pursue my writing career, I thought about what I might lose if I didn't ever become an author—my dream, my chance to fulfill my purpose, my opportunity to realize my potential and inspire and help others. I examined my vision and thought about a life in which I failed to obtain my dream. This adjusted my attitude. Seeing my possible future from the flip side—how failure would detract from my life—motivated me more than seeing success. I began working harder and got moving faster. I knew I had to accomplish my goal, no matter what. I refused to fail.

I began taking the steps—whatever steps I could find or learn. I spent time on social media, I spoke every chance I got, I wrote for magazines, and I blogged five days a week or more. Even if I didn't like what I was required to do, I did it knowing it was getting me where I wanted to go. I could make (and still do) any task bearable—even pleasant—by believing it was necessary to my success, deciding to do it because it would help me succeed, and then actually doing it.

Michelle, one of my students, considered what she might lose if her novel—which she planned to self-publish—failed. She listed the following items.

- Credibility (with a small but growing audience of blog readers and fellow writers, several published)
- Patience from my family, given the time waste of having me spend months not earning an income
- The ability to go on (?)

But Michelle already was developing (or had) an Author Attitude. Her last response got her thinking more positively. She related, "If my first book fails to sell, or sells an average amount, this means I lose:

- Nothing, other than the time and resources spent on the indie production.
- Nothing, provided I learn from the process and change my promotional work or other things and produce a new book or change the current one.

In other words, it could be a gain, provided I learn from it and go on.

MANUAL

I later learned that this approach to changing behavior is the same one used by Third Wave Psychologists. They employ approaches consistent with much of the training given to life coaches and Neuro-Linguistic Programmers (NLP), which focuses on acceptance and awareness of negative emotions and thoughts and commitment to alignment of values, beliefs and goals. When you commit to something, you adopt an emotional state—an attitude—of obligation. You feel emotionally compelled to move forward to achieve what you value *for yourself.* Basically, if you know your negative beliefs, thoughts, and feelings and how these affect your actions and results, you can adopt an attitude that helps you choose (decide upon) new behaviors (actions) that align with your new values, beliefs, and goals.

If you haven't felt willing to do what it takes, this type of activity and focus can help you develop the necessary will. Every day, look at your vision, see what you stand to lose if you don't make the right choices, and choose to make decisions and take actions that align with your goal. Be *willing* to go over these things *every day.* That's having an Author Attitude.

I think Jonathan Winters had an Author Attitude. He said, "I couldn't wait for success, so I went ahead without it." That's *chutzpah.*

Use what you have learned in this chapter, and success might have to catch up with you, too. You still need to evaluate your book idea, though (and you'll evaluate yourself again later). In the process, your "personal training" and Author Training continues as well. *WOOT!*

Reading Suggestions:

Outliers by Malcolm Gladwell

Mindset: The New Psychology of Success by Carol Dweck

The Success Principles™: How to Get from Where You Are to Where You Want to Be by Jack Canfield and Janet Switzer

What Got You Here Won't Get You There: How Successful People Become Even More Successful by Marshall Goldsmith and Mark Reiter

Learned Optimism: How to Change Your Mind and Your Life by Martin E.P. Seligman

How Successful People Think: Change Your Thinking, Change Your Life by John C. Maxwell

Goals!: How to Get Everything You Want—Faster Than You Ever Thought Possible by Brian Tracy

Eat That Frog!: 21 Great Ways to Stop Procrastinating and Get More Done in Less Time by Brian Tracy

Write That Book Already! The Tough Love You Need to Get Published Now by Sam Barry and Kathi Kamen Goldmark

Write It Down, Make It Happen: Knowing What You Want and Getting It by Henriette Anne Klauser

The 4 Disciplines of Execution: Achieving Your Wildly Important Goals by Chris McChesney, Sean Covey, and Jim Huling

MANUAL

STEP #2

Know What Your Book Is About and Why Someone Would Want to Read (Buy) It

Most aspiring authors think they know exactly what their book is about and why someone would want to read it, which, unless you plan to give your book away for free, means "buy" it. In truth, they typically possess only a general idea.

When I work as an editor critiquing manuscripts, proposals, and pitches at writers conferences, most writers who enlist my services spend at least three to ten minutes explaining their books' subject to me. Novelists go into great detail about their main character, describe secondary characters, and reveal every single twist and turn of the plot. Nonfiction writers offer me the full spectrum of content they plan to include in their books. I'm privy to every minute detail including why *they* want to *write* the book. Almost all of them fail to explain why *readers* might benefit from *reading* their books or to mention the angles or themes they have taken with their subjects or stories that make their book unique compared to other books already on the market.

These writers haven't honed their story or subject. They haven't thought carefully enough about what makes their books different to articulate this idea. They don't fully understand why someone would want to read or buy their books. They haven't become so familiar with their subject matter and their angle that they can tell me in under a minute the gist of what they are writing or have written. They can't answer their readers' primary question: "What's In It For Me?" (WIIFM?)

That's a problem. Some of these writers plan to pitch their books to agents or acquisitions editors while at these conferences. They may have three to five minutes total to do so in a "speed dating with agents" session and to conduct a follow-up conversation about their book. They will use all their time describing their book idea before receiving any feedback.

In general, if you can't speak or write about your book idea in a pithy and compelling sentence or two, known as an elevator speech, book pitch, or log line, you don't have a way to communicate that your idea has the potential to be:

- a sound business proposition
- a book that adds value to lives
- a story worth reading
- information your readers need or want
- a totally new idea or never-before-told tale

That's what agents and acquisitions editors have to hear before they "buy into" a book idea, but it's also what makes potential readers carry a book to the register. The ability to condense your idea into a sound bite easily understood from both a business and creative perspective, therefore, helps *you* gain clarity on your idea and determine if your project is viable. That's why you need to learn how to write a book pitch.

You typically find a book pitch in the "Overview" of a book proposal because this section does just what it says: It provides a big-picture view of your entire project. It explains in a condensed manner what the book is about and justifies its publication—i.e., it explains why it is marketable. Thus, writing a pitch and an Overview provides important starting points for any book project and essential elements in your book's business plan.

The Overview: Justify the Writing and Publishing of Your Book

Step #2 of the Author Training Process, *Know What Your Book Is About and Why Someone Would Want to Read (Buy) It*, asks you to accumulate the information necessary for the Overview of your business plan. The Overview serves as the first page or two of your business plan, just as it serves as the first page or two of a formal book proposal. Your Overview will include your hook, your pitch, a summary, and information about word counts, special features, photos or illustrations—everything an acquisitions editor will quickly need to know to feel compelled by your idea. I will walk you through exercises to help you gather the information necessary for your business plan's Overview, which we will assemble together at the end of this chapter. These steps include:

1. Write a book summary.

2. Determine the angle or storyline of your book.

3. Write a theme statement.

4. Compose a list of benefits.

5. Develop a purpose statement.

6. Decide on a title.

7. Create a compelling pitch.

8. Consider special features.

By creating an Overview, you will gain clarity about your subject or story, justify the writing and publishing of your project, discover your book's true angle and theme, identify your book's benefits to readers, train yourself to see your idea from a business perspective, and develop confidence in your idea. If you aspire to become traditionally published, the Overview in your book proposal attempts to entice a literary agent and then a publisher—a venture capital partner for your project—to discuss your project further. The Overview is the first thing an agent or acquisitions editor reads in a book proposal; therefore, it must sell your book idea to them. (A query letter entices an agent to ask for a book proposal, if you write nonfiction, or a manuscript, if you write fiction; the agent then sends a query to an acquisitions editor, who again asks for a proposal for nonfiction or a manuscript accompanied by a proposal for fiction.)

If an acquisitions editor at a publishing house gets excited about your idea, your Overview provides the basic initial details used by the editor at the weekly editorial board meeting to justify purchasing your book idea and establish you as a publishing partner. The rest of your proposal provides further justification.

Whether you self-publish or traditionally publish your book, you need to train yourself to evaluate the business plan you write through the eyes of everyone on that board—the acquisitions editors, publisher, marketing team, salespeople, and publicist. They all have to buy into your project—and into you. Like them, you must discern if your Overview (and, ultimately, every section of your business plan) provides justification for the writing and publishing of your proposed book. If you self-publish your book, your Overview must justify to you the writing and publishing of your proposed book. It must make you feel confident that you will earn back everything you will invest in your book. You must feel convinced that your book idea represents a viable business proposition—that it is marketable. As an indie publisher, you serve as the editorial board, unless you recruit others to serve on it with you.

If you plan to ask others to invest in your project, such as with a kickstarter.com or indiegogo.com campaign that allows you to crowdsource the funding for your project, you also want to approach the writing of this first section of your business plan with objectivity—with an Author Attitude. You will benefit by determining if your Overview (and later your whole business plan) offers a compelling argument and enough benefit for you or others to want to back your project.

This type of an "idea evaluation" increases your confidence in your book concept. You need that confidence—confidence backed by hard facts obtained as you continue your Author Training and refine the Overview. When completed, your Overview should convince you that your book will be salable because you will write it keeping in mind the criteria used by an editorial board or even just one acquisitions editor.

Also, the Overview serves as an important part of the road map for your book. It concisely details what you plan to write about and why anyone would be interested in reading your book. As you create this document, your vision of what you need to do to arrive at your final destination—a successful book—becomes clearer and clearer. Whether you write nonfiction or fiction, your Overview should describe the scope of your concept so anyone can understand it.

For this reason, your Overview, much like your vision for success, serves as inspiration as you progress through the Author Training Process and then as you write the actual book. Review this one piece of your plan before each writing period to remind yourself of the promises you must keep to your readers and what you intend to accomplish. When you get confused or veer off track, reread this document to remind yourself of your book's subject, angle, theme, story line, benefits, and purpose. This puts you back on the track to success.

What Is Your Book About?

The ability to write your Overview, including a pitch, will determine if you know your book's subject or story. If you can't describe your book in a brief, compelling manner, you don't know what it's about. (And if you can't write about it in a compelling manner in a short amount of space, you can feel certain readers won't buy it.) However, there are some steps you can take prior to actually writing your Overview that will help you figure out what your book is *really* about. These include writing a summary and identifying your book's idea, angle, and theme. Once you have done this, you can move on to identifying your book's benefits and purpose. Then you can determine the best title and pitch for your book. At that point, you will be ready to write your Overview.

Your Book Summary

To begin, take some time to write a short description of your book. You may do so in your journal using the exercises in the back. I call this your "book summary." Describe your non-fiction book or summarize your novel, and for now, try to write it in less than three paragraphs. For nonfiction, this is about how long a summary might be in your Overview. In fiction, a synopsis will be a paragraph or two at most in your query letter or a full page in a separate synopsis. For now, keep it under three paragraphs.

Pay attention to whether or not you find this exercise difficult or easy. Obviously, if you can summarize your book in one or two paragraphs quickly and easily, you probably know what you are writing about. If you struggle with this exercise, you've got a bit of work ahead of you, but keep working through the steps. It will get easier.

Your Book Idea and Angle

As you write your summary, you want to keep your idea and angle in mind. You can even define them and include this information in your business plan for reference. For example, a nonfiction book begins with an idea. This could be defined as an opinion, conviction, view, belief, or principle. Your idea might be quite broad, such as "saving money," "spirituality," or "leadership." However, every nonfiction idea needs an angle, or a narrower topic, such as "saving money in your sixties," "Kabbalistic meditation practices," or "leadership tips for women." A subject angle serves as a book's primary organizing principle and helps your book become unique and interesting to the most people or to a particular set of people.

Let's say you want to write about training dogs. Dog training serves as your book's general idea. You must now find one aspect of dog training about which to write, such as how to train dogs without using treats. That becomes your book's angle.

The broad idea for this book was "How to become a successful published author." The more specific angle on that idea was "How aspiring authors can train to become successful published authors using the nonfiction book proposal as an evaluation tool for themselves and their ideas."

Novels begin with a different type of idea—the idea for a story or the idea for a character. Your fiction idea will be angled based on genre. Other details of your story, such as place, inciting incident, age of reader, theme, and moral of the story (or even morals of the characters) will affect the angle as well. You might, for instance, have the general idea for a romance novel. You angle that idea by writing a romance novel involving a love triangle between a duke, duchess, and knight that takes place in Scotland in the 1700s.

MANUAL

Your Book's Theme

Your book will also have a theme, a unifying or dominant idea. This provides an overriding emotional, philosophical, or universal aspect to the story. The theme statement for your dog-training book might be: "Human encouragement and love quickly and easily accomplish canine training goals." For this manual, it might be, "Learning to see yourself and your book objectively through the lens used by publishing professionals provides the key to successful authorship," or, more simply, "Learning to develop an Author Attitude provides the key to success as an author."

Novels and memoirs tend to stress themes. If you have written a romance in which a woman "heals past hurts" or "reclaims her self-confidence," these are themes that benefit other women. The broad idea for your romance novel might be: "A woman goes to New York and has an affair with a man." The angle of your novel might be: "A failed actress travels to New York after asking for a separation from her husband, has a fling with a young actor, and realizes the bright lights of Broadway now have less allure than her marriage." The theme of this novel might be: "Old dreams sometimes cloud current realities." See how an angle is more specific but a theme is deeper and more meaningful? Angles make your book unique. Themes give them value. Within themes lie benefits, and benefits sell books.

How Will Your Book Benefit Readers?

To create a successful book—one that sells to many readers—you must conceive your idea with the "What's In It For Me?" factor in mind. The WIIFM? factor represents the value your book adds to your reader's lives or how your book caters to their interests and needs. Your book must focus on providing readers with benefits. Think of benefits as concrete "things" you will "give" readers in the pages of your book. You can also consider them the promises you make to your readers.

In his book *Sell Your Book Like Wildfire: The Writer's Guide to Marketing and Publicity*, Rob Eagar suggests people purchase books that appeal to their self-interest. "If you miss this fundamental principle, you will fail to create the sparks needed to sell books like wildfire," he writes. He explains that when potential readers ask what your book is about, "actually they are wondering, 'What's in it for me if I buy your book? Is it in my best interest to read what you've written?'"

As you write the business plan for your book, concentrate on how to conceive your book with your readers' interests in mind. Once you can write and talk about those benefits in a concise manner, you can later write your book with your readers' interests in mind as well.

Your job, therefore, involves discovering the benefits your book might offer a reader. Fiction books sell on uniqueness and story, but they often have benefits embedded in their stories. You might provide value to readers by exploring relationships, challenges, places, history, language, lifestyles—all from within the pages of your novel. Diana Gabaldon's Outlander series offers readers a history lesson (and a *Gaelic* lesson) along with romance and the possibility that time travel is real. Beverly Lewis shows readers what it is like to live an Amish life in her romance series, Home to Hickory Hollow, The Rose Trilogy, and Seasons of Grace. In *The Harbinger: The Ancient Mystery That Holds the Secret of America's Future*, Jonathan Cahn tells a story based on a mystical interpretation of a biblical verse, giving readers a chance to gain a different perspective on historic events. Jasinda Wilder's best-selling novel, *Falling Into You*, tells readers a story about how a person can heal from grief by entering into another relationship.

However, nonfiction books sell directly on their uniqueness, value, and benefit. Through the pages of your book, you help readers do or achieve something, solve problems, answer questions, fulfill desires, or learn something new. Think of timeless nonfiction bestsellers like Richard N. Bolles' *What Color Is Your Parachute?* or Dale Carnegie's *How to Win Friends and Influence People*, or consistently best-selling authors, such as Deepak Chopra, Suze Orman, Wayne Dyer, and Jack Canfield. They all use these formulas. However, your nonfiction book doesn't have to be a how-to book to add value to readers' lives. Even best-selling memoirs, such as *Wild: From Lost to Found on the Pacific Crest Trail* by Cheryl Strayed, solve problems and add value. Strayed shows how someone can pick up the pieces of a broken life and put it back together. In his memoir, *Proof of Heaven*, neurosurgeon Eben Alexander shows us why we should believe in life after death.

Think of current bestsellers, like *Outliers* by Malcolm Gladwell, which offers readers benefit by explaining why some people succeed and how readers can, too. Or consider *The Power of Positive Thinking* by Norman Vincent Peale, which stayed on *The New York Times* bestseller list for 186 weeks and provided the benefit of advice on how to have a positive attitude and achieve better results because of it.

The benefits of the book you want to write must resonate with readers emotionally. If you can make your readers feel something, they typically will purchase. What they feel is more important than what they think. That's why, for example, considering what they stand to *lose* if they don't read your book can bring up a totally different set of benefits than what they stand to *gain* by reading your book. To figure this out, ask yourself, "What will my readers lose if they don't read my book?" Instead of receiving benefit or value from reading your book, what hindrances, handicaps, or disadvantages will they discover they have because they are not privy to the information in your book? Looking at the issue from this perspective can provide a more emotionally driven answer than the opposite question, "What will my readers gain if they read my book?"

Create a list of your book's benefits. These can include anything you feel adds value to readers' lives, including a good belly laugh. If you cannot create a list of at least three to five benefits—preferably five to ten—this means your book does not add value to readers, and you'll need to rethink your concept. If you want to produce a successful book, you must be willing to objectively and tenaciously retool your idea until you conceptualize it in a way that offers high value to readers.

Megge, a student of mine, admits that when she finished her Overview she thought she'd completed that section of the plan and the Author Training Process. "When I came to the part of Nina's plan that asks for the benefits of this book, I sort of stalled out. No, I actually balked," she says. "Benefits! Of a memoir? C'mon, girl."

I explained to Megge that even a memoir could provide benefit to the reader. To make it marketable, her transformative story should have some sort of universal lesson, inspiration, or personal insight for the reader. What will the reader learn? What will they apply to their own life after reading the memoir? "Once I connected back to what originally propelled me into this book in the first place, I had more benefits than I could possibly fit on the page," Megge says. (That initial reason for writing her book likely corresponded with her purpose, which we will discuss next.)

It was easy for Deborah, another student, to find benefits in her self-help book. Yet, the process of writing an overview, which forced her to adopt a businesslike view of her book, helped her clarify the added value to her readers. "It's like applying for a job: It's better to approach it from the perspective of what benefit you provide rather than what you get out of it yourself," she related. This sentiment points out how you must move out of Step #1, in which you focused on how your book might affect you—your vision of success—and fully into Step #2 (and most of those that follow), which ask you to focus on how your book will affect *your readers*.

Does Your Book Have a Purpose?

Like many writers, you might believe writing a book fulfills a sense of personal purpose. Or maybe you think your book has its own purpose to fulfill. That purpose could be an extension of your personal purpose and is what gives your book a reason to exist.

Your book's purpose includes the benefits it provides to readers. For example, Seth Godin's bestseller *Tribes,* has a simple purpose: to inspire readers to lead. He states it this way: "We need YOU to lead us." Godin's book promised to make readers "think (really think) about the opportunities for leading your fellow employees, customers, investors, believers, hobbyists, readers."

The back of Mark Victor Hansen and Robert G. Allen's bestseller, *The One Minute Millionaire*, features a list of concepts you will learn from reading their book. Among these are "the power of one great idea, how to develop multiple streams of income, six forms of leverage, and the essentials of marketing success." These constitute three of seven benefits promised to the reader. The back cover copy of *The One Minute Millionaire* also says,

> "In every city, often behind the scenes, there are thousands of enlightened millionaires who acquire their wealth in innovative and honorable ways—and then give back to their communities. This book will show you how to become one of them ... more quickly than you ever imagined."

The outcome of the author's promise—its purpose—is that readers will quickly learn to become enlightened millionaires who can give back to their communities.

"Purpose" speaks to why you think your book must exist, why people must read your book, and why you must write it. Your reasons have to resonate with those you ask to invest in it—publishers or other backers and your buyers (readers). If you strike an emotional chord with your work, readers will hear it. You need only read the first pages of Brené Brown's bestseller, *Daring Greatly*, to find yourself feeling what she has felt. Who likes to feel vulnerable? No one. Her book's purpose lies in showing us how we can succeed in all areas of life by learning that vulnerability makes us stronger and more capable. That's the benefit it promises to give us.

Malcolm Gladwell's bestseller, *The Tipping Point*, promises to explore and illuminate "the tipping point phenomenon" and how it changes the way people "think about selling products and disseminating ideas." The purpose of the book, found in the introduction, is to answer two questions: "Why is it that some ideas or behaviors or products start epidemics and other don't? And what can we do to deliberately start and control positive epidemics of our own?" This is also the benefit it delivers to readers.

Most novels won't make such clear promises because they don't have a strong purpose statement, but you might find something similar if you search. On the back cover of John Irving's *The Fourth Hand,* for instance, I discovered this:

MANUAL

> While reporting a story from India, New York journalist Patrick Wallingford inadvertently becomes his own headline when his left hand is eaten by a lion. In Boston, a renowned surgeon awaits the opportunity to perform the nation's first hand transplant.
>
> But what if the donor's widow demands visitation rights with the hand? In answering this unexpected question, John Irving has written a novel that is by turns brilliantly comic and emotionally moving, offering a penetrating look at the power of second chances and the will to change.

Answering the question "*What if the donor's widow demands visitation rights with the hand?*" represents the novel's purpose. The fact that the book takes "*a penetrating look at the power of second chances and the will to change*" also serves as the author's promise to readers and serves as a "WIIFM? statement." Readers of the novel benefit by exploring these themes.

I found a statement of purpose on the back cover of Fyodor Dostoevsky's *Crime and Punishment*:

> In this greatest psychological novel of all time, Dostoevsky illuminates the irreconcilable dualism of mankind, the conflict of a soul possessed by good and evil.

In best-selling author Lisa Scottoline's most recent novel, *Don't Go*, she tells the story of a soldier who "discovers what it means to be a man, a father, and ultimately, a hero." This is the purpose of her book, and that purpose benefits readers, who also discover what it means to be a man, a father, and a hero in the process of reading the story.

As mentioned in Step #1 of the Author Training Process, when you create clearly definable goals, you increase your chances of achieving them. Your book's purpose represents a goal. It's what you and your book set out to accomplish.

When you can clearly define this purpose, you will have an easier time fulfilling it. If you keep the purpose in mind while writing your book, then you will have kept your promises to your readers when you have finished. It's important, therefore, to write a statement of purpose for yourself and your book. Determine why you feel the need to write your book. (You can answer this in your journal, along with other questions we will cover here.) What will you accomplish by writing a book? Examine the goal you want readers to achieve; why do you think it's important for them to do so?

Once you've written this statement of purpose, keep it handy. Read it often—especially before each writing period. It will become part of your book's business plan.

Although you still lack a few elements—a good title and a pitch—with a summary, unique angle, list of benefits, and purpose statement, you've got the start of a convincing justification for the writing and publishing of your book.

Create a Title for Your Book

Now it's time to take the work you've completed and create a title for your book. You may already have a title in mind, but more often than not the first—or even second or third—title you come up with doesn't represent the best title. Just as with everything else about your book project, your title must promise readers that the book you've written will add value to their lives in a way that they seek desperately, or that it will fulfill a desire, tell a compelling story, or in some other way serve their interests. It has to answer the question: What's in it for me?

When creating a title for a nonfiction book, you might use:

- a play on words
- alliteration
- a popular phrase
- slang
- your subject's name or title

You might try to highlight something unique about your subject. If your book falls into the self-help genre, you want your title to:

- identify the reader's problem
- offer a solution to a problem
- give readers hope
- be specific and to the point
- cut straight to the chase

Readers shouldn't wonder what nonfiction books are about; the titles should clearly tell them. For example:

- *Change Your Thoughts, Change Your Life* by Wayne Dyer
- *Secrets of the Millionaire Mind* by T. Harv Eker
- *Secrets of Silicon Valley* by Deborah Perry Piscione
- *Unsinkable* by Debbie Reynolds and Dorian Hannaway

- *Give and Take* by Adam Grant
- *Killing Kennedy* by Bill O'Reilly and Martin Dugard
- *Salt Sugar Fat* by Michael Moss

John Kremer, author of *1001 Ways to Market Your Books,* recommends titles that are no more than five words "because short titles are more memorable. You can add a subtitle to give more information. Having a number in the title can be good, too—particularly the number 7 as in *The 7 Habits of Highly Effective People.*

Here are other book titles that contain numbers:

- *101 Things You Need to Know* by Julie Mullarkey-Gnoy
- *The Seven Spiritual Laws of Success* by Deepak Chopra
- *10 Secrets for Success and Inner Peace* by Wayne Dyer
- *The Five Dysfunctions of a Team: A Leadership Fable* by Patrick Lencioni

In *Write the Perfect Book Proposal*, Jeff Herman and Deborah Levine Herman say a book title can be longer if the first few words "provide emotional appeal." Book titles that evoke an emotion do tend to sell well. Readers must feel as if they can't live without the information within your book's covers. Additionally, titles that create what the Hermans call "a motivating visualization" also draw more readers; if readers can "see" in their minds' eyes the end result that will come from reading your book, they are more likely to carry your book to the register.

Kremer says, "Consider coining a word of your own as John Naisbitt did with *Megatrends.*" Or follow the lead of other fiction and nonfiction authors who made their titles "brandable," like:

- Jack Canfield and Mark Victor Hansen's Chicken Soup for the Soul series
- Joshua Piven's *The Worst Case Scenario Survival Handbook*
- Jay Conrad Levinson's The Guerilla Marketing series
- J.K. Rowling's Harry Potter series
- Stephenie Meyer's Twilight Saga
- Ian Rankin's Inspector Rebus series
- R.L. Stine's Goosebumps series
- James Patterson's Alex Cross series
- Stan and Jan Berenstain's Berenstain Bears series
- Ann Rice's The Vampire Chronicles

MANUAL

You can write a much longer subtitle, especially if your title is short or witty and needs further explanation. I like these:

- *Lapsing into a Comma: A Curmudgeon's Guide to the Many Things that Can Go Wrong in Print—and How to Avoid Them*
- *Damn! Why Didn't I Write That? How Ordinary People are Raking in $100,000.00 … or More Writing Nonfiction Books & How You Can Too!*

Fiction titles that offer a sense of story, evoke emotion, or provide a motivational visualization work well, too. Look at some recent bestsellers:

- *Walking Disaster* by Jamie McGuire
- *Fever* by Maya Banks
- *Starting Now* by Debbie Macomber
- *The Host* by Stephenie Meyer
- *Breath of Scandal* by Sandra Brown
- *Bones Are Forever* by Kathy Reichs

It's possible to get a sense of their storylines or a feeling for what they might be about, especially if you know the category or genre in which the author writes. Novels with titles that convey a storyline are a good choice as well, such as:

- *The Boy in the Suitcase* by Lene Kaaberbol and Agnete Friis
- *The Husband's Secret* by Liane Moriarty
- *Under the Dome* by Stephen King
- *The Longest Ride* by Nicholas Sparks

Fiction titles tend to be shorter than Kremer suggests, often just two or three words. Many use genre-recognizable words, such as *blood* for vampire stories, *death* or *killer* for thrillers, *dragons* for fantasy, and *kiss* or *lust* for romance.

If you plan to write a series or have spinoffs, you might want to brand yourself with your book titles (more on this in Step #7). Think J.K. Rowlings' Harry Potter series and Kathy Reichs' *Bones,* and even Janet Evanovich's Stephanie Plum series, which is easily recognizable by the titles (*One for the Money, Two for the Dough,* etc.).

It's also important for book titles to be "searchable" and "discoverable" on the Internet. Therefore, if you can include keywords or keyword phrases in your title, which are the words people use when they conduct Internet searches for topics, you increase the chance your book will be found when potential readers look online for something related to your subject. Nonfiction books often have quite long subtitles in an attempt to include as many keywords as possible. Novelists are using this tactic more and more often.

Training yourself to write a marketable title and subtitle represents an important part of Step #2 in the Author Training Process. It requires seeing your book not just creatively but from a business perspective. The marketing team in a publishing house makes the decision about a book's title. If you self-publish, you must make this decision based on what title will help your book sell the most copies, not on what you like.

Successful books require great titles. Of course, to some extent you never know what will sell or why. Who would have thought books with titles like these would become big hits?

- *The Effect of Gamma Rays on Man-in-the-Moon Marigolds* by Paul Zindel
- *Who Moved My Cheese?* by Spencer Johnson
- *The Happy Hooker* by Xaviera Hollander
- *Eats, Shoots & Leaves* by Lynne Truss
- *The Ominivore's Dilemma* by Michael Pollan

By writing an appropriate title, you will increase the odds of selling your book. Go ahead and use the training exercises in this book. Since you know what your book is about and its benefits, writing a title should come easily at this point, but play around anyway and come up with many options before whittling them down to the perfect title. If you are still not sure what your book is about, this exercise will feel difficult. If this is the case, simply keep working through the Author Training Process and return to this section later. The training exercises and questions will be there when you're ready!

Writing a Pitch or Elevator Speech for Your Book

I was once told, "Nina, if you can't write the subject of your book on the back of a business card, then you don't know what you're writing about." This was my introduction to the concept of a book pitch. Even though you've already written a summary of your book, it's time to hone that to a pitch. Then you'll discover if you *really* know what your book is about.

Start with the business card test. Get a business card, or something the same size (2" × 3½"), turn it over, and write, "My book is about…," and fill in the rest in the amount of space you have. Write in words large enough to be read by anyone without a magnifying glass. Can you do it?

Now, try something a bit longer. Just as you did at the beginning of this step, describe your book's subject, but this time do so using all the information you now possess about your book idea, including the angle, theme, benefits, and purpose. Try to fit this book summary or synopsis into 150 to 300 words. Include your title in this description. (You can go back to your original summary and rewrite and revise it if you like.) Think of this exercise as answering the question, "What is my book about, and why would someone want to read (buy) it?" Produce a concise summary or description of your book. Save this. You will come back and edit or revise this description of your book several times.

Next, save a copy of your summary as a new document. Then edit what you've written down to 100 words and then down to a 50-word book pitch. The final word count doesn't have to include the title. You will use this concise, pointed pitch many times and in many different circumstances—not just at conferences, where you will pitch to agents, but also when you pitch the media, when you provide a book description on Amazon (or other book distributors), when you write guest blog posts or articles, when you create press releases, or when you tell the person sitting next to you on an airplane about your book (and hopefully sell them a copy). Your pitch appears in a query letter, too.

Keep in mind that there is a difference in pitching fiction and nonfiction; memoir, while nonfiction, can be pitched more like fiction because it reads like a novel. Both genres can and should stress the benefits your book provides.

Nonfiction writers should focus a pitch on what the book is about and why it is unique, timely, or needed. The rule of thumb for nonfiction pitches is to answer three questions: Why this book? Why now? Why you?

You should also include information on your market, your book's unique features, and any comparison you can make to another best-selling book, if possible.

Fiction writers should provide the narrative arc in the most creative way possible to hook the listener. Katharine Sands, agent and author of *Making the Perfect Pitch: How to Catch a Literary Agent's Eye*, recommends that a pitch "distill aspects of your work in such a way that it creates alchemy." When pitching fiction, she says, include three elements: Place (setting), Person (who), and Pivot (inciting incident or event).

Chuck Sambuchino, author of *Create Your Writer Platform* and the editor of *Guide to Literary Agents*, offers a four-step pitch formula: Offer the details of your book, such as genre, title, and word count, then a one-sentence log line, a pitch, and a description of your character arc.

James Scott Bell, author of *Self-Publishing Attack! The 5 Absolutely Unbreakable Laws for Creating Steady Income Publishing Your Own Books*, teaches a pitch formula with three sentences.

For nonfiction writers:

- Sentence 1: most gripping question + the specific answer
- Sentence 2: In [title of book] + you will learn …
- Sentence 3: about the author (Who the heck are you?)

For fiction writers:

- Sentence 1: character name + vocation + initial situation
- Sentence 2: when + the doorway of no return (inciting incident)
- Sentence 3: now + death overhanging (physical, profession, or psychological death)

And Rob Eagar, author of *Sell Your Book Like Wildfire: The Writer's Guide to Marketing and Publicity*, says that no matter what you do when pitching, do not answer the question "What is your book about?" Only answer the question: "What's in it for me?" (That's right; it's that WIIFM? factor again.)

I thought the following was the final version of my pitch for this book—49 words (without the title and subtitle).

> *Evaluate Your Book for Success!: 9 Steps Every Writer Must Take to Guarantee an Idea Has What It Takes to Attract Readers and Publishers,* will be the first book to show aspiring authors how to use the step-by-step process of compiling the information necessary for a nonfiction book proposal to evaluate themselves, their ideas, their book proposals, and their manuscripts or books so they can produce traditionally or independently published books that sell.

I felt I needed the extra words to be more specific, but later I reduced it to 28 words this way.

> *Evaluate Your Book for Success!: 9 Steps Every Writer Must Take to Guarantee an Idea Has What It Takes to Attract Readers and Publishers* will show aspiring authors how to evaluate themselves, their ideas, their book proposals, and their manuscripts so they produce traditionally or independently published books that sell.

MANUAL

Before my agent submitted the book proposal to Writer's Digest Books, I took another crack at the pitch because I had, in fact, re-angled the whole idea and the title to make it more marketable. (Agent Katharine Sands thought that the word *evaluate* in my title might turn some readers off and suggested I come up with another title.) That suggestion generated this 42-word pitch:

> *The Nonfiction Author Training Manual: 9 Steps to Create Ideas Readers Crave and Become the Partner Publishers Seek,* will be the first book to show aspiring nonfiction authors how to ensure both they and their ideas have what it takes to succeed—that they know how to produce traditionally or independently published books that sell to readers and to publishers.

I reworked the subtitle after the book sold—*9 Steps to Prepare You and Your Book Idea for Publishing Success*—to increase marketability and search optimization. Writer's Digest Books dropped *nonfiction* from the title, and the marketing team finalized the subtitle to what you see on the cover, keeping salability and search-engine optimization (SEO) in mind. (You will learn how to do this in future steps and come back to refine many of the pieces of your Overview.)

"Writing a great pitch forces you, as one writing teacher once told me, 'to give up your darlings,' and get to the heart's core of the writing project," Megge shared. "Everything else is chaff for the wind." Indeed, she related, "Working on my pitch and Overview has taken months and given me invaluable insights. As I shape and edit, I get closer and closer to what I really want to say."

Create an Overview of Your Book

To finish the Overview step of the Author Training Process, take the 150- to 300-word book summary or description you wrote earlier, your book pitch, and your list of book benefits, and combine them into one document that you will place at the beginning of your business plan. You can also include your theme and purpose statement if you wrote them. Later, when you have compiled the information on your markets and your competition and you've written your table of contents and chapter summaries, you will return to this document to add or revise this information.

A formal Overview for a book proposal includes, in this order:

1. **A hook**—this is similar to an article's lead paragraph.

2. **A book pitch**—the short summarization of your book or story with a slant toward reader interest or benefit; for fiction, this could be one short sentence, sometimes called a log line. As stated earlier, this sometimes includes your title, purpose, and angle in a catchy way.

3. **A synopsis**—a one- to five-paragraph summary of your book, going into further details about what you plan to offer the reader.

4. **Book features**—a word count, special features, illustrations, as well as the back matter (glossary, appendix, etc.) you expect to include in your book.

5. **A description or list of benefits**—these two bulleted lists are most commonly found in nonfiction proposals but can be used for fiction as well.

Remember, you are creating a marketing document with the intention of selling your book "idea" to a publisher or to yourself. Later you will sell it to readers.

If you plan to include any special features in your book, describe these in your Overview as well. Special features might include things like end-of-chapter questions, epigraphs, meditations, tips, exercises, charts, photos, etc.

Use everything you have learned and created in this step to put your Overview together. When you are done, you should have a two-page document that accurately describes your book. It should read like marketing copy. Most important, it should sell your book.

"Defining the subcomponents of an effective book Overview is exactly the process I needed to help me get beyond the beginning of my own book proposal," claims Victoria Hudson, author of *No Red Pen: Writers, Writing Groups & Critique*. "Even though I was using excellent resources for how to write a proposal, I found the examples and descriptions lacking, as often too much information or experience was assumed. As an emerging writer and first book author, I needed to drill well down into the procedure in order to understand what I was trying to create when writing the book proposal or business plan."

Read your Overview carefully, whether it is in "rough-draft form" for your business plan or written more formally for a proposal. Ask yourself if this is the book you plan to write—and want to write. Ask yourself if you think readers want this book, or, better yet, *need* to read this book. Does it address their interests? Does it answer their real question: WIIFM? Ask yourself if this document provides enough compelling information to make a venture capital partner (a publisher) want to read the rest of your business plan and if it provides enough justification for the writing and publishing of your project to entice a publisher to ask to see more or for you to proceed with the project as an indie publisher

MANUAL

If so, you've competed the first step in the proposal process and are on your way to conceiving a successful book.

If not, your idea may have a low likelihood of success at this point, which means you may need to go back to the drawing board. Or you might need to revise your idea, find another use for it, or start fresh. It's also possible you need to adjust the content you include in your book; in this case, keep moving forward through the steps and see what happens as you flesh out your concept.

You must determine the source of the problem, however, and resolve it. If that's not possible, you may need to give up on this particular book idea and come up with a new one. If you need help evaluating your idea objectively, hire a professional book doctor, a book coach, or an author coach. Asking someone with a different perspective than yours to look at the "big picture" can help you find the answers you seek—a new angle or theme to your book idea or even a new market or structure. It may be easier for an "outsider" to see your idea from a business perspective.

Hopefully, at this point you know exactly what your book's about and why someone would want to read (buy) it. That means you know what benefit your book will provide readers, and in turn, when you begin writing you'll know what commitments to keep to them. Plus, anytime someone asks you what your book is about, you can tell them—and it won't take more than thirty seconds to do so. It also means you've trained yourself to think like a successful author. You've begun to look at your project with an Author Attitude. *WOOT!*

Reading Suggestions:

Crafting Titles by Elizabeth James

 # Book Title Tweet Book01: 140 Bite-Sized Ideas for Compelling Article, Book, and Event Titles by Roger C. Parker

Making the Perfect Pitch: How to Catch a Literary Agent's Eye by Katharine Sands

STEP #3

Analyze How Many People *Really* Might Buy Your Book

I've often heard this advice: Write the book you want to read. It's good advice if you want to read a book many people want or need. However, if you are the only one, or one of just a few people interested in reading such a book, its not advice you want to follow.

Maybe you are one of those writers who doesn't care if your book has a market or any prospective readers. You simply have an idea for a book and want to write it. You feel passionate about your topic. You feel you *must* write your book no matter what—even if only a few people end up reading (buying) it. I call this writing "the book of your heart." In this case, it may not matter to you if you sell one copy or one hundred because you probably define success as writing and publishing the book you want to write.

I pass no judgment on you or any other aspiring author with this goal. Everyone has his or her own idea of success. You should write the book you feel passionate about writing. However, I believe that if you explore your motivations further, you'll probably find you write because you want to be read and to impact readers' lives. It's fine to express yourself with no thought of who will read your work or if anyone will ever read your work, if you want to keep a journal. However, writers who author books typically do so to have someone read what they write—the more people, the better. That's why you must be concerned with more than self-expression if you want to produce a successful book.

Assuming you want to achieve the goal of successful authorship, at this point you must train yourself to see your idea with your book's target market in mind and consider the impact market size will have on your potential book sales.

What's a Market and Why Do You Need One?

As a writer who wants someone *in addition to yourself* to read your work, you need an *audience* for your book. You can't write "the book you want to read" and make it successful unless lots of other people are just like you or have the same interests as you. This means that *before you write your book* you have to discover if, indeed, it will have an audience.

In the publishing industry, your audience—these "other people" who might be interested in reading (or buying) your book—are called your book's "market" or "target market." In Step #3 of the Author Training Process, *Analyze How Many People* Really *Might Buy Your Book,* you will train yourself to see if your book idea has the kind of market that makes it a viable publishing project. As you do so, you find your readers and get to know them. This requires:

- Identifying your audience
- Profiling your readers
- Familiarizing yourself with your readers
- Identifying how many potential readers exist for your book
- Determining where your readers "hang out" both virtually and in the "real" world

If you want to publish a successful book, you must have a market that produces enough book sales to reach your own sales goals or those of a publisher. Many aspiring authors write their books without first evaluating markets to determine if enough interest exists to support sales of their books and, thereby, publication. Or they propose books to publishers without doing so only to be rejected because no market exists for their books or the market is too small.

Training yourself to look at your book's market critically accomplishes five things:

1. You discover if enough potential readers exist for your book; if so, you can move forward with the project.
2. You get the chance to consider new potential markets to target.
3. You can re-evaluate the angle of your book to target larger, more profitable markets with your content.
4. You can identify how to adjust your promotion plan in order to target larger markets.
5. You can write for your reader.

From a publisher's perspective, the bigger the market for your book, the better. The reason is simple: The more potential readers for your book, the more potential buyers for your book; the more potential buyers for your book, the more potential money your book might earn over time. Your venture capital partner, the publisher, might earn back his investment and make money—and so might you. If you self-publish, you might earn back the money you invest in your own project. Low risk is a good thing for a potential book project.

Can You Describe Your Market?

I edited a proposal for an aspiring author who had written a memoir about her escape from Egypt to America. The original document simply said the book would be of interest to Muslims as well as to Americans interested in the news about the Arab Spring. Additionally, since a woman had written the book and the book was about a woman, she felt it would have appeal to female readers. That's all the information she offered about markets.

All of that was true, but the information was not specific enough to really determine whether her book had the potential to sell well. She needed to do more research to find out how many people might actually purchase her book—how many people comprised the markets she mentioned.

We did that research and discovered the following statistics based on a study conducted by the Pew Research Center's Forum on Religion & Public Life and released in 2011:

- The world's Muslim population is expected to increase by about 35 percent in the next twenty years, rising from 1.6 billion in 2010 to 2.2 billion by 2030.
- If current trends continue, Muslims will make up 26.4 percent of the world's total projected population of 8.3 billion in 2030.
- In the United States, the population projections show the number of Muslims more than doubling over the next two decades, rising from 2.6 million in 2010 to 6.2 million in 2030.

Those statistics prove a market exists for the book—a large market any publisher should find propitious. We also found market statistics on the secondary women's market the author planned to target:

- Women buy 72 percent of all books given as gifts, according to a 1991 Gallup survey, and considering the fact below, this likely hasn't changed much.
- Women bought 64 percent of all books sold in 2009, according to a study conducted by the publishing research firm Bowker.
- Women make up 55 percent of the U.S. population.

Again, the market for her book is more clearly defined by these figures.

Carla King wrote about her adventures riding motorcycles in her self-published book *American Borders: A Solo Circumnavigation of the United States on a Russian Sidecar Motorcycle*. This might seem like a memoir that wouldn't interest too many people. In fact, her audience includes some six million people who have motorcycles registered in the United States. The exact number of motorcycle riders could be larger since some riders are passengers and not owners. Many people also ride off-road bikes, and these do not require a license. Some estimates put the number of people in the United States who ride motorcycles at least once a year at seven million.

Surprisingly, a good portion of those people are female—a good thing for King. The Motorcycle Industry Council reported in 2009 that the number of female motorcycle operators in the United States increased to about 7.2 million out of 27 million overall riders. About one in ten owners at that time were women. The American Motorcyclist Association has about 225,000 members as of this printing. While the number of female members is under 10 percent, the number of new female members is increasing.

According to King, *American Borders* enjoys a significant number of nonmotorcycling readers, as will her upcoming *China Road Motorcycle Diaries*, such as those who like adventure, travel, and women's issues. "One woman who read it recommended it as being 'part *Zen and the Art of Motorcycle Maintenance* and part Harlequin Romance,'" she says.

Yet, many men purchase *American Borders*, especially around the holidays. "I make the most money at motorcycle shows that take place around Christmas, when lots of gift buying is happening. A book about a woman adventure motorcycling is very popular with guys who are trying to get their gals on a bike. It's better than buying lingerie!" she claims. Her online holiday sales correspond with that holiday trend as well.

A book does not have to have a huge market, though. It's possible to sell a lot of books by targeting your work to a niche market. Self-publishing expert and author Dan Poynter provides a good example of an author who has written books for small niche markets. He self-published *The Parachute Manual: A Technical Treatise on the Parachute*. About 350,000 people complete more than three million jumps in a typical year. There are about four hundred skydiving centers scattered across the United States. Most are located on smaller outlying airports. That's not a huge market by any means, but it's an engaged market that spends a fair amount of money on its hobby, he says. And, more important to the author, these people are easy to find and reach.

A book that might seem to have a small audience might still be a viable project. A small hobby or interest could have hundreds of thousands of potential readers—and that's just in the United States. If you also consider the potential of selling your book internationally, the audience grows larger.

A novelist can and should consider target markets as well. The rise of the chick-lit category, for instance, came out of the market for those books, which can be described as smart, fun fiction for and/or about women of all ages. Knowing how many women purchase books, it's obvious why mom lit has grown into a category of its own, too. There are novels targeted at those who enjoy reading about female detectives, time travel, particular time periods, and even knitting.

Recently, paranormal fiction has sold well because so many people are interested in things like telekinesis and clairvoyance. Such people—young and old—represent a target market. Novelists can choose almost any target market—Generation X, people who love to travel, adults or children who love to cook, those who have elderly parents living at home, individuals touched by suicide, parents with gay children, or singles who adopt pets—and write novels to target these markets. You need only craft stories that include characters, themes, and details that relate to those readers' interests and experiences.

Traditionally, novelists have not done much market analysis, but such research will help you write a better book and sell more books—to both publishers and readers. Novelist C.S. Lakin lets a publisher know what market she plans to target when she writes a book proposal. For example, here is a market statement describing her Sacred Sites series:

> The Sacred Sites books are written for a wide audience with sophistication of language and themes that will find much appeal with both Christian and mainstream fantasy readers. And although these books deal with scriptural themes and use biblical Hebrew, they are written so those of any (or no) faith will enjoy them.

Keep in mind that market interests change quickly and what seems like a hot topic right now probably has already turned cold for most publishers. As agent Verna Dreisbach points out, "Take, for example, the DaVinci and vampire type books. Once they are out, the market has probably already changed. That's when a lot of novice writers start writing a vampire book. By the time agents get that manuscript, that market has come and gone, and publishers are way over it—considering time spent writing, pitching, acquiring, editing, marketing, and getting the book to print. By then publishers have moved on to zombies. Writers can't necessarily write to the current market. They have to be ahead of the game, finding new markets and interests, too."

This happened with books on yoga, for example. Booksellers were overstocked and had too many choices. "That meant publishers weren't buying any, which meant if you wrote a yoga book, you were out of luck," says Dreisbach.

To stay up on what types of books publishers are purchasing now, you must watch industry trends. Read *Publishers Weekly* (the free or paid subscription), read industry blogs and columns, and keep an eye on what bookstores carry. Then try to be a trendsetter rather than riding on the coattails of current bestsellers or trends.

You Need Actual Figures to Determine the Size of Your Market

An agent or acquisitions editor who receives a query or proposal for a book with no discernable market or a market that appears too small will send a rejection to that author even if the idea is a good one or the writer is skilled in his or her craft. A platform and promotion plan will not save the idea. To whom would the author promote the book? With no market, the author has no potential book buyers, no potential readers. Remember, the publishing industry revolves around selling books. No market means no one will buy the book.

As you create a market analysis for your book, be specific. Use numbers to describe your market size. In Lakin's example above, she could add statistics on Christian and fantasy readers, as well as spiritual fantasy readers, to bolster her market description.

Imagine if you were an agent or acquisitions editor and received a proposal for a book about creating change in people's lives, and the author described her book's market this way:

> In the general self-help market, a huge and ever-popular area of publishing, [Book Title] will appeal to all readers wanting to improve their ability to receive their desires, fulfill their purpose, develop a connection with God, raise their consciousness, or manifest what they want in their lives. Anyone looking for a way to better themselves, move farther along the spiritual path, or improve their current conditions will find this book useful.

What might you think? Would you be inclined to back this project? As an indie publisher, would this be enough information to make you feel secure that your book has potential buyers, confident enough to put your money into the project?

The author's market sounds pretty large but also somewhat broad. It's hard to *really* know if her market is large enough or targeted enough.

What if the same author sent you the following information instead?

> "[Book Title], which offers readers concrete steps to learn how to make time work for them, not against them, will appeal to those interested in the Law of Attraction, personal growth, and all forms of manifesting dreams and desires. It targets the same 70,000+ people who attended Oprah's Internet class with author Eckhart Tolle to discuss his last book, *A New Earth*. Its market also includes the same readers who purchased over 21 million copies of Rhonda Byrne's best-selling *The Secret*; that book and film grossed $300 million in sales, according to a January 15, 2009, article by Forbes. Additionally, the market for this book includes cultural creatives, a group of people who in the last half century have grown from 50 million in number to hundreds of millions around the world.

If the author wanted to take this further—which she did—she could also tell an agent or publisher that her book targets women. And, as we know, women purchase the majority of books in the United States and make up more than half of the country's population.

Brad Henderson could have described the market for his proposed book on grammar this way:

> *Grammar Rocks* will target the large number of adults who need grammar help in their professional and personal lives.

Or this way, as he actually did in his book proposal:

> *Grammar Rocks* is designed to be a just-in-time solution for adults who have completed their education and now need review and additional instruction in grammar to acquire the missing pieces either skipped or skimmed by modern schools. As such, the 129 million American adult men and women, ages nineteen through forty-nine, who are products of a post-1960s holistic writing education that skipped grammar essentials make up the primary market for this book.

The second description offers specifics that a publisher—indie or traditional—will find useful.

Sometimes you may not know the exact number of people who make up a market—you may not have the statistics. Other available figures, however, can support a market for a book as well. This is where Google and other search engines "become your friends," as the saying goes. Begin inputting short questions or keywords (search terms) into the search engine, and see what you discover. Play around with the keywords and keyword phrases you use in your searches, such as "Generation X," "number of Muslims living in US," or "How many motorcycle owners in US," and see what comes up. (Just make sure the figures you use come from a reputable source.) No matter what genre describes your book, you can discover market statistics of some sort—how many people or large groups of people who would be interested in purchasing your book.

Consider paranormal fiction, like the books best-selling author Amanda Hocking writes. I did a Google search at the time of this writing for "paranormal forums" and found 116,000 to 10,200,000 results (depending on whether I put quotation marks around the words), and Facebook has pages of listings for paranormal groups. A Google search for "paranormal blogs" brought up 41,300,000 listings, and almost every state in America has a paranormal association of some sort, as do most European countries. You can find ghost conferences and UFO groups almost anywhere in the world. If you did some digging, you could come up with the number of people who attended those conferences or joined the associations.

With this information, you can avoid saying, "Hocking's books sell well, so mine will, too." Instead, you could say, "Here's the reason there is a market for my novel, which, like Hocking's books, is about vampires." (You could also include the number of books that Hocking and other authors in that category have sold.)

If Catharine, the author with the self-help book, singled out a particular type of person who wants to create the specific personal change she wants to write about, she could make the book's market appeal more apparent with specific figures like those mentioned above. This would involve pinpointing the book's angle and how it targets the market or markets. In this case, the author has singled out readers who "want to control time, use time, manage time, or have time work for them." No statistics are available to indicate the size of this market, but the Google Keyword Tool indicates that 823,000 global monthly searches and 246,000 local monthly searches are conducted for the phrase "time management." A Google search on "time management" shows the popularity of the subject—1,980,000,000 results. The aspiring author could use these figures to demonstrate that her book addresses a common interest; it answers the WIIFM? question for both men and women.

If you wanted to write a book about how to grow a particular type of orchid, you could use a search engine to discover how many people purchase that particular orchid or how many people purchase orchids each year. I did just that on Google with the keyword phrase "how many people purchase orchids," and here's what I discovered, thanks to the University of Michigan Department of Horticulture Orchid Research Program.

> Orchids are currently the second most valuable potted crop in the United
> States with a total wholesale value of $144 million in 2005. ... In 2005, 18 mil-
> lion potted orchids were sold at wholesale, with an average unit value of $8.00
> (USDA 2006b).

Now, not all of those were sold in the United States, and the information was not current. Yet, given that I purchase orchids and know other people who purchase orchids, I realize that orchid lovers are extremely engaged in orchid growing and buying and that they spend a lot of money per year on products related to orchids. They also attend orchid shows. Even if you don't know much about specialty orchids, you need only visit a grocery store to see that orchids are a popular plant to purchase. If you were writing a nonfiction book on orchids (or on one particular orchid), you could make some phone calls—to the University of Michigan or to the American Orchid Society or to any one of the many orchid shows across America, for instance—and get current sales figures as well as additional statistics that would help you create a picture of your market size (the number of people who attend orchid shows each year). This is how you determine or indicate the size of your market.

Let's apply this orchid example to a novel. Imagine you are writing a thriller in which the killer leaves an orchid bloom at the scene of every crime. Each bloom is from a different type of exotic orchid plant. Now you can tell an acquisitions editor that your book will appeal to the many readers interested in thrillers and also to the 18 million people who purchased orchids in the United States in 2005 alone.

If you write a novel about a dancer, your target market could include the millions of people who watch *Dancing with the Stars, So You Think You Can Dance,* and *Dance Moms.* You could research the number of people who actually call in to vote for contests on certain shows that allow voting. Or Google each television show's ratings. I easily discovered that in 2010, *Dancing with the Stars* had 21.3 million viewers, causing it to rise above *NBC's Sunday Night Football,* according to Nielsen ratings, which estimate what people are watching based on a group of paid viewers. I also found out that in 2012, *Dancing with the Stars* aired to 18.5 million viewers.

If you were to write a detective series in which the main character has a sidekick who is a dog, you could target dog owners and veterinarians. A Google search for "how many dog owners in the US" led me to this data: According to the 2011–2012 APPA National Pet Owners Survey, 46.3 million U.S. households own a dog. When I did a similar search for the number of veterinarians in the United States, a *New York Times* article reported roughly 91,000 working vets in the country.

Re-Angle Your Market for Success

Once you know the market size—whether it's big or niche—it's time to evaluate your idea with that market in mind. Determine if your book idea seems viable or how to make it viable based on the information you have accumulated. Should you:

- continue forward with your project?
- go back to square one and conceive a new idea with a bigger market or a more viable niche market?
- rework or re-angle your current book idea to fit a market, thus making it a salable project?

Those book ideas that have no market at all or are indefinable as far as specific figures go are best abandoned—that is, if you want to produce a successful book by publishing industry standards. If not, you can pursue ideas as indie projects—and books of your heart. However, an agent or publisher will not take on a project unless it has a promising market. As part of your training, you need to learn to evaluate your project objectively with this in mind. Know that you are taking a risk if you choose to proceed with a book that has no market—a risk a seasoned publishing professional most likely would not take.

Small publishing houses might be willing to take a risk on a book with a small or niche market—if some other factors are in place as well, such as a strong author platform and promotion plan. Additionally, an analysis of competing books must indicate that your proposed book might meet or exceed their sales figures. (We will go over such analyses in forthcoming steps.) Knowing this, if you want to have your book traditionally published, you will need to look at your market statistics and make an objective determination about what type of publisher to approach.

If you have a market with promising figures, moving forward may seem like a no-brainer. However, sometimes a large market isn't necessarily the best thing. An agent or acquisitions editor might look at your book idea and think, "This book might not sell well because the market is *too* large. It's not unique enough to gain traction there." Saying "*x* number of millions of people are buying thrillers" isn't specific enough and is a very broad statement. What kind of thrillers? By what kind of authors? Use your book's angles and themes to narrow it down for publishers. In such a case, a smaller market serves your book better. This could also lead you to change the angle of your book to target a more unique market.

I was asked to do this with a book I wanted to sell about making Jewish Sabbath observance meaningful and spiritual. My agent told me I would have an easier time selling the book (to a publisher and to readers) if I angled it to the Jewish women's market. This way I could target the real book buyers in the Jewish market. So before we submitted to acquisitions editors, I re-angled my book proposal.

Sometimes, however, it's good to go broader with your market. Prior to landing an agent for my Sabbath book, I approached a few small independent publishers on my own. One of them asked me to broaden my market by including all religions that celebrate the Sabbath. In this way, they felt they could sell more books. In their eyes, the book was a less risky project if they could sell it in a more general religious category or to all religious faiths. As you can see: one book, many market options, many ways to write it.

Remember the aspiring author who intended to target his book to the single-mother market? When he discovered some of the mothers for whom he was writing were actually married but perceived themselves as parenting alone, he not only targeted a much broader market—mothers in general—he also had to change the language he used as he wrote the book.

Charlene originally wanted to write a self-help book for women. When she realized corporate readers, including men, might be interested in her work-life balance concepts, she changed her target market. She also changed the title of her book and some of the content. Her author platform also supported this change.

Market research conducted during her Author Training helped Rhonda determine the best audience for her memoir and narrow the time period and subject matter she would address. She began thinking her book's market was people involved in adoption, but she later expanded it to people who have experienced grief and loss, as well as adoption. "When it comes to memoir, which is a slice of life focused on specific theme and plot, writing to my market helped me pare down my story to reach an intended audience," Rhonda explains. "I was buried with too many thoughts and angles. Looking at my market helped me determine what needed to be included in this slice of life. I went from drowning in too much information to a framed idea that would reach my audience."

Penney and Dawn, who were planning to co-author a book on social media, discovered that in 2009 there were 27.5 million small businesses in the United States, according to the Office of Advocacy. "This was the most current number we could find, so I'm sure that the number of small businesses that were started in 2012 is even larger. Once we saw this number, we knew we made the right choice to target small business owners," says Penney. "Since both of us work as social media consultants, we realize that almost every small business owner can find a reason to use social media to help them grow their business. Seeing these numbers assured us that we have a large audience available to purchase our book."

MANUAL

Write for Your Market

In these examples, after re-angling book ideas to meet a bigger (or different) market, the writers needed to write their books in a way that targeted their new or enlarged market. This is a key point. You need to ensure you write your book in such a way that you do, indeed, make it relevant to all the people in your market. More simply said, write for your market—or all of your markets.

This involves knowing not only the size of your market but also who makes up your market. At this point, you need to actually get to know individual readers. Instead of looking at the size of your market, break it down into the readers for whom you are writing so you can write with clarity and purpose.

Find ways to get to know your ideal reader by:

- listening to conversations in online groups
- asking questions in online forums
- having conversations on Twitter
- responding to queries on LinkedIn
- participating in Google Plus groups
- attending events
- joining organizations
- conducting online research

From your time spent on these activities, determine your readers' demographics, spending habits, lifestyle, income, etc. Then describe your reader in detail—as if you were creating a character in a novel. When you can do this, you can write for your reader, and all the many people in your market will find your book relatable.

When Rhonda started networking online with potential readers of her memoir, she claims her writing changed—it relaxed, and she began to feel she was writing a letter to the reader. "Joining social networks, following blogs, and interacting with those in my audience deepened my focus and direction and allowed my writing to become interesting to others. Until I was able to focus on the reader, my writing was too vague," she explains.

As you look at your markets, don't be so wedded to your idea that you aren't willing to consider a new angle for your book or new potential markets. Take a big-picture view—an objective view. Could you write your book so it hits the best market, the one that makes your book the most viable—the most attractive to publishers and to the most readers? Train yourself to see more than the initial readers and groups you thought you would target. Be willing to create a book idea and to write a book that targets the market or markets that will help you and your book become the most successful it can be. Once you have completed your research, be sure to write a target market paragraph that's similar to the ones found earlier in this section (using specific figures and demographics), and place it in your journal. When you can do this clearly and effectively, you have completed Step #3 in the Author Training process. *WOOT!*

Suggested Reading:

Blue Ocean Strategy: How To Create Uncontested Market Space And Make The Competition Irrelevant by W. Chan Kim and Renee Mauborgne

The Handbook of Online Marketing Research: Knowing Your Customer Using the Net by Joshua Grossnickle and Oliver Raskin

Marketing Research Kit for Dummies by Michael Hyman

MANUAL

STEP #4

Compare the Competition and Discover If Your Idea Is Unique and Necessary

Most aspiring authors believe their ideas are unique and that readers absolutely need to read their books. Like these writers, you probably feel convinced that your book idea is new, fresh, timely, different, and essential. You may feel certain that readers must read the information you have to offer, the arguments you want to make, or the stories you have to tell. You might even possess a sense of urgency to write and publish now, and if you don't want to do it as an indie publisher, you may feel sure a publisher will want to take on your project and get it into print ASAP. Great!

I often have felt that way about my book ideas, and I still do when an idea first strikes. It's great to feel passionate, enthusiastic, and confident when the proverbial lightbulb goes on, but those feelings—and your conviction—simply aren't good enough reasons to publish a book. You must have the facts to back your convictions, facts that unequivocally prove your idea is unique and necessary in the marketplace. These facts must convince a literary agent first, and an acquisitions editor second. They also must convince you, especially if you plan to self-publish.

Unfortunately, your passion, intuition, or gut instinct (and I'm a big believer in all three) are not enough when it comes to making decisions about book publishing—at least not if you want to publish a successful book. If you simply trust your gut or take inspired action, you may not sell many of your self-published books, and that means you won't make back your investment. A publisher likely won't take a risk on your book if you can't show hard data and research to back up these emotional responses to your project. That's why Step #4 in the Author Training Process asks you to do the evaluation necessary to *Discover If Your Idea Is Unique and Necessary* enough to succeed in the target market you chose in Step #2, *Know What Your Book Is About and Why Someone Would Want to Read (Buy) It.*

A book-coaching client of mine shelved one book idea for another (in the time frame of just one week) as she followed her passions and interests. This second book idea resulted from a talk she had been asked to give for an organization. She was excited about this speaking opportunity and the topic, which related to the overall subject matter about which she originally wanted to write. She said she would come back to the original book idea, but now she wanted to pursue this newer concept, which she believed was singular.

Preparing for her presentation made her realize she had the foundation for a book, she says. The process of determining what she would talk about required her to go through a similar process to outlining the contents of a book; she'd even come up with an acronym she liked and that she thought worked well. Indeed, she had most of the elements that comprise a book—if she angled it correctly for her market, which was women who want to assume leadership roles at work.

Here's the problem she faced: This writer had no idea how many other books already existed on the topic of women and leadership—16,774 were listed on Amazon when I looked. She hadn't even thought to look at similar books in a bookstore or on Amazon.com. Not only that, she had not considered:

- how her book would be different from other books written and published on the topic
- how her book might complement other published books in some manner
- if the particular category of books required another book on this topic
- how to make her book stand out from the pack

Why? She felt certain it was unique and necessary because she'd thought of it and was excited and passionate about it. She assumed her book would be different, unique, and necessary, especially since she worked with and spoke with the women in her target market—those who were leaders or wanted to become leaders in business. She had large plans to boot. She wanted to expand her market to men as well, yet her acronym, which she planned to include in her book title, was rather feminine and would likely turn off most men at first glance (if not some women as well).

"I don't think you'll attract many men with a book directed toward women or with that title," I said. Her smile faded. "Have you checked out any other books on the market that are like yours?" She shook her head and looked down at the stack of papers she had printed out to show me—her PowerPoint presentation.

The more I explained how her book had to be different, unique, necessary—how it had to "fill a hole on the shelf in the bookstore"—the more her excitement turned into disappointment.

Like her, you have to determine if there is, indeed, a space on the shelf where your book would sit in a brick-and-mortar bookstore, a space where a book is currently missing, a book that has not been written yet, a book that is needed and that is unlike all the other published books in its category, such as self-help, history, science fiction, or women's studies—a unique and necessary book.

The Competitive Analysis and How It Helps Angle Your Book

As I explained all of this to my client, she felt that her great idea no longer sounded quite so good.

In fact, it still might have been a good—even great—idea. Targeting men could have worked if she did it strategically. But that word—*strategically*—is the key. She needed to evaluate her project against the competition, something required if she intended to sell her idea to an agent or publisher, and necessary if she planned to self-publish. She would have to prove how her idea stood up against the books already published. Not only that, she would have to show how it would rise above the competition.

To discover if your book will fill a hole on the bookstore shelf—or if there even is a hole waiting to be filled—compare your project to existing books in its category and evaluate the pros and cons of the competition so you can highlight your project's pros. Compile a list of books—at least ten or fifteen—that will directly compete with yours. Later you should narrow this down to five key books, but start broad and narrow it down later. Based on this comparison, you can determine if you can do a better job with your subject than authors who have come before you. Indeed, if you can produce an objective "competitive analysis," you can evaluate how you need to change or tweak your book concept to make it matchless in its category and indispensable in its target market.

To conduct a competitive and complementary book analysis, take a trip to both online and physical bookstores. Look for books that are similar to yours. Do this online using search terms that are the same or similar to your book topic in search engines and related sites. Try these websites:

- Amazon.com
- BarnesandNoble.com
- WriterDigestShop.com
- Goodreads.com
- LibraryThing.com
- Google.com search
- NetGalley.com
- BookDepository.com

In a physical bookstore, look in the appropriate category or ask a salesclerk, "Where can I find books like ... ," and describe your book. (Try using your pitch!) The clerk will direct you to the right section and shelf. There you can begin exploring. Bring a pad and pencil, and take notes. This research will be the foundation for your comparative analysis.

This competitive analysis parallels the nonfiction book proposal section called "Competing Books" (or sometimes called "Competitive Analysis"). In this section of your proposal, you provide agents and acquisitions editors with a detailed look at what traditionally published books have been written on your topic and how your book compares to them. (Publishers don't care about self-published books.) This convinces a publisher that the book you plan to write is different and will add something new that existing titles don't offer. For the sake of the Author Training Process, if you plan to self-publish your book, your analysis might benefit from an evaluation of best-selling indie books that compete with or complement your book project.

My student Marianne was looking for competing books on a particular type of holiday giving—creative gifts that support families in need. When she had trouble finding competitive titles, we discussed studying books with similar themes, such as supporting families in need, creative gift giving, and making holidays meaningful. Like her, you might need to be creative and look at the themes and angles you have taken with your book. Or you might need to look only at complementary titles. (More on this below.)

List these competitive books by bestseller status or by publication date first. Also, gather information such as title, subtitle, author, publisher, copyright year, number of pages, paperback or hardcover, and price.

From your research on the books, write two statements (they do not have to be full sentences) that reveal the positive and negative aspects of each book, explaining what the book offers the reader and what it doesn't. Focus these statements on how each book's content is similar to your idea or different, how they help readers (by answering their questions or solving their problems) or don't, and how their structure is different or the same. Finally, include a paragraph comparing these books to your proposed book, and you as an author to these authors, if relevant. When you have done all of this, you have completed a general competitive analysis. You can complete this activity using the training exercises in this book and your journal. We will look at a more detailed example later.

The "Complementary Books" section of a proposal, which typically follows the Competing Books section, offers a chance to evaluate your book in relation to similar books on the market rather than direct competition. Competitive and comparative titles may sound like the same things, but there's a difference: Comparative books may resemble your project in general subject matter, category, or even storyline but won't contain the same specific information, advice or tools, personal experiences, journey, or story. You might or might not find them on the same shelf. For example, a book about how to write a book proposal is complemented by a book on how to write query letters.

A man e-mailed me with a question about his memoir on the topic of dating, relationships, and healing a broken heart. Other memoirs on these topics or similar topics written by a man would represent direct competition. Complementary books for his book project would be any of the many similar stories told by women or the prescriptive nonfiction books about dating, relationships, or healing from a broken relationship. (Surprisingly, I only found twenty-seven memoirs on Amazon when I searched with the keywords "memoir romantic relationship," and only three were written by men.)

For my client with the business book for female leaders, competing books include the thousands I found on women and leadership, such as *Lean In: Women, Work, and the Will to Lead* by Sheryl Sandberg and *How Remarkable Women Lead: The Breakthrough Model for Work and Life* by Joanna Barsh, Susie Cranston, and Geoffrey Lewis. *Her Place at the Table: A Woman's Guide to Negotiating Five Key Challenges to Leadership Success* by Deborah M. Kolb Ph.D., Judith Williams Ph.D., and Carol Frohlinger JD and *Stiletto Network: Inside the Women's Power Circles That Are Changing the Face of Business* by Pamela Ryckman would represent complementary books for her project because they are about specific aspects of leadership and women—negotiating and power circles.

In the Complementary Books section of your business plan, list five to ten books. Include the same basic information you included for the books you deemed competition (title, subtitle, author, publisher, copyright year, number of pages, paperback or hardcover, and price). Provide an analysis for each that compares your book to these books or compares you as an author to these authors, if the latter is relevant.

Do not underestimate the importance of this step in the Author Training Process. And if you don't think your book has any competition, look carefully at complementary books (although most books have at least some competition). Don't, however, skip this step. It's a rare book that is "the only one" of its kind, which is why agents and publishers cringe when they see a proposal that says, "This book has no competition." Such a statement is a tip-off that an aspiring author hasn't done her homework or suggests a lack of market for her project. If you want to create a successful book, you need to go to the trouble of producing a competitive analysis for your business plan.

Why a Competitive Analysis Is So Important to Your Business Plan

I have twice (that I know of) had publishing houses reject my proposals because of the Complementary Books section—not because I hadn't researched or written it well or excluded it but because they felt the books I listed hadn't sold enough copies. As I mentioned before, sales are very important to publishers and publishing companies. That is why you must train yourself to look carefully at the competition your book faces. The list of competing (and/ or complementary) books included in a book proposal indicates the sales potential of your book. In other words, the sales track records of books similar to the one you are proposing show how well your book might sell in the same category or markets.

You may think stiff competition, such as several best-selling books, bodes poorly for your book idea. In fact, that isn't true. The fact that there are many bestsellers in your category proves a market exists for books like yours; people are purchasing those books consistently. If you can evaluate these other books and ensure your idea is unique and that it offers new benefits to readers, you can demonstrate to a publisher (or to yourself) that it will sell just as well—if not better. You want to consider how you can capture those same readers and some new ones, too. If you can't do that, your book won't get the nod from a publishing house, which means it should not get the nod from you as an indie publisher either.

Let me give you two clear examples of this concept. Recently my literary agent pitched an idea to a midsize publisher. While several of the competing books had sold well, only one had become a bestseller. The acquisitions editor came back with this response:

> We had our editorial meeting this afternoon, and I presented Nina's book idea. I was told that, except for one outlier, BookScan shows the competing books in this area selling only about two thousand hard copies during their first year and then trailing off after that. We believe a substantial portion of the books' sales

> come from Kindle sales, which we can't track. So my director of trade sales and marketing wasn't able to give me a sales projection for such a book. But, given the inevitable low price of such books, it would be risky for us to take a 'flier' on it (as we say) anyway."

Note that the price of e-books was also taken into account, as would be the price of the hardcover books in the list of Competitive Titles I provided.

Two years ago, my agent proposed a different book to a large publisher. This response came back: "Sales of the competing books weren't as strong as I had anticipated, so it would be tough to make a sales case to bring this one through acquisitions."

The lack of sales produced by the competing books I had chosen, which were the closest ones I could find, indicated:

- too small a market for my book
- a market with not enough interest in my subject
- potential readers who saw no benefit or value in the topic

Thus, my financial backer, the publisher, wasn't interested in investing in similar books because the type of book I wanted to write represented too large a risk. Let me point out that in this second case one of the books on that list was Michael Larsen's *How to Write a Book Proposal*, which had sold well over 100,000 copies and was about to be released as a fourth edition. Still, it may have been the only book on the list that had sold well. The others could have been low performers as they were in my last example.

When my agent proposed the same project to a specialized midsize publisher, the book was purchased with less issue. This demonstrates how different types of publishers see competing and complementary books differently—and so must you, especially if you plan to self-publish. Larger publishers want and need to sell more books. Small and midsize publishers have smaller sales goals. A specialized publisher can see the uniqueness of an idea and how it meets a need in a category it knows well. You need to go back to your goals—your idea of success. Then determine to the best of your ability if the competitive environment seems favorable for moving forward with your project.

A category with few books and little competition does not mean your book won't succeed or shouldn't be written and published. It could represent an opportunity for you. A small amount of competition doesn't mean a publisher won't feel a market exists for your book. You could dominate the niche with your book if you can prove your book is unique and necessary and that a market exists for it.

This, again, is the most important factor: If you can prove that people are ready and willing to purchase your book—that people need your book—then your project could still be viable despite the lack of competition or too much competition. You might look at complementary books to see if you can find proof of need for your book.

How to Gather Data for Your Competitive or Complementary Analysis

It can be hard for authors to obtain the same sales figures to which publishers have access. Nielsen BookScan provides the publishing industry with reasonably accurate point-of-sale data, but according to Harvard Library, the service represents only 75 percent of all retail sales. BookScan is the sales data provider service publishers use, but most aspiring authors do not use it due to subscription costs. Authors are granted access to BookScan data concerning their own books via Amazon Author Central accounts, but they can't access other authors' book data.

Another resource is *Publishers Marketplace*, which offers a free and a paid subscription. You might garner some information here in articles and book reviews.

You might be able to use Google to obtain sales figures on some of the more popular books. Some books' sales figures are mentioned in articles, especially if the book has been a *New York Times* bestseller. (*The Times* compiles data from a selection of bookstores and generates rankings. However, such lists don't indicate how many copies have actually sold or the relative sales among books on the lists. And e-book sales are difficult to track.)

You can use the Amazon.com bestseller list as a way to discover which books are selling better than others. This list is updated hourly and is based on BookScan data. You can find the list by inputting "Amazon Best Seller List" into the book search engine on the site. Then click through the category list on the left until you find the category for your book.

This list is not user-friendly; it can take a while to hit on the correct category for your competition. For an easier way to navigate to this list, find a bestseller in your category. Go to its page. Scroll down until you see its best-seller ranking under "Product Details." Then click on the link to the list. Peruse the appropriate bestsellers in the category.

You can also use KDPCalculator.com to make some educated guesses about competitive book sales in your category. Input the current Amazon Best Seller Rank of any book on Amazon (Kindle, paperback, or hardcover). You can find the Amazon Best Seller Rank under the book's "Product Details." This site tells you how many copies per day a book sold on that particular day. You then can estimate how many copies sell per week, month, or year

MANUAL

based on that one day. (Note that some Kindle books will sell more copies if they are being offered free on a particular day or selling for $0.99 rather than $2.99 or higher.)

According to the Harvard Library, you can find historical statistics for particular books in *A Guide to Book Publishers' Archives,* which identifies archival collections from actual publishers—a reliable source of sales data.

Now it's time to take a close, detailed look at the competing and complementary books you've previously discovered. Let's call this your "Competitive Book Tour." You can do much of this research using the "Look Inside" program offered by Amazon.com and BarnesandNoble.com. Or you can go to a bookstore or library and peruse the books in more depth.

If you are in a physical store, find those titles you've already identified and begin studying them. What are they about? How are they organized? What tone does the author use—humorous, informative, business professional, cynical? Train yourself to look at these books critically. Evaluate your book against the others. You don't necessarily have to read every competing or complementary book. But you do need to study:

- their tables of contents
- the promises they make on their back covers
- their introductions

Also notice:

- how these other books differ from your project
- who wrote the foreword, if there is one
- the author's bio
- any special features, such as quotations, a workbook element, case studies, or tips or tools

As you look at each book, answer these questions:

- How is it different from the book you want to write?
- How is it similar to the book you want to write?
- Is the scope of the book different? How so?
- Does it have different benefits? What are they?
- What are its pros and cons?
- How would you improve it?
- What do you like about it? Dislike? And how can you apply this information to your book?

- What promises does the author make to readers? What promises does the author fail to make that he could or should make? Are these promises you can make or want to make?
- What are the author's credentials (or lack of credentials)?
- How do your credentials compare to the authors?

As you do your research on competitive and complementary books for the Author Training Process, you do not need to stick to the confines of what would go into a book proposal. Take copious notes on these other books as you do your evaluation. Go beyond what I've detailed here. You will find your notes helpful if you need to apply your findings to revising your idea, angle, theme, or the content or special features you decide to include in your book.

When I do a competitive analysis, I typically purchase the top five books I consider competition for my book project. I also purchase the top few I feel complement my idea. This way I can read them or study them more carefully. If you are low on funds, you can borrow them from the library, borrow them virtually from the Kindle Prime program, or buy them from used bookstores.

How to Use Your Competitive Research to Improve Your Book Idea

Once you've accumulated your research, whittle your lists of competing and complementary books to five each. It's time to determine if your book project can truly compete with similar published titles—or, if not, what you can do to make it more competitive. If the competition has made you doubt the viability of your idea, you may not have to give up on it completely; you may simply have to retool it—re-angle it—so it is unique and necessary in a particular market and either fills a gap on the bookstore shelf, complements existing books in some way, or tells a new story. This still means being willing to make some changes as you objectively look at the information you have accumulated and consider how to create a salable book.

The man who e-mailed me about his memoir would have to determine how many other men have written memoirs on healing relationships and also if his story is different from theirs. The client who wanted to write the book about leadership for women would have to evaluate how her content would differ from the other successful books on the market and fill an unmet need for those readers. She would also have to consider changing the book's market back to the original, more specific one she had first chosen—technical women. A novelist who asked me how to ensure her young adult novel stood out from the pack needed to evaluate her plotline, story location, characters, and themes against other novels in the YA category.

MANUAL

If you have separated your research into two categories, competing and complementary books, first look at the complementary books. Readers who purchase complementary books will likely purchase your book as well. When evaluating the complementary titles, train yourself to consider how you could best serve this audience. How can you interest these readers and get them to purchase your book, too? If, for example, you want to write a book about Zen meditation, you might include a chapter on Buddhist retreat centers, the history of Buddhism, and why Buddhism appeals to so many people. This would attract those readers generally interested in learning about Buddhism but who didn't set out to buy a book on Zen meditation. If you write novels about zombies but want to expand your readership, you could include a vampire in your next book. This would attract all those readers interested in stories about vampires.

Next, you should consider how you can affiliate or become venture partners with the authors of the books on your complementary list. These authors are your allies. You can sell your books together, which is why Amazon often suggests that readers who purchased one book might also buy another. Train yourself to think this way. If a reader buys your book, what other books might he buy?

You might want to reach out to these authors in some way:

- Ask to teach a course or produce a small product together.
- Suggest interviewing the author on a teleseminar or podcast.
- Offer to have the author write a guest post that you feature on your blog.
- Ask if you can promote his or her book on your site.
- Ask the author to write your foreword.

Rhonda says that after doing her complementary analysis, she connected with several authors. "Since I had already read their memoirs, it was easy for me to post reviews for their books, and they, in turn, are interested in reading my memoir," she says. "Each of us is coming from a unique angle of our personal experience that complements the other's story."

Now focus on the competing books. These are the most important to consider because these are the books readers might buy *instead* of yours. With the research you have done, can you honestly say your idea is unique and necessary? Does it have benefits or features that the other books lack? Is it a new take on an old idea? Are you offering readers of these other books something the other authors have not delivered? Are you telling a different story? Does your plot or your character development offer readers something uncommon? Or not?

My student, La Donna, spent time researching her genre before determining how to write her romance novel. "I checked out how much [other novelists] were charging for their e-books, paperback, and hard copy. I wanted an idea of how they valued their work. I read their book descriptions. I read the first twenty reviews (if they had that many)," she says. "The reviews told the real story." She learned that romance readers want fast storytelling and engaging characters, so she looked at her plot and writing and catered to readers' desires.

Based on the competitive analysis for their book on social media, Penney and Dawn decided to publish an e-book first. "With an e-book, we'll always be able to stay up to date. People who buy our book will be able to download the updates when Facebook makes another change to the news feed or a new scheduling program gets launched," Penney explains. "Our research showed that most of the social media books published did not provide updated information."

Additionally, their competitive analysis helped them target their market to a need in their category. Here is an excerpt from their query letter: "Most of the competing books were directed towards a social media manager or marketing director. Where was the book to help the small business owner understand how to use social media marketing?" Penney queried. "We've fine-tuned our content of creating a guideline to help small business owners take that 'overwhelming feeling' out of using social media marketing. This e-book will show the small business owner how they can find time in their already crazy busy day to stay on top of social media and to make it work for their business." (If you recall, their market research gave them confidence that small businesses would provide be a good strategic market to target.)

Don't forget to also look at the authors' bios carefully and compare yourself to them. Consider:

- How are you different or similar to them?
- Will it help you or hurt you to have different qualifications or similar ones?
- Are you equipped to join the ranks of these other authors?
- What else might you have to do to make your bio and qualifications stand out?

Once you've thought about this, keep your answers in mind (or written down and saved) for Step #9: *Weigh Whether You Are the Best Person to Write This Book ... Now.*

Based on your research and your evaluation, decide if you need to make changes to your concept. Objectively evaluate whether or not your book:

- Tells a fresh story
- Offers a different perspective from other authors

MANUAL

- Provides a compelling argument other authors have not made
- Gives a different set of data or more current information
- Shows a new angle on a tried-and-true topic
- Takes readers on a singular journey

Ask yourself: "What else can I add to my book, or how best can I angle it to provide information or a story no other author has offered?"

It's a good idea at this point to go through Step #2 and #3 one more time. Revision lies at the heart of writing a book and at the heart of preparing to write one as well. As you revisit Step #2, edit what you wrote for your book's pitch, summary, and benefits. Mike Larsen, author of *How to Write a Book Proposal*, likes authors to compare their books to others in the second line of a pitch; this can be a helpful descriptor, but it requires a competitive analysis. You might find that your pitch and overview change considerably with this new research, especially if your benefits have changed.

As you go through Steps #2 and #3, see if any of your answers to the questions posed in the chapter or training exercises differ now. Your idea might have changed significantly, and if so you will need to alter your title or subtitle to better capture your market or to show how the benefits of your book will make it unique and necessary. Sometimes it's a good idea to start from scratch … relook at your idea, angle, and theme. You may want to edit your title, pitch, summary, and benefits, or even reconsider your market. Then move to the next step in the Author Training Process. The next step is a creative one: You get to plan out the actual content of your book. *WOOT!*

Suggested Reading:

Top Dog: The Science of Winning and Losing by Po Bronson and Ashley Merryman

Competition Demystified: A Radically Simplified Approach to Business Strategy by Bruce C. Greenwald and Judd Kahn

Outthink the Competition: How a New Generation of Strategists Sees Options Others Ignore by Kaihan Krippendorff

STEP #5

Examine the Structure of Your Book

Remember Alice from *Alice's Adventures in Wonderland*? She didn't have a map. No destination. That's why she wandered around and didn't care where she ended up. At this point in the Author Training Process you have the information you need to design the creative map for your book. If you've left your Alice Attitude behind and adopted an Author Attitude, you can complete Step #5, *Examine the Structure of Your Book*. Additionally, you can make sure you arrive at your destination: a successful book—one that sells to readers and to a publisher as well, if that is your goal.

You've made it halfway through the Author Training Process, and this step asks you to apply your research, evaluations, and training to create the table of contents (TOC) for your book. In a book proposal, this would be called the "List of Chapters," and it represents the structure of your book's content. It also represents an important part of the writing guide you are creating. You can consider it a map for writing a successful book because it begins to put all the pieces together—unique and necessary content based on your idea and targeted to your category and market.

If you feel uncertain at all about creating your book's structure or developing a map to take you (and readers) from its beginning to its end, take a deep breath and drum up your courage. You will find many tips and tools in this chapter to help you figure out what will end up on the pages of your book. What you first thought you would write about may, indeed, have changed by this point in your Author Training. You can firm up your summary, pitch, list of benefits—in fact, your whole book idea—after you have completed your TOC, if need be. (You'll have another chance to review all of these elements again after you complete Step #6.) Soon you'll have a well-defined map anyone can understand—you, agents, editors, or readers.

At this stage of the Author Training Process, however, the TOC is just a list of chapters you *plan* to include in your book, each one named appropriately and listed in an order that seems to make sense from a storytelling or conceptual standpoint. If you provide descriptive chapter titles, such as those found in nonfiction books, anyone can look at your TOC and see the reasonable and effective path you've charted to get to your planned destination. Your pitch, summary, and list of benefits provide a description of that destination.

But you should think of Step #5 as a chance to build and strengthen the structure of your idea, changing it from a general overview to a defined map. The TOC holds up your book and gives it form, much like a backbone. Without a strong TOC, your book ends up crooked, bent, or unable to stand. When an agent or acquisitions editor looks at the List of Chapters in a book proposal, they "see" your book—or they don't. If your TOC is weak or too general, your idea remains amorphous.

The TOC is often the next logical thing for agents or acquisitions editors to look at after the Overview, where they can find a complete and concise description of a book idea. A look at a TOC can help an agent or acquisitions editor determine if your book will have substance, contain pertinent information, tell a complete story, and carry out the promises you made in your Overview. They can tell if it has the strength to hold up all aspects of your content, takes a logical path, and gets your readers where you say you want them to go.

The TOC is particularly helpful for evaluating the soundness of a nonfiction book. These books tend to have chapters descriptive of their content. As such, the TOC easily shows if the creative plan for the book will hold up the proposed content and get readers where they need to go. However, if a novelist writes chapter titles that allow readers to glimpse the storyline (without revealing important twists or climaxes later on, of course), the TOC can provide an agent, editor, or reader with the same ability to gather this information about a novel. Memoirists should keep this in mind because it can help readers (and agents or editors) make early purchase decisions about their books as well.

Think about it: When you go into a bookstore and open a book to its TOC, you know if it appeals to you and if it contains the information you need or want or a story you would like to read. You must prepare your book idea for that prospective reader's first glance.

How to Create Your Table of Contents

As an author in training, you want to approach your TOC as both a creative and business process. In the first case, writing your TOC offers you a chance to get inspired and help your idea take shape. Have fun when creating the titles of sections and when shaping the bare bones of the content readers will find within your book's pages. In the second case, you have the opportunity to evaluate your TOC from a business perspective to ensure it lines up with your target market as well as with your angle, theme, purpose, pitch, summary, and benefits. You determine if each section and chapter you have proposed will:

- fulfill the promises you made to your readers—provide them with benefits
- be unique—differ from your competition
- be necessary—answer questions or solve problems
- hit readers emotionally—allow them to relate to what you have written
- tell a compelling story—entice the reader.
- target your intended markets—be written for your readers

Not every writer begins writing with a TOC as a map, although many do. Others like to write "by the seat of their pants," allowing their books to flow out of their heads with little planning. (Some refer to this as "mappers vs. pantsers.") I recommend both fiction and non-fiction writers develop a TOC because it provides organization, direction, and focus as you write. It also reduces some need to revise and cut in later drafts of your manuscript.

To develop a TOC, however, you must organize your story or information into chapters.

Delineating Chapters

Whether you are starting from scratch or have your research at hand, you are at the right place in the process (as long as you previously have completed Steps #1 to #4) to begin breaking down your book idea into the steps (or chapters) needed to fulfill your promises to the reader. You can create your TOC in a variety of ways. For nonfiction, which often has about ten to fifteen chapters, for example, you can:

- Create a list of ten to fifteen topics you know you want to cover in the order you want to cover them. Write a compelling title for each topic; later you can refine what you come up with, but for now this becomes the chapter title.
- Think of ten to fifteen common questions you want to answer for your readers. Then write creative chapter titles for each one of those questions; another option is to leave the titles as questions.

- Think of ten to fifteen pressing questions you want to answer for your readers. Then write creative chapter titles for each one of those questions; these could be "how-to" titles.
- List ten to fifteen benefits you want to offer readers. Write titles that draw readers into those chapters by explaining what's in it for them—the added value that speaks to their interests.

To create a TOC for a memoir:

- Create a time line. Draw a line with the start and end date of the period about which you plan to write; place dates that indicate major events you want to include in your story on the line. Then organize these into chapters.
- Plot vignettes on a storyboard. Storyboards are graphic organizers most often combining both images and descriptions of a scene. Some writers simply describe scenes on them. Once you have organized them in chronological order, identified themes, and determine the narrative arc, write your TOC.
- Create an outline. List the events you plan to include, and then organize them logically with lesser events placed after more important events. (In all these cases, add in flashbacks in the places you feel appropriate to recount them, not necessarily in real time.)
- Organize your memories into topics of interest.
- Make a list of ten to fifteen significant moments or turning points in your life, and relate them to your themes; locate them on a time line. Write each turning point in a scene, creating chapters from these core stories.

To create a TOC for fiction:

- Profile your characters. Give them backstories and motivations so you get to know them before you set them within the dramatic or comedic arc of your creation. Then outline your storyline. Place the scenes you plan to include on that story line (like a time line) with your characters. Consider how your novel's themes play out on that storyline and where the dramatic arcs occur. Then break this down into chapters, and create a TOC.
- Create a storyboard. Break this down into chapters and then a TOC.
- Number the lines on a sheet of notebook paper, and put one word (be it an action, place, person, object, or symbol) that best represents what you want to happen in each chapter. That becomes the working chapter title. Then make notes about specific events that will occur in that chapter as well.

• Use an Excel spreadsheet to block out chapters and the scenes within them. Move events around as necessary. (You can also write character biographies as part of this exercise.) Then create a TOC.

Speaking of Excel, you can find lots of proven creative tools to help you organize your research and, later, your work. Some can be used on your computer or online. For example, you might explore these programs:

• Scrivener
• Evernote
• Dropbox
• Box.net
• Google Drive

Most Internet browsers, like Firefox, Internet Explorer, and Google Chrome, allow you to bookmark pages into folders you create and save them in those browsers. You can then organize your online research into folders named for each of your book's chapters, which makes it easy to find the websites and web pages you have used for your book research.

You can also create a folder on your computer in which to save and organize research. Use your book's title as the name of your primary book project folder. Create subfolders within that one for research, your manuscript (and separate chapters), book design, or anything else related to your book (including your business plan). You can save information you find online to the research folder by copying and pasting links and information to Word files. You can even scan research into files and save them into these folders. The same holds true for audio and video files and other snippets of information, including screenshots of web pages.

Many writers prefer old-school organizational methods, such as putting their research or ideas on 3" × 5" index cards and keeping them in those little index card boxes, putting papers in folders in a filing cabinet, creating piles, or saving information in boxes. Dan Poynter, author of *How to Write Nonfiction*, talks about creating the content for books with a "pile method"; each pile later becomes a chapter.

As you organize chapters for a nonfiction book, consider placing them in order like this:

Book Subject (or title and subtitle)

Chapter 1 Topic
> Subtopic
> Subtopic
> Subtopic
> Subtopic

Chapter 2 Topic
> Subtopic
> Subtopic
> Subtopic
> Subtopic

For fiction (or memoir), consider something like this:

Book Title

Chapter 1 Primary action or development
> Scene
> Scene
> Scene
> Scene

Chapter 2 Primary action or development
> Scene
> Scene
> Scene
> Scene

Whatever method you use to organize your TOC, make sure it is clear, well-defined, and as categorized as it needs to be for someone who doesn't know anything about your book to look at your TOC and immediately see—and understand—what you are trying to accomplish.

How to Mind Map Your Book to Create a TOC

Another method I like to use to create a TOC is called "mind mapping." Although quite creative, writers—especially nonfiction writers—tend to think in a linear fashion. Mind mapping allows you to move out of the left side of your brain, where you might develop an outline for your book (or write a business plan), and tap into the right side, where you can inspire the free flow of thoughts.

Also, mind mapping provides an exercise for brainstorming chapter ideas and storylines as well as content within nonfiction chapters, scenes within fiction chapters, and subheadings that delineate nonfiction. It allows you to drill down beneath your chapter titles to the actual content. You end up with a clearer idea of what you actually will write about in each chapter and what will appear in your completed manuscript.

You can purchase mind-mapping software or download free software, such as: xmind. net, mindmeister.com, freemind.sourceforge.net (http://freemind.sourceforge.net/wiki/ index.php/Main_Page), and mindjet.com.

The easiest way to complete the exercise, though, involves purchasing a large posterboard and some colored sticky notes, such as Post-it Notes. I like the square or rectangular Post-its you can use to mark pages in a book as you read. You need ones made of a material you can write on.

Write your topic or title on a larger Post-it Note and place it in the middle of the board. Then start writing related topics, events, memories, or characters on the smaller sticky notes. I like to use one color for this part of the exercise. Just stick them all over the board. Don't worry about where you place them unless you are certain they are related topics. In that case, you can group them together.

I call this a "brain dump." Simply allow yourself to put everything you can possibly think of onto the board. Free-associate. Empty your mind. Fill the board to capacity without thought of organizing anything. When you think you are finished, think again … and again.

When done, organize the notes. Look for related topics, time periods, events, themes, or storylines. Pick up the notes and move them around. See which groupings are well suited to become chapters. More than likely, the ones with the most information or most scenes will work as chapters, but you may have to break some of them into more than one chapter if you have an overabundance of notes. Use a different-colored Post-it Note at the top of each grouping to delineate it as a chapter, and place a title on that note. As you group the Post-it Notes, you might get additional ideas. Add these into an appropriate group or chapter. (You might even brainstorm a whole new chapter in the process.)

As you complete the exercise, you should have created a number of chapters—hopefully ten to fifteen, if you are writing nonfiction. If you are writing a novel or memoir, you might have more. Now type each chapter name or subject into a TOC. Each of the sticky notes in the groupings below the chapter title becomes a topic, event, scene, or issue to cover in that particular chapter. (Hang onto this information for Step #6, when you flesh out your TOC into chapter summaries.)

As indicated above, you can mind map a novel using the same basic process. Place all the events or ideas for the story on various Post-its, and then move them around, combine them into scenes, and organize the scenes into chapters. Basically, you mind map a storyline.

One writer I know told me she does a modified mind-map exercise prior to writing her novels. She gets a bunch of blank paper and cuts each sheet in half. She then blocks in what will happen in each chapter on different-colored sticky notes and puts them on the pages—one blank page for each chapter. "This way I can move events around, add new ones, or get rid of things," she says. "These pages are my outline. It's a bit bulky and messy looking at times, but boy, oh boy, does it ever work for me."

Once you've typed up your fiction TOC, evaluate if each chapter has a dramatic arc, carries out your themes, shows character development, etc. In Step #6, you will use this additional information you accrued during the process in Step #5 to write your synopsis or chapter summaries.

As you might have guessed, those writing memoirs can also use the mind map successfully. Brainstorm all the different events that happened during the time period you want to cover in your book. Let your mind wander so you can remember as many events as possible. Put them all on the board. Include the flashbacks you plan to write about. This exercise may even jostle some new memories. Then organize these events into a time line. Place the flashbacks in places that enhance your storytelling. Look at the time line for a narrative arc, a dramatic arc, themes, and, most important, transformational events. Then break the time line into chapters. Type these up into a TOC.

Some people like doing mind maps on a posterboard by writing down their ideas with colored pens or pencils; this is the traditional methodology that requires going though the same basic exercise described above, except when you are done brainstorming, you circle items and link them with lines. I find this rather confusing in the end; it can be hard to follow all of those lines and circles. You can do it more neatly on a white board using colored markers because you can erase items and move them around.

Evaluate Your Book's Structure

Once you have completed your TOC, it's time to continue your Author Training by looking at what you've created from a publishing business perspective—as if you were an acquisitions editor. You already have some training in this particular type of evaluation because you purchase books based on a TOC. Put this ability to use and evaluate your book's TOC.

First, take a step back and imagine you are a potential reader of the book you want to write. Imagine that it already exists and you have found it in a bookstore or on Amazon.com. You pick it up or click to download it.

Go back and read what you wrote in Step #2: your book pitch, summary, and list of benefits. These are your promises to the reader. This is what you are trying to accomplish. Imagine this is the back-of-the-book copy; i.e., what you see written on your book's back cover. Maybe it is more condensed and polished, but it's something close to the marketing copy you view when you click on the "Look Inside" feature on Amazon.com or when you turn over the book in your hand. Reading this material, you know what the author promises will be inside the covers.

Now flip to your TOC, and see it through the lens of agents or acquisitions editors. They will consider what you wrote in Step #2, your promises and premise, and determine if your TOC follows logically, if you have followed through on everything you said you would while also targeting your market and providing unique and necessary content in your chosen category. Will a publishing professional think your TOC carries out everything you described in your Overview?

To see your TOC through the lens of an agent or editor, evaluate if your TOC:

- easily shows what your book is about, why it is unique, and why it is necessary
- provides an order that reflects a beginning, middle, and end of your subject or story
- illustrates a compelling, unique topic or story with depth
- keeps your promises to the reader and matches your Overview

Books need structure. Plenty of room exists for creativity, but a book without a clearly defined TOC won't get readers where you want them to go and won't fulfill the premise laid out in your Overview. Remember: The TOC provides the map for your book as well as its structure. You'll use it to ensure you get to your destination. Write the book you set out to write, get your readers where you want them to go, and make sure they receive the information you promised they would receive.

When you have a strong TOC, you have an essential part of the writing guide you are creating during your Author Training Process. If your TOC evaluation proves you've accomplished that step, move on to the next one, where you will learn to provide directions—summaries—to go with that map.

MANUAL

But if your TOC evaluation proves that you do not have a strong enough idea, that your proposed steps don't align with your Overview, or that have holes in your proposed TOC, go back through the steps in this chapter again—or revisit Step #2, *Find Out If You Know What Your Book Is About and Why Someone Would Want to Read (Buy) It.* You might need to get more clarity on your idea. Remember that each step builds on the next; you are involved in a process. Run back through the process with the research you have accumulated, if necessary. If you must repeat steps a few times, so be it—this is what you need to do to create a successful book and achieve your goal of successful authorship. That means you have trained yourself to have an Author Attitude. *WOOT!*

Suggested Reading:

Finish What You Start: How to Set Priorities, Organize Your Thoughts, Defeat Procrastination, and Complete Outstanding Projects by Kerry Gene

Mind Mapping for Writers: How to Improve Productivity, Overcome Procrastination, Get Creative and Finish Writing That Book Using Your Lack of Focus as an Advantage by David Lynch

STEP #6

Decide If Your Book's Content Matches Your Initial Vision

At this point in the process, you get to do some real writing. Whoo hoo! How much writing you do in Step #6, *Decide If Your Book's Content Matches Your Initial Vision,* depends on how you plan to publish and what you plan to write. You will write more at this point if you plan to self-publish or if you write fiction than if you hope to traditionally publish or if you write nonfiction.

Before you dig in and begin composing any amount of your manuscript, you now want to add more detail to the map you created in Step #5, *Examine the Structure of Your Book.* In this step, you add directions for those using that map, your TOC. In the language of a book proposal, this step involves writing the section called Chapter Summaries for a nonfiction book or the synopsis for a fiction book. This section is necessary for your writing guide, which is why I recommend both nonfiction and fiction writers produce a chapter-by-chapter synopsis. To complete Step #6, you will write a synopsis of each and every chapter you listed in your TOC and place it in your business plan.

For all nonfiction books, this is included in a proposal even if your nonfiction manuscript is complete, and it should be included in your business plan if you self-publish. It allows an agent or an acquisitions editor to quickly scan not just your proposed chapters but the content of your book to determine if the book has substance, is unique, flows, makes sense, is necessary, and is compelling. It allows the editor to judge if you have carried through on the premises you laid out in your Overview and TOC. Your chapter-by-chapter synopsis helps publishing professionals determine if they are interested in your project without having to read the whole manuscript. In fact, for nonfiction, agents and acquisitions editors rarely read the whole book unless it is a memoir; they usually just read one or two chapters, or about twenty to thirty pages of your manuscript, along with the chapter summaries.

Even if you don't plan on seeking a traditional publisher, write a chapter-by-chapter synopsis for your business plan so you can evaluate your content just as a publishing professional would.

For fiction, your synopsis is typically a short (usually a page or two at most) description of your entire novel that details the most important information about your story, such as plot, theme, characterization, and setting. It allows an agent or acquisitions editor to get an overview of how these elements coalesce to create a compelling story without reading the entire novel. Most agents and acquisitions editors will ask novelists to send a synopsis and three consecutive sample chapters prior to sending the whole manuscript, which they request only if they find the synopsis compelling. However, I've known agents who ask for three pages, thirty pages, a chapter-by-chapter synopsis, or just a synopsis. Be prepared to give them whatever they prefer. Writing a chapter-by-chapter synopsis now will accomplish this task and also help you write the full synopsis by clarifying the heart of each chapter, and as a result, the book as a whole.

By "fleshing out" your novel with chapter summaries, you will know exactly what material must go into each chapter and if your story works. As I mentioned earlier, the chapter-by-chapter synopsis offers a superb writing guide even if an agent or editor never gets to see it. You are developing that guide as part of your Training. (More on this later.)

If you're writing nonfiction, keep your summaries for each TOC section to no more than a page each, preferably just a paragraph, thereby forcing yourself to be as specific as possible. For fiction writers, try to keep each chapter summary to a paragraph or two. Your full synopsis will only be a page or two long, so brief summaries help you cut to the heart of what you are trying to say. Write your summaries now.

Bring Your Book to Life

In the last chapter, I said the TOC gives your book form, like a backbone, thereby allowing an agent or acquisitions editor to "see" your book taking shape. Imagine the TOC as a skeleton, the most basic outline for the body of your book. But as you write each chapter synopsis, you "flesh out" your ideas so the skeleton of your book idea gets muscles, tendons, organs, and limbs. It comes to life. Unlike a parent who sees her child as perfect at birth, you must look at the book you bring into the world, the idea you create, with critical eyes—just like an agent or acquisitions editor. It is not yet perfect—far from it—and that's okay for right now. The detail provided by your chapter-by-chapter synopsis gives you the opportunity to clearly see the content you plan to write and determine if your book matches your initial vision. You can also evaluate if it has the constitution and character to survive in the world (in the market) or if it has some inherent problems that will cause it to struggle to stay alive or to suffer an early death. Those are the things you must look for and focus on, just as agents or editors will if given the chance.

Writing chapter summaries may give you new insight into your book idea. Rhonda made many changes to her memoir idea during Step #5, and during Step #6, as she wrote each chapter synopsis, she continued to revise and improve upon her idea. In fact, during the two-step process, she broke her initial idea into several books instead of one, and she began the Author Training Process again. My client David realized he had fleshed out a different book than the one he outlined in Step #5 and also had to start the process over.

Without chapter-by-chapter summaries or a synopsis, it's hard for an agent or acquisitions editor to visualize your book's final form. It doesn't come to life for them otherwise. Most of the editors and agents who read my students' business plans (some of which I will include later in this book for your benefit) were only given a TOC (no chapter summaries). Agent Sheree Bykofsky commented that she could not really offer feedback on the TOC of the memoir she reviewed because the TOC was not descriptive enough. She needed chapter synopses.

I dislike composing chapter summaries and synopses, and I dread this part of the Author Training Process and of proposal writing. I write nonfiction and find chapter-by-chapter synopses a monotonous exercise. One colleague completed this part of her nonfiction book proposal first because she said "it scared her"; she's primarily a novelist. Fiction synopses are difficult for me as well—cramming a long story into three to five paragraphs can feel painful.

The worst nonfiction chapter summaries are those that simply say, "In this chapter, readers will ..." The best ones are crafted creatively to give readers a sense of the book's angle, how they will benefit from reading it, and what the author's voice sounds like. Try to use active sentences. If you plan to polish your business plan into a book proposal, these summaries are particularly important.

For the Author Training Process and your business plan, you need only jot down a few sentences or a paragraph that describes what you will include in each chapter of your book. After you evaluate the content and determine if it is sound, this section of your business plan

MANUAL

will act as a written reminder of the content you plan to include in your book and a phenomenal writing guide. You can review it before writing any chapter to remind yourself of what you plan to include. It also becomes part of a larger writing guide. (More on this later.)

Final Content Evaluation

No matter what type of book you plan to write, once your chapter summaries or your synopsis is complete, evaluate everything you have written thus far. If your summaries don't sync up with previous steps, you need to go back and repeat those steps until it does. Otherwise, the structure of your book will not be solid, and the content you produce will not result in a marketable book. At this point, however, your content should be closely aligned with your original idea, angle, theme, market, etc. To evaluate if you have indeed succeeded at this exercise, answer these questions one at a time:

- Does your content match your TOC?
- Does you content match your pitch?
- Does your content provide the benefits you claimed your book will offer readers?
- Do you have enough to say to fill a whole book?
- Is the content unique and necessary? How so?
- Is there anything that feels unnecessary? Why?
- Does your content target your market? How?
- Will your content interest your ideal reader? How so, and why?
- Does your book fill a hole on the shelf in its category? How or why?
- Have you told a compelling story?
- Will it take readers on a new journey? How so?
- Is your book marketable? How so?

Having considered these questions, determine if you need to re-angle, retarget, or retool the work you did in Step #2 ... one last time. Take another look at your angle, theme, and purpose. Edit your pitch, summary, and benefits based upon your TOC, chapter synopses or synopsis, or both. Make sure all of these elements (pitch, summary, and benefits; TOC; chapter synopses; full synopsis) still target your market—that the market remains the best one based on your content—and that your book still falls into the same category you have chosen and, therefore, your competition continues to be the same. If so, at this point your book should fill an empty spot on the shelf.

As you review your Overview, add another 100 to 300 words to the summary of your book, bringing it up to 300 to 500 words. By expanding and refining this part of your business plan, you should now discover you really *really* know what your book is about. When you initially wrote the summary, you may have had only a general idea of what you were going to write about. Now you *know.* Your TOC provides a rich source of information on your book's content, but the chapter-by-chapter summaries or full synopsis provide a more in-depth description.

At this point in the Author Training Process, most aspiring authors feel confident about writing their books. After finishing Step #6, my client Deborah says she could see her book's structure, and she felt secure about filling each chapter of her nonfiction book with valuable content. She was glad to have the precious moment that came after writing chapter summaries. She now felt eager to begin writing.

Of course, your content might change as you produce your manuscript, but what you have created in these steps is as close as you can get to a solid description of your book's content prior to writing the actual book.

I made some major changes to the first chapter of this book. My business plan, or proposal, described "business hats" and "special glasses" that would help writers see themselves and their projects from a publishing professional's perspective. A few students in my Author Training 101 class, who served as beta readers of the manuscript, told me the concepts were confusing. As I began editing chapters, I realized they were right; these concepts didn't work well. So I rethought and revised; I combined "hats" and "glasses" into Author Attitude. That required a fair amount of rewriting and reworking of several chapters. It happens to all of us, so be prepared and make sure you take on the upcoming challenges with the correct Author Attitude.

After completing Step #6, you may discover you have made significant changes to the work you did in Step #2. That is why I advise *not* writing your sample chapters or your manuscript until this point in the process. It is also why I advise starting the Author Training Process when you first get an idea instead of sitting down to write each time a book idea pops into your head.

Also, if your book idea changes drastically for any reason, restart the process from scratch. For example, Charlene began her book about finding work-life balance with the idea of targeting a general self-help market. She then put the book aside for several months before beginning her coaching sessions with me again. In that time, she changed jobs and decided to re-angle her book to align it with her new work position, which required speaking to entrepreneurs and corporate employees. If you recall, she also retargeted her market, this time

MANUAL

choosing a business-related one. Her book's focus remained work-life balance, but she needed to change its title and subtitle, create a new pitch, write a new summary and list of benefits, conduct new market and competitive book analysis, and rework her TOC and chapter synopses—all to fit the new angle of her book. With her revised business plan, she could move forward to create a marketable book that better served her new audience.

It's almost time to begin writing. First, make one last pass through the work you completed in this step and make sure you have done the following:

- evaluated your chapter synopses and/or your synopsis
- made any necessary changes based on your evaluation of your chapter summaries
- made any necessary changes to the work you did in Step #2 so you have synched up your pitch, summary, benefits, TOC, and chapter summaries/synopsis so they all align perfectly—and all target your market and make your book unique and necessary in your category

This is now the point when you should feel, "I now know exactly what my book is about, why someone would buy it, who will buy it, what it will look like, what will be in it, and I'm ready to write it!" You have a map with great directions. And you've got an Author Attitude.

Knowing How Large Your Book Will Grow

As you prepare to write, it's handy to know approximately how many pages and words your book will be when complete so you can use these estimations as guides for writing your book. You'll need to have a word or page count in mind if you plan to approach a traditional publisher with a nonfiction book, and you'll be required to provide this estimate in a book proposal. It's just as important to know these numbers in advance if you plan to self-publish.

To estimate the cost of book production, you will need to know the length of your book. The longer your book, the more expensive it is to produce. A book that costs more to produce must sell more copies before it becomes profitable. As an indie publisher, this is important to consider since it's your money you need to earn back.

You must consider other factors as well, and sometimes a longer book actually proves more financially feasible than a shorter one. I tend to think readers prefer shorter books—many people are busy and enjoy a book that can be read in less time. I used to think a shorter book would prove less of a risk for a publisher, so I proposed several short books (under 40,000 words) to Writer's Digest Books. However, the shorter books weren't getting approved at the pub board meetings. The consensus among the marketing and production team members was that I needed to write at least 50,000 words to make the book financially feasible. Only when I agreed to write a longer book did I receive a contract.

My publisher, Phil Sexton, explained that the larger physical shelf presence of a longer book gave the sales team more confidence that the book would be seen. "Once a book is spine out, it's the only real estate you have to work with when it comes to customers who are browsing the shelves," he told me. "A spine that's very thin is easily overlooked. Also, a larger book justifies a larger retail price, which can make a big difference in how the profit and loss statement works. So one reason is financial; the other is more practical." You'll want to consider these same issues when you plan your self-published book.

Fiction writers usually know the final word or page count of their books because they must finish their manuscripts before they submit to agents or publishers. Those who self-publish might want to estimate the length of their novels and try to stick close to that number because going over means you will go over your production budget and increase your financial risk. If you plan to traditionally publish your novel, you can easily include a word count in your proposal if your manuscript is complete. Of course, having an idea of your book's length—how long a publisher expects a book to be, or how long you (as the publisher) expect it to be—will help you work smarter, not harder.

That said, how long should a book *really* be? The general answer is that each manuscript should be long enough to adequately tell its story or provide the information required. Thus, one could say each manuscript should be as long as it needs to be. Tell your story or share your knowledge in as many words as necessary—no more, no less. Of course, if you independently publish, you have the ability to make this decision. If you traditionally publish, you can propose the length of your book, but the publisher has final say.

The average nonfiction book, such as something in the how-to or self-help category, runs anywhere from 40,000 to 80,000 words. Memoirs tend to be about 60,000 to 90,000 words long. Biographies or historical texts sometimes run upwards of 200,000 words, but be sure you have a contract in hand before you write that much. You don't want to spend years on a book only to find out that it won't sell or that someone else beat you to the punch.

The average mainstream adult novel is 60,000 to 120,000 words (on the lower end for new authors), while YA novels tend to be 40,000 to 80,000 words long. In terms of mainstream adult fiction, the YA novel equates to a novella.

Still unsure of how long to make your book? Go out and find similar books to the one you want to write, and determine how many words are printed from cover to cover. Then model your manuscript after that book. If you want to write a memoir, for example, look at four or five similar memoirs and determine their word counts. Then produce a manuscript that

MANUAL

falls within a similar range. If you plan to traditionally publish, check out the length of the books produced by the publishers you plan to approach. Having a model is always a good idea.

E-books vary widely in length. An e-book might be quite short—3,000 words, or as short as you can get away with—or as long as a full-length book. In fact, many long-form printed books are turned into e-books, and according to a study released in May 2013 by Mark Coker of Smashwords.com, longer e-books actually sell better. He reports, "For the second year running, we found definitive evidence that e-book readers—voting with their dollars, euros, pounds, krone, krona, and koruna—overwhelmingly prefer longer books over shorter books. The top 100 best-selling Smashwords books averaged 115,000 words. When we examined the word counts of books in other sales rank bands, we found the lower the word count, the lower the sales."

Here's a handy tool I learned from agent Michael Larsen, author of *How to a Write Book Proposal*: He used to recommend that the number of lines written for each chapter summary in a book proposal equate to the number of pages written for each chapter. Of course, if you haven't written your book yet, you won't know the length of each chapter. You can take an educated guess based on the number of lines in your chapter summaries. I find this method makes me write a tighter chapter-by-chapter synopsis. A typical double-spaced one-page summary might have eighteen to twenty-four lines of copy on it. That's 3,750 to 4,500+ words per chapter. If I were writing a nonfiction book with twelve chapters, I could now easily estimate that it would be at least 50,000 words in length.

That also gives me an estimate of page count. The average Word document (with 12-point Times New Roman font, double-spaced) has about 275 words per page, making a 50,000-word document approximately 180 Word document pages long.

Determining how many actual pages will be in your published book can only be done accurately if you know your page size, font style and size, paragraph and line spacing, header sizes, the spacing and style of boxes, charts, bullet lists, and of course, the total number of words. The book may also have an index, and front and back matter will be added to the final product. However, Kristen J. Eckstein of Imagine! Studios, LLC, claims that if you format your Word document using 12 point Arial (or Helvetica), and 1.5 spacing with 1" margins, you can arrive at almost the exact final page count for a 5.5" × 8.5" or 6" × 9" standard book (given that there are no charts, graphs, bullet lists, etc.). (Keep in mind that most agents and editors will ask to see a full double-spaced manuscript for fiction or several chapters for nonfiction, and this will help them get a sense of the book's length.)

You can also determine page count and word count based on the number of chapters you plan on including and the estimated length of each chapter. Write a sample chapter or two, for example. See how long they are. Most often, books contain chapters of similar length. If your first two chapters are about 3,000 words long, you can assume the others containing the same amount of information or content (based on your chapter-by-chapter synopsis) will be that length as well. This is yet another way your TOC and summaries will come in handy. Multiply the number of chapters by the average chapter length, and then take the total and divide by 275 to get the number of manuscript pages. For published book pages, repeat the calculation above. If you write several sample chapters and chapter length changes considerably, you know you need to re-evaluate your book's length.

Or calculate your word count based on the number of scenes per chapter or vignettes per chapter. How long will each one be? Multiply that by the number of chapters in your book. This will give you an estimated word count, which you can then also convert into a page count.

Write Some Content!

Finally, you are ready to write. Depending on the publishing path you have chosen and the type of book you are writing, you can write:

- sample chapters for your nonfiction book (if you plan to traditionally publish and to write a book proposal)
- your whole manuscript (if you are writing fiction and want to traditionally publish or to self-publish, or if you are writing nonfiction and plan to self-publish)

The work you have done up to this point provides you with a phenomenal writing guide you can use to easily, if not effortlessly, produce a manuscript. Here's how you put the pieces together to help write your book.

Take the Overview you created in Step #2 (pitch, book summary, and list of benefits) and Step #5 (TOC) and this current step, Step #6 (chapter-by-chapter synopsis or stand-alone synopsis) and put all of them into a document labeled "[Book Title] Writing Guide." If you wrote a purpose statement include that, too. Next, copy and paste each chapter summary individually into a new computer file and save it as "Chapter X." Also, copy and paste your pitch into that document and place it above the chapter summary. This will remind you of your overall message before you begin each chapter.

If you are writing nonfiction, take each chapter summary (in the individual file) and break your sentences or paragraphs into smaller segments using subheads or bulleted points. Think of these as little chunks of content you need to flesh out and develop.

MANUAL

If you are writing fiction and have written a chapter-by-chapter synopsis, break these into scenes. You can do this by leaving space between the paragraphs or sentences or by using bullets.

Then use this five-step process each time you write:

1. Take out the first document, "[Book Title] Writing Guide."

2. Read the Overview, which contains your pitch, book summary, and list of benefits. Also read your purpose statement. This reminds you of the job you must do—the book you must create—and your promises to your readers.

3. Open the chapter document you are working on today and begin writing, going from bullet point to bullet point, scene to scene, or section to section as dictated by your summary until you get to the end of your chapter.

4. Reread the complete summary of "Chapter 1" (or whatever chapter you worked on); determine if you achieved all your goals.

5. Reread the first page or two of the guide (pitch, book description, and list of benefits); ensure you delivered on your promises in this particular chapter.

If breaking your chapter summaries into smaller chunks does not work well for you, then simply leave the full summary at the top of the first page of your chapter and refer back to it as you write. It still serves as an effective writing guide.

In this way you include all the material you said you would cover in each chapter—and without needing to wrack your brain to remember what you said you would write. Not only that, you will write according to your readers, your market, the book's description, and the benefits you promised to provide.

This process will help you maintain your Author Attitude as you write, too. You get to be creative, and at the same time you retain a big-picture business view of your book—the identical view an agent or an acquisitions editor would have of your manuscript. In this way, you won't get lost as you write but will continue steadily following your directions and map toward your destination—a completed, salable manuscript. *WOOT! WOOT!*

Suggested Reading:

Fiction

Outlining Your Novel: Map Your Way to Success by K.M. Weiland

Manuscript Makeover: Revision Techniques No Fiction Writer Can Ignore by Elizabeth Lyons

Ready, Set, Novel!: A Workbook by Chris Baty

The Plot Whisperer: Secrets of Story Structure Any Writer Can Master by Martha Alderson

The Plot Whisperer Workbook by Martha Alderson

Writing the Breakout Novel Workbook by Donald Maass

Writing a Killer Thriller: An Editor's Guide to Writing Compelling Fiction by Jodie Renner

YA

Writing Great Books for Young Adults by Regina Brooks

Writing Irresistible Kidlit: The Ultimate Guide to Crafting Fiction for Young Adult and Middle Grade Readers by Mary Kole

Memoir

Writing the Memoir: From Truth to Art by Judith Barrington

Writing and Selling Your Memoir by Paula Balzer

Journey of Memoir: The Three Stages of Memoir Writing by Linda Joy Myers

The Memoir Project by Marion Roach

Writing About Your Life: A Journey into the Past by William Zinsser

Nonfiction

Telling True Stories: A Nonfiction Writer's Guide by Mark Kramer

Creative Nonfiction: Researching and Crafting Stories of Real Life by Philip Gerard

Writing Creative Nonfiction by Carolyn Forche and Philip Gerard

The Truth of the Matter: Art and Craft in Creative Nonfiction by Dinty W. Moore

Follow the Story: How to Write Successful Nonfiction by James B. Stewart

Writing Nonfiction: Turning Thoughts Into Books by Dan Poynter

MANUAL

STEP #7

Discover Ways to Brand Yourself and Earn More Money

Now that you have created a map and directions for the completion of your manuscript—and possibly even your first chapter or full manuscript—the Author Training Process asks you to extend your vision of success beyond the publication of your first book. In this step you consider how to support your book and further your writing career. There's more to reaching your goal—successful authorship—than producing a manuscript. And your map (for your business plan, and later on a formal book proposal) needs to include these details, too.

Step #7 in the Author Training Process, *Discover Ways to Brand Yourself and Earn More Money,* is often overlooked by writers who fail to see the big picture, which in this case includes the longevity of their own career as writers and of their book's sales life. They simply see themselves as authors of one book—the one they would like to write at this moment.

If this describes you, remove your blinders. An Author Attitude involves seeing the big picture of your book, yourself, and your career. It means conceptualizing how you want readers to think about you and your book, or books, and how you want to build a career in writing. To earn a living from your book, you have to become a savvy entrepreneur and discover ways to build a business around your book. This entails viewing yourself and your books as a brand rather than just as a writer or an author. It also means having the potential to become more than a one-book wonder.

While your current book project requires you to focus your energy and attention on it if it is to succeed, you also must think beyond this particular book. Agents and publishers consider your future as a writer when they look at your first book idea, and so should you. This long-term vision, which you created in Step #1, is part of your business plan. (If you didn't include additional titles in your vision of success, go back after you read this chapter and rewrite your vision to include the elements discussed here.)

When you visualized your career, how many books did you see yourself writing? Where did you see yourself in ten years? Where did you see your book? Did you see yourself continuing to receive income from it for many years? Or possibly forever? Did you see yourself speaking and teaching on topics related to that book? Did you see yourself writing additional related books?

Your vision—and your map—needs to extend beyond the completion of your manuscript and beyond the release of your published book. That's just one destination—not the final one—if you want to become a successful author and create a career as an author. Step #7, *Discover Ways to Brand Yourself and Earn More Money*, corresponds with several optional sections in a book proposal called "Spinoffs," "Subsidiary Rights," and "Resources Needed to Complete the Book." These sections ask you to consider:

- additional books you might write
- additional products and services you might offer
- the money you need to complete your current project and begin earning additional income

Developing additional books and products constitutes platform-building and promotional activities for serious writers and authorpreneurs. These activities require that you think about what readers will naturally want from you after the publication of your first book. Publishers want to know how you plan to keep the momentum going to sell the first book. You might accomplish this with your second book or with additional products.

Write More, Sell More

In the first section, Spinoffs, you provide a list of the follow-up books or series you would like to write, including a short pitch for each one. If you include this in a book proposal, it shows a publisher you have a long-term view of your career as an author and the creativity and stamina to create that career. A series of books on a topic or a novel with sequels can build a brand for an author. A brand makes you more recognizable to readers and more "discoverable" on the Internet; it generally helps sell products. That's attractive to any publisher, including a self-publisher.

The more you write and publish, the more products you sell. This is known as the Long-Tail Effect. If you want to know more about this, read Chris Anderson's October 2004 article, "The Long Tail" in *Wired Magazine*, or get the book he wrote based on this article, titled *The Long Tail: Why the Future of Business Is Selling Less of More.* Here's how the Long-Tail principle might work for you: If your first book sells well enough for a publisher to want you to write a second book, and that second book sells well enough for you to write a third, it's possible your third book might become a bestseller. Then people who never heard of you before will discover your first two books and start buying them, making them bestsellers. Not only that, a book you self-published four years before your first traditional publishing deal, which you never bothered to promote (causing it to sell only about two hundred copies in the last ten years) suddenly gets discovered by some of your new fans. Thus, that book starts selling one hundred or so copies per day. This is the Long-Tail Effect in action, and this is why agents and publishers look for writers with plans to write many books.

Novelist Chris Cleave provides a good example of how the Long-Tail Effect works. When his novel *Little Bee* became a bestseller, his previous books were then reissued in paperback with new covers. This helped him sell more copies of all of his books.

Sheree Bykofsky and Jennifer Basye Sander explain in *The Complete Idiot's Guide to Getting Published (5th Edition)* that publishers look for fiction writers who can "go the distance"—write ten to twenty books in ten to twenty years—because it "takes time and money to build an audience for a new novelist. Once that audience exists, the sky's the limit. People who read fiction read their favorite writers. And when they find a new writer, they read everything that writer ever wrote—as well as everything he or she goes on to write in the future. This makes successful novelists an excellent investment for publishers. It more than makes up for the initial investment required to build an author's name."

The co-authors write, "That's why it's not enough to show the publishing world you can write one great novel. You have to convince them you can do it over and over. Show them that you, too, are in it for the long haul and that you can keep them turning pages through ten or twenty books over ten or twenty years."

Michael Larsen calls spinoffs "the hottest tip" in the fourth edition of his book *How to Write a Book Proposal.* He explains that by coming up with multiple book ideas, you use niche craft to create a career out of your book idea. "Agents and editors don't want literary one-night stands," he says. "They want to discover writers, not just books. Writers who turn out a book a year, each book better and more profitable than the last, are the foundation of successful agents and publishers."

I love spinoffs and have a long list of them for myself in my business plans. In most cases, each book idea is clearly conceived from another; they follow logically one to the next and serve as a map for my career path. I actually have many interests, though. I've grouped some of these interests together to create two distinct subject areas in which I work and write: writing/authorship/blogging and personal growth/spirituality. Although there are some books I'd prefer to write now, I'm traveling along the map in a logical manner. By taking the time periodically to review my spinoffs with my branding in mind—and my vision—I can determine how to bridge the gap between my two areas of interest. And my readers, hopefully, will come along with me. In this way, I can build my brand and my readership for both types of books at the same time. I also can make my vision a reality.

That said, I didn't know that much about branding when I began my writing journey. So I wrote a few short books—twelve actually—without a complete map. Luckily, they were self-published. I can go back, revise them, and put out new editions that fit my branding.

Carla King considered spinoffs in her business plan and has branded herself successfully. She says sales of her *American Borders* has trailed off because it was released in 2010, but her new book will help support her brand, Motorcycle Misadventures. "I expect that when *China Road* hits, I'll gain more awareness as an author. If readers like *China Road*, they'll buy *American Borders*. I'll have an ad for it in my new book, maybe with a discount code," says King. "And those who like *American Borders* will buy *China Road*, of course."

King, who goes by "Miss Adventuring" on social media, named her publishing company Misadventures Media. She explains, "It can be the umbrella for motorcycling, 4×4 off-road vehicles, scuba diving, aviation, and even my *Self-Publishing Boot Camp*," a book and a course she teaches. "I'm writing a specialized version of *Self-Publishing Boot Camp* for the travel market, titled *Self-Publishing Safari*."

King has kept spinoffs and branding in mind as a way to help her and her books succeed. "I have consciously branded myself as an adventure traveler focusing on adventure motorcycling at first and branching out into other adventures."

Having ideas for spinoffs helps present you as a good publishing partner because they demonstrate your future plans to produce books, whether traditionally or via self-publishing. A partner's investment in you has more potential to pay off if you publish multiple books. That's why best-selling indie romance writers like Bella Andre, author of the Sullivan Series, ended up with a groundbreaking print-only deal with Harlequin last year. She wrote multiple books following a successful theme or in a high-interest genre and retained all e-book rights, foreign translation rights, audio rights, and film rights in the seven-figure print-only deal and will continue self-publishing the Sullivan e-books with all major retailers.

Other authors who use spinoffs and common-thread themes successfully to brand themselves and increase sales include Lorraine Chittock, a female adventure author and photographer who wrote a series of animal-related books, including *Cairo Cats*, *Dogs without Borders*, and *On a Mission from Dog*; Joseph Berk, who writes books that examine useful topics including manufacturing processes and vehicles, such as *Systems Failure Analysis, Cost Reduction and Optimization for Manufacturing and Industrial Companies, The Complete Book of Police and Military Motorcycles,* and *Total Quality Management: Implementing Continuous Improvement*; and Edwidge Danticat, who writes stories about Haiti, where she was born, but also creates nonfiction spinoffs, such as *Create Dangerously: The Immigrant Artist at Work. Breath, Eyes, Memory* was an Oprah Book Club pick.

Crossing genres while continuing to write about one theme or topic is another superb way to produce spinoffs and brand yourself. Or if you are a fiction writer, consider writing a nonfiction book about your craft or about the particular subject in your novels. A writer of crime novels may consider penning a nonfiction book about his or her favorite criminal, mobster, detective, or period in crime history, and vice versa. You can create a brand, but you don't have to repeat yourself. Having a brand and writing spinoffs is about expanding your creativity, visibility, and marketability rather than limiting yourself to one book.

When readers know you for writing about something in particular, they will seek you out over and over again for books on that subject or for that "something" for which you are known. I love books on human potential and spirituality. I often read the same authors, like Wayne W. Dyer, who has become known—branded—as the "father of motivation."

I've also read quite a number of Jack Canfield's books. While most writers think of him as the originator of the Chicken Soup for the Soul series, which fostered the emergence of inspirational anthologies as a genre, he has become known as "America's #1 Success Coach." That's his brand. His other books include *The Success Principles* and *The Aladdin Factor.* He offers numerous products and services from his website that also brand him as a success coach.

On a smaller scale, Mignon Fogarty, also known as "Grammar Girl," has done a nice job branding herself with eight self-published books in her Grammar Girl Series, including *Grammar Girl's Quick and Dirty Tips for Better Writing, Grammar Girl's 101 Misused Words You'll Never Confuse Again*, and *Grammar Girl's 101 Troublesome Words You'll Master in No Time*. Not only that, she has an app, podcasts, coffee mugs, and T-shirts. When you think of "grammar," you think of Fogarty.

Go to her website or pick up one of her books, and take a look at how Fogarty presents her topic of using good grammar, a topic that can often come across as boring. Instead, she makes it fun. Her site is different and has personality. Her style and the attitude she brings to her topic is part of branding, too.

Or there's Dana Lynn Smith, known as the "Savvy Book Marketer," with seven e-books in her Savvy Book Marketer series, including *How to Get Your Book Reviewed, The Savvy Book Marketer's Guide to Successful Social Marketing, The Savvy Book Marketer's Guide to Selling Your Book to Libraries,* and *Facebook Guide for Authors.* She also has two training programs. If you want savvy marketing tips, you think of Smith, who also lends her topic a personality and style all her own—practical and businesslike but friendly and accessible.

Martha Alderson has created a brand with her Plot Whisperer books. She started with four successful self-published books, including *Blockbuster Plots.* Then because of her successful blog, Plot Whisperer for Writers and Readers, and her success record as an indie publisher, she received a traditional deal for *The Plot Whisperer.* She now has three books in that series, including *The Plot Whisperer Book of Writing Prompts* and *The Plot Whisper Workbook: Step-by-Step Exercises to Help You Create Compelling Stories,* because Adams Media wanted to build her brand.

Additionally, take a look at Chris Guillebeau, author of *The $100 Startup* and *The Art of Nonconformity.* He has a number of "Unconventional Guides," an Art of Nonconformity blog, groups, and a summit. Want to do it differently? See Guillebeau.

In the fiction category, it's harder to find good examples of branding. Most authors rely on writing many spinoffs in one genre to accomplish a good brand. Visit R.L. Stine's website to see great branding by a novelist. This children's fiction author, known for his Goosebumps series, incorporates creepy music, a Funhouse, a Rainy Night Theater, and a note that welcomes you to "Horrorland" on his website. There's no question about the genre of his books.

Or look at Cindy Woodsmall's website. She writes Amish romance stories. The banner on her site features a beautiful Amish farm scene, and while promoting all her books, she offers Amish recipes and quilt giveaways from the site.

How to Spin Your Book into Multiple Titles and a Brand

You'll be amazed by what you can come up with if you take the time to brainstorm additional book ideas. Think of new ideas for books related to the one you've worked on during the Author Training Process. Then try a mind-mapping process. Put your current book title or subject in the middle of the mind map, and see how many related book topics you can create. Make a list of books that support each other, and develop spinoffs or a series.

Think of all the other subject areas that interest you. Think of all the different topics you'd like to write about and what it is you "do" or would like to do in a broader sense. Ask yourself questions like:

- Who am I as a writer and a person?
- How do I want to be known?
- How can the books I write support me in becoming who I want to be?
- How can the books I write help me fulfill my purpose as a person as well as a writer?

Is there a central theme running through all your answers? Can this theme help you create spinoff books?

Group your book ideas by subject matter, and find a theme that would serve as the umbrella for all the topics. Then try to devise a brand for yourself as an author, and let the books support your brand.

I spent considerable time on this exercise. It took me over a year to hone my brand, and like other businesspeople, I have refined my brand's message over time. I worked with a media coach as well as with a friend to try and target what I do, what I do for others, what I want to do, what excites me, how I wanted to be perceived, and what I wanted to be known for. I decided on *Inspiration to Creation Coach* because it encompassed both areas of my work (writing/publishing and personal growth/spirituality), and I was able to pull in my last name with an acronym: **A**chieve **M**ore **I**nspired **R**esults. In both pieces of this branding, you can find the elements of all that I "do" and all that I "am." It may not be explicit, but it's there. I then created a website (ninaamir.com) to serve as an umbrella for my other sites. This is my branding site and a way for readers or the media to easily find me and my other sites.

As you develop your branding and your spinoffs, each new book idea you create should ideally relate to the last. For example, maybe your new idea picks up where the last book left off, or maybe it goes deeper into a concept introduced in an earlier book. You might touch on the concepts you plan to write about in your next book, or you could write each chapter with the idea of expanding them into separate books later. In this way, one book feeds into another. You want to introduce concepts in your first book that make readers want to purchase your next book but that also make you the expert on that topic or create a name for you in your genre.

The manual you are reading provides a great example of this principle. In my previous book, *How to Blog a Book*, I introduced the concept of the "proposal process." I have a chapter that discusses this process and shows readers how to use it. This book expands on that particular chapter by discussing only the proposal process concept, which I renamed the Author Training Process. Hopefully, people interested in the first book will want to learn more about the process and purchase *The Author Training Manual*. Also, readers of this book might want to read *How to Blog a Book* as a way to build platform and write a book. The two books together enhance my expert status in the area of writing and publishing. However, one of my students told me she purchased my self-published book, *The Priestess Practice*, after buying *How to Blog a Book* and then began to follow my blogs. That's how she also ended up taking my course, Author Training 101. You never know how a reader will find you, but this example demonstrates well the Long-Tail Effect.

If the idea of planning two or three spinoff books feels overwhelming, or if branding seems too large a concept for you right now or doesn't work with the type of writing you do, simply keep your current book in mind when completing this step. This should be easy since you've just finished planning its content. Then think about *one* book that could logically follow it. This becomes the one spinoff you include in your business plan.

However, if you plan to write a novel you know you will make into a series, in Step #7 you could write pitches for the next few books in the series. Or if you don't plan to write a series, maybe you have one character you could write a book about after the first is published. Diana Gabaldon is best known for her Outlander series but has also written numerous books about Lord John Grey, a secondary Outlander character. If you plan to write a book for a specific audience, like a book on business tips, you could pitch books for several related niche markets, like business for women, teens, or first-time entrepreneurs. If you plan to write a book for an elementary-level audience, you could pitch books for intermediate and advanced audiences, not to mention elementary-, middle-, high school-, or college-level readers. A children's book could be adapted for the young adult market or even for adults (and vice versa). Here are some other ideas:

1. Build on the ideas mentioned in your book or expand a chapter to a full spinoff, as I mentioned earlier.
2. Write a series that centers on a secondary or minor character in your novel.
3. Write a similar nonfiction book directed at a new market.
4. Write nonfiction books about the themes or issues in your novel, or write a novel based on a nonfiction topic that interests you.

Don't think that because you write novels you are excluded from building a business around your book with products, services, or other books. If you put on your business hat and consider the themes and issues in your book(s), you can pull these out and discuss them in the same way nonfiction authors do. Novelist Anita Diamant is a good example of this principle at work. She wrote the international bestseller *The Red Tent*, a book about the biblical character Dina, as well as three other novels featuring Jewish characters or based on events in Jewish history. Plus, she wrote *The New Jewish Wedding, Living a Jewish Life,* and five other Jewish-related nonfiction books. She also has a CD of songs she wrote.

Many novelists compose nonfiction about writing, such as Chuck Wendig and James Scott Bell. Bell also has two nonfiction books on unrelated topics, *How to Achieve Your Goals and Dreams* and *How to Manage the Time of Your Life*. He offers writing workshops.

If you are still having trouble thinking how you might produce spinoffs, look for authors you know who have written more than one book, have written in multiple genres or formats, or who have also built a business around their books. Here are a few examples:

- Suze Orman, the personal finance guru (and not even a writer first) has ten books all related to money or money and women. Orman also has twenty-five different products related to her books, like a Protection Portfolio and an Identity Protector.
- Organizational and personal productivity expert David Allen has written five books. On his website he offers these bundled in a variety of ways along with numerous productivity products (too many to count), services, educational opportunities, and much, much more.
- Deepak Chopra has sixty-five books (with twenty *New York Times* bestsellers in both the fiction and nonfiction categories), all of them about physical, mental, emotional, spiritual, and social wellness—and also books for children. Additionally, he has numerous products related to this subject area, including supplements, herbs, jewelry, gifts, videos, CDs, and even a new line of products with Oprah Winfrey.
- Dan Millman has eleven books, including two children's books, nonfiction and fiction, all based upon his initial hit, *The Way of the Peaceful Warrior.*
- J.K. Rowling has written eleven books, seven in the Harry Potter series, plus three short related books and one adult novel. Additionally, her company sells numerous Harry Potter games, figurines, and related products, including the Wizardly World of Harry Potter at Universal Orlando Resort in Florida, Pottermore Website with Sony, and Wonderbook: Book of Spells for Playstation 3.
- Wayne W. Dyer PhD. has over thirty books, many audio programs and videos, and three children's books.

- Nora Roberts has written two hundred romance books since her first book was published in 1980. Multiple TV movies are based on her work. She has created the Nora Roberts Foundation (to support literacy), and she even created a jewelry line based on her books.

If two hundred books seems a bit out of your realm, no worries. Few writers are that prolific, and no agent or editor is going to be interested in all two hundred of your book ideas when they look over your proposal. The point is to start thinking beyond your first book because one of the questions agents and editors will ask themselves is, "Is this author a one-book or multiple-book wonder?" Publishing professionals tend to be less interested in single-book authors. Agents, in particular, invest a lot of time and energy into clients for little financial reward (15 percent of an advance, which these days could be as little as $2,000, and on sales. The average book, if you recall, sells only about 250 copies). Assuming you have much better-than-average sales, the publisher will want to see a second or third book from you to make the initial investment more worthwhile. With three books out, you can achieve more sales over time, plus you become better known.

To factor your spinoffs into your business plan, produce a list of two to five book titles, including subtitles, and a 50-word pitch for each one. You don't have to polish these to a high shine. Just brainstorm until you come up with a few titles that support your current book idea or indicate the path you plan to take as an author. If you really want to do a more complete version of this list, write a one-page proposal for each new idea. Include details on the market, competition, and how you will promote the book. Or show how you can promote it in a way that helps sell the other previously published titles and build your career around these books.

Become an Authorpreneur

You also can help brand yourself as an author by becoming an entrepreneur, or an authorpreneur. Consider turning yourself into a brand, like Nike, which began with a pair of running shoes and expanded to clothing and a variety of other products. If you are like most people, each time you see the "swoosh," you think, "Nike." Not only that, you think, "Just do it." That's how you want readers to think of you—you want them to associate your name with something meaningful and to know they can come to you for more than just one book or several books; you want them to know you have a variety of products related to those books.

MANUAL

You will make the most money as an author if you become an authorpreneur. If you have developed a trusted brand, then your readers will purchase your books, products, and services because they relate to them and to you—to your image or to your company and what it stands for or means to them. They will know, like, and trust you—and want to buy whatever you offer.

Suze Orman is a great example of an author who has successfully transformed her name into a brand. If you think of personal finance, you think of Orman, and she has a variety of products and services to offer on her website. Dr. Mehmet Oz has become a household name when it comes to personal health. He has ten books in print and a television show. Both Orman and Oz surely make money from their books, but they have done more than that. They have built recognizable brands and businesses around their books, as well as around their expertise, with a wide range of products.

Although novelist Stephen King's fifty books branded him as a contemporary horror, suspense, science fiction, and fantasy author, he also has five nonfiction books on writing. He writes magazine colums, produces e-book singles, and writes television and movie scripts. In fact, he broke out of publishing when his books began to be adapted as screenplays. Now he writes television shows, like *Under the Dome.*

Or you could follow Joanna Penn's lead. She started out with a self-published nonfiction book called *Career Change: Stop hating your job, discover what you really want to do with your life, and start doing it!* Then she decided to self-publish thrillers under the name J.F. Penn. However, because she blogged about her self-publishing process—and then about the process of also landing an agent—she branded herself as an expert on becoming a self-published novelist and writer entrepreneur—a writerpreneur. Indeed, she has multiple books—three to date in her Arkane thriller series. She also has at least eight different programs for writers who want to learn how to write or publish a book or make money with products related to their books.

Many products based on books fall into the Subsidiary Rights section of a book proposal or contract. These are rights granted to publish or produce in different formats additional works based on your original work, such as a paperback edition of an original hardcover book or a motion picture based on a novel. More often than not, you won't find this information in a book proposal, although it used to be fairly standard. You want to include this section in your business plan if you have an entrepreneurial spirit and plan to build a business around your book by manufacturing products and services. You can call it Products and Services if you like, since you may not plan on selling rights, especially if you aim to self-publish. Typically agents negotiate, and even write up, the Subsidiary Rights section in a proposal. In a contract, audio, video, film, television, courses, apps, games, and other products spun off a book fall under the auspices of Subsidiary Rights and provide another way for authors to become more attractive to publishers. These creative ideas for book-related products help increase book sales and expand your brand. Therefore, if you know you plan to create such products, mention them in a proposal to illustrate that you are a serious businessperson who can sell books in numerous ways. For a publisher, every book is a business center, and anything that sells books or makes money off a book is one more reason to purchase that manuscript. The same goes for you as an indie publisher; see this section as another way to increase the attractiveness of your investment, and consider creating many business centers.

Put simply, products and services related to your book represent opportunities to merchandise your book and increase book-based income. I want you to make money from the books you author—even if the majority of the income doesn't come from book sales, which it typically doesn't. As an authorpreneur, you can profit from writing a book in many ways, so take the time to evaluate your ability to make money as an author.

For each of the following suggestions, envision your book as you've detailed it thus far in the Author Training Process, and then consider how you might transform the book into the products on the list. How would your idea fit each product? How would your audience use this new product? Write a few sentences in your journal:

- audiobook
- courses, webinars, and teleseminars
- movies
- a television show
- action figures, clothing, jewelry, etc.
- membership sites
- keynote speeches
- online streaming videos

Have fun with this exercise because you never know when a silly idea might suddenly become plausible or even profitable. Including a list of products and services that might become offshoots of your book proves to a publisher and to yourself that you can do more than write. These items can give you additional ways to generate income as an author, and your likelihood of selling a decent amount of books and creating a career as an author grows if you produce more than books.

MANUAL

Ready and Able to Write and Publish?

The last part of Step #7 involves evaluating if you have the financial ability to move forward with writing and publishing your book and if you have the funds to create the products, services, and branding discussed earlier. Another section that has fallen out of use in a book proposal is called "Resources Needed to Complete the Book." It includes information about the costs associated with finishing a proposed book project, such as permissions. While it is used less often in book proposals, this section remains vitally important to your business plan, so be sure to include it. To complete this section, consider what expenses you might incur when producing your book—and if they will stop you from moving forward.

For instance, you might have the expense of:

- permissions from publishers for quotes or photos
- traveling for research purposes
- hiring editors, proofreaders, and/or designers
- hiring proposal consultants or editors
- hiring indexers
- buying cover art or interior photographs
- e-book conversion
- printing

Have you determined the costs of these things? If not, you need to do so. Finding exact costs for each of these, as well as the other items to follow later in this chapter, may be difficult because fees vary greatly. Consulting friends in the industry often provides the most helpful method, as they may refer you to reliable and affordable professionals. Otherwise, perform a Google search for manuscript editors or book doctors, and get a sense of their fees. Do the same for local designers, print-on-demand publishers, e-book services, etc. Persistent research and patience will eventually lead to acceptable estimates or even exact figures.

You also need to determine what marketing and PR you will need to do and what it will cost. You may need:

- a website or blog
- business cards
- a publicist or PR agent
- a professional headshot
- help with social networking
- assistance with a virtual book tour

Then you need to determine if you are able to pursue an agent or publisher or if you are ready to self-publish your book. If you are planning the indie-publishing route and are low on funds, you might need to produce an e-book first and earn the money for a print book. (However, you still need the funds for cover design and editing with an e-book.) Or if you are taking the traditional-publishing route, you might need to save the money for a proposal consultant to ensure your query and proposal are top-notch before you can seek an agent. Maybe you are ready to do what is necessary right now to publish your book or approach an agent or publisher.

As for your spinoff products and services, a few costs to consider include:

- website or blog site design and hosting (a blog can serve as a website)
- setup of an online store
- logo design
- branding help
- any type of product-creation assistance, such as transcription, video editing, or audio editing

Determine which products you want to pursue first, and then find out what it will cost to produce them—and if you will need help. You may be able to do all of it yourself if you are willing to take on the work and learn the skills; just apply your Author Attitude to these tasks.

If you feel stumped after this exercise because you don't have the resources to complete your book and/or produce your products and services, consider the following crowdfunding options:

- a kickstarter.com campaign to raise funds
- an indiegogo.com campaign to raise funds
- raising money on your blog or website with a PayPal button
- using a company like Pubslush.com, which only crowdfunds for book projects.

Jim Kukral wrote a book about crowdfunding the financial resources for your book: *Book Marketing for Kindle Authors: How I Raised Over $30K in 30-Days to Write My New Kindle Book (Crowdfunding Tips & Tricks for Authors)*.

Any of the elements from the list above, should you choose to use them, go into your business plan once you finish your evaluation.

Keep in mind that all three evaluations discussed in this chapter—multiple spinoff and branding books, products and services that financially support and brand your book, and resources required to move your project forward—provide essential information for your

MANUAL

business plan. Your ability to become a multiple-book author and brand yourself with those books will increase your potential to sell more books and succeed as an author, so look at this element carefully. Your ability to produce products and services that help you further that author brand and create additional income streams around your books gives you the ability to earn a living as an author. By examining the financial component of what it takes to produce your book, you can move forward with your project as a savvy businessperson ready and able to bring your book into the world. *WOOT!*

With that in mind, it's time to see *yourself*, rather than your book project, through an agent's or publisher's lens.

Suggested Reading:

Reinventing You: Define Your Brand, Imagine Your Future by Dorie Clark

Make a Name For Yourself: 8 Steps Every Woman Needs to Create a Personal Brand Strategy for Success by Robin Fisher Roffer

Be Your Own Brand: Achieve More of What You Want by Being More of Who You Are by David McNally and Karl D. Speak

You Are A Brand!: How Smart People Brand Themselves for Business Success by Catherine Kaputa

Managing Brand You: 7 Steps to Creating our Most Successful Self by Jerry S. Wilson

From Entrepreneur to Infopreneur: Make Money with Books, e-books and Information Products by Stephanie Chandler

Damn! Why Didn't I Write That?: How Ordinary People are Raking in $100,000.00 ... or More Writing Nonfiction Books & How You Can Too! by Marc McCutcheon

Official Get Rich Guide to Information Marketing: Build a Million Dollar Business Within 12 Months by Robert Skrob

Click Millionaires: Work Less, Live More with an Internet Business You Love by Scott Fox

The 4-Hour Workweek: Escape 9–5, Live Anywhere, and Join the New Rich by Timothy Ferriss

The Well-Fed Self-Publisher: How to Turn One Book into a Full-Time Living by Peter Bowerman

STEP #8

Weigh Whether You Are the Best Person to Write This Book ... *Now*

Like most aspiring authors, when inspiration hit, you probably assumed you were the right person to carry out your idea from start to finish. You also probably wanted to complete and publish your book as soon as possible. You saw yourself writing the manuscript, getting it traditionally or independently published, and then holding the bound book in your hands as you proudly showed your friends and family your name printed on its cover.

But are *you* really the best person to write your book ... and should you write and publish it *now*? These important questions need answers, even if you don't want to ask them or don't yet understand why you should have a response.

At this point in the process, you are adept at evaluating yourself—especially through the eyes of those who are more critical or have a business perspective. It's time for you to do this type of assessment one last time. When you first wrote your pitch in Step #2, I suggested that you address three related questions: "Why this book, why now, and why you?" It's time to get clear about that third point: *Why you?*

In Step #8 of your Author Training Process, *Weigh Whether You Are the Best Person to Write This Book ... Now,* you determine if you are ready and qualified to write your book at this moment, or if you need more qualifications, a higher expert status, an expert co-author, or more platform.

If you are a novelist, knowing if you are the right person to write your book may seem like a no-brainer. You may think that as long as you can write well and have a new story to tell, it's yours to tell. However, if you choose to write about crime, for example, you must know how criminals or cops act. If your criminals steal pieces of art, you must be an expert on art and art museums—or become one through research. If you possess an expertise, put it to use in your fiction. Know that even novelists, like James Patterson, for example, use co-authors to help them churn out so many books per year; you might consider finding one that offers you expertise or platform.

If you are writing a memoir, no one else is more qualified to write your story. However, your story must be extraordinary, and, again, you must excel at your craft.

If you write any other type of nonfiction, you need a marketable idea you can put into easily read and enjoyed words and the credentials or expertise to make readers or publishers trust you enough to purchase your book or believe what you have written.

As in most endeavors, timing is everything. Publishing is no different. For many reasons, it may be the right or wrong time to approach agents or publishers or to self-publish. You may want to be first to market with your idea, or it may be timely, necessary, or in the news, for example. Yet, you might still need to improve your craft, build a bigger platform, or obtain additional credentials. This step in the Author Training Process asks you to take a hard look at these issues.

You actually began this particular evaluation in Step #4 when you did your competitive analysis. At that time, you looked at yourself in comparison to the other authors who have written similar books to the one you plan to write. You also thought about it in Step #1 as you delved into your willingness to take on the many tasks necessary to succeed as an author, such as platform-building and promotion.

At this point, take these evaluations further. Try to drill down deeper as you: 1) create and evaluate your author biography (or bio, and 2) create and evaluate your author platform description.

Together, these parts of your business plan give you a tool for assessing your ability to write your book and sell it to readers right now.

Who Are You?

You will need an author bio for many reasons. You'll place one inside or on the back cover of your book; on your website or blog; on all of your social-media sites such as Twitter, Face-book, or Google Plus; at the bottom of every guest blog post you write, for a blog tour or virtual book tour when your book is released; on your Amazon Author Central page, and of course, in your book proposal (if you write one). You will need different lengths of bios for different purposes, such as for introductions when you speak, or for the bio at the end of a magazine article. Yet they should all be consistent to help your branding.

Once you have your bio written, it's easier to see what might be missing from your experience or background that could hold you back from achieving the "job" you desire. In this case, that job is "published author." See your bio as your résumé or a curriculum vitae. The training in this step requires seeing yourself through the eyes of a prospective business partner: an agent or publisher. Imagine they are reviewing your bio to determine if they want to go into business with you. How will they see you—as a good or bad partner, a qualified or unqualified partner, a highly trained or poorly trained partner?

To begin this training exercise, write a one-page, third-person bio about yourself. (The only place you might choose to use a first-person bio is on your website or blog.) Include all the pertinent information that proves you are qualified to write your book and become a publishing partner for an agent and, ultimately, a publisher. Write with this in mind even if you plan to self-publish; indie publishers need to view their credentials just as critically. Include your most important or relevant credentials first and then all other details in descending order of importance. Be sure to include the following:

- education
- personal background
- life experience
- business (if relevant)
- interests
- passions
- books you have published (along with the publishers and sales figures, if impressive)
- awards
- special skills
- conferences you've attended or participated in
- contests you've won
- professional memberships

Have someone help you with this exercise. They might offer a more objective view of your strongest credentials and experience. Or ask a variety of people who know you and what you have accomplished that they think qualifies you to write your book. Add these things to your bio.

You also can briefly mention family, interests, hobbies, and where you live. At the end of the bio, include a list of quotes or reviews about your work from publications or opinion makers, or include letters or publicity that others would find impressive.

Once you have your one-page bio, whittle it down to a 150-word bio, a 100-word bio, a 75-word bio, and then a 50-word bio. You might also try a 140-character bio for Twitter.

These shorter bios can act as brief promotional pitches. Think of them as your own personal elevator speeches or branding statements, not your book pitch because it's all about *you* this time. Who are you? How do you want to be known? Are you "The XX Expert" or "The XX Coach"? This relates to the branding you did in the last step. Consider the spinoffs you think you might write. How would they help brand you? Will you write just fiction or nonfiction or both? How can you put all the books you write under one umbrella that people will recognize immediately by name—and will it be your name or a brand name? For example, I'm known as the "Inspiration to Creation Coach." I write about a variety of topics, but they all inspire my readers to create something in their personal or professional lives as well as to fulfill their potential. Joan Stewart is "The Publicity Hound"; everything she offers has to do with publicity, and her logo is a hound. (I assume she can sniff out the best story!)

Once you have written these shorter bios, take an objective look at them. What do you see? Do you see someone qualified to write the book you have outlined and described in previous steps of this training manual? Will your experience instill trust in a publisher who's considering investing money in you? Yes, investing in *you*. After all, you must produce, or create, the project the publisher will sell. The idea is yours, but the publisher isn't buying just the idea; he is buying a finished manuscript. Your experience has to instill trust that you can write a valuable book—that you have something worthwhile and credible to say—and that you can say it in a unique, compelling, believable, new, and well-crafted manner. (And that you will help sell the book after it has been published.)

Go back to your notes about the authors of competing books in your category. How do your credentials measure up to theirs? Are they all professionals, such as PhDs, rabbis, priests, ex-athletes, doctors, or CEOs of companies? Or are they just average people who had interesting life experiences? Where do you fall on that spectrum? Do you have more or fewer credentials, and are your credentials unique?

If you are having doubts about your credentials, you don't need to throw away your idea. You might still find a way to write your book. You may just need to look at other options or ways to write it. For example, to gain the expertise you need, you could:

- interview experts and conduct research
- find an expert co-author
- get an expert to write the foreword

If you are worried about your writing ability, you can:

- hire an editor or "book doctor"
- hire a ghostwriter
- dictate your project (and have the transcripts edited)

It's possible that you simply need to take some time to get more experience. Maybe you need six months to hone your craft. Maybe you need to seek out an expert co-author or someone to write a foreword so you and your book gain some authority or credibility. Or maybe you need to get some extra credentials, like a life-coaching degree or a teaching certificate.

When examining your credentials, consider one other factor before making the decision to move forward with your project: author platform.

What Is Author Platform and Why Do You Need It?

A literary agent introduced me to the term when I submitted my first proposal to Sheree Bykofsky Associates, Inc. I got a call from Janet Rosen, a literary agent, who told me she loved my idea, my book title, my writing, and even my proposal (the first I'd ever written), but … "You have no platform," she said. I had no idea what she was talking about and asked her to explain. "No one knows who you are," she said simply. "So no one will buy your book."

Remember, agents and publishers make money from book sales—your book sales. If you can't help sell books, they don't want to partner with you or invest in you. It's too risky. Smaller independent publishers and even some midsize publishers are less risk adverse. The size of your platform, to some extent, indicates how well you can help sell books; it's a built-in audience. And while there is much discussion about how much time should be devoted to platform-building and at what point in an author's career, most publishers want to see an author platform above many other things, especially for nonfiction authors. Although this is not a book on platform or platform-building, I will go over a few basics to help you understand what platform is, why you need it, and how to evaluate yours.

First things first: What does "author platform" really mean? According to Chuck Sambuchino, author of *Create Your Writer Platform*, "a platform is your visibility as an author" and "your personal ability to sell books right this instant." That's why publishers want to know if you have one—and why you need to evaluate whether you are ready to become an author *now*.

Michael Hyatt, author of the best-selling *Platform: Get Noticed in a Noisy World*, defines it as "the thing you have to stand on to be heard." In an interview in *Publishers Weekly* in May 2012, Hyatt says, "Until about six years ago, having a platform meant having a radio or TV show, a newspaper or magazine column, a best-selling book, or celebrity status. Today, a platform is about leading a tribe of engaged followers."

Seth Godin popularized the word *tribe* in his book *Tribes: We Need You to Lead Us,* when he introduced the concept of creating a group of engaged followers to lead. (If you recall, Godin says you don't create a tribe overnight. You must begin several years before the release of your book.)

I like the definition provided by Jane Friedman, web editor of the *Virginia Quarterly Review* and former publisher of Writer's Digest (F+W Media). She says agents and editors are "looking for someone with visibility and authority who has proven reach to a target audience." In the online world, there's lots of talk about "visibility" and "reach" and "authority," which is also called "influence." Yet, this applies to the offline world as well. Here's how these elements work when it comes to building platform in general:

Visibility: You do and say things that make people in your target market aware of you. This includes speaking, getting published in online and traditional publications, appearing on radio and television, and using social media, including social networks, blogging, podcasting, etc. Making yourself visible helps people get to know you and your work as well as to trust and like you. They become your fans, followers, peeps, subscribers. They become part of a community, or tribe, whose common denominator is you.

Reach: What you do and say gets shared or talked about. People mention you in social or traditional media. Your posts and status updates get tweeted, liked, +1'd. Thus, the ability you have to contact or touch people extends further than your current location or circle of acquaintances and beyond the bounds of your immediate community.

Authority: Your credentials and expertise give you authority in your field. Coupled with your visibility and reach, you gain authority in other areas as well and become influential.

Influence: You gain an ability to engage and affect others. They sign up for your mailing list, subscribe to your blog, follow you on social networks, take up your causes, listen to what you say, believe in you, agree with your opinion or what you write, and do what you ask.

Online, it is said that visibility + reach = influence, but this is true offline, too. If you can apply all of these elements—visibility, reach, authority, influence—to your target market, you create a platform. Therefore, having a platform means you become visible to the target audience you want your book to reach, your audience sees you as having authority, and your audience engages with you at a high level, thereby giving you influence in that market.

My definition of platform is: visibility, authority, and engagement with your book's target audience that gives you influence in that market.

But how big does your platform have to be?

Publishing houses look at the size and elements that make up your platform to determine if they want to offer you a book contract, but that doesn't mean you need a huge following to land a deal or to produce a successful self-published book. A huge following might help sell books … or not. Yet, midsize and large book publishers still look for a large, engaged platform because successful authors often have them—and they usually have Author Attitude.

What publishers don't realize but that you should know (especially if you plan to self-publish) is that a small, engaged platform could serve you just as well—if not better. In 2009, researchers showed that large numbers of followers on social networks did not always equate to "influence" or sales. For years, marketers have touted the idea that the more fans and followers you garner on social networks, the higher likelihood you have of actually selling something—in this case your book. Today, this is called "The Million Follower Fallacy." More researchers have gone on to study social-networking behavior and have corroborated the fact that those with the most followers don't always have the most influence. Greater influence goes to those social networkers whose status updates get shared and whose followers mentioned them.

The researchers came to the conclusion that "influence is not gained spontaneously or accidentally but through concerted effort. In order to gain and maintain influence, users need to keep great personal involvement." Take note: You need to work tenaciously at building platform.

An author platform also equates to how many people know and associate you and your name with something of value to them. Remember when you created a list of benefits? You made sure they were benefits your market wanted and needed and that no other authors had previously provided. This ties into authority—your expertise and credentials. Readers purchase books because they know and trust the author and associate value with that author. They don't purchase because the author has four million followers. Content marketing,

MANUAL

which includes giving your work away for free, and social media are based upon the idea of getting people to know, like, and trust you. That's engagement. That's platform.

Building that trust through a platform takes time, dedication, effort, money, and passion. Maybe you have worked on this, but maybe not … or maybe not enough. List all the things you've done to build your platform, and then list the things you plan to do in the next six to twelve months, such as:

- speaking engagements
- teaching
- teleseminars
- radio appearances
- television appearances
- blogging
- social networking
- podcasting
- hosting a radio show
- starting a forum or membership site
- writing for publications
- joining or participating in professional organizations

Make a record of the number of people in each of your social networks, on your mailing list, on your blog's subscriber list, etc.

When you are done, you should have a list of pertinent information with dates, places, names of organizations, titles of talks or articles, and numbers associated with your different activities. Is there anything missing? Share these lists with a friend, loved one, or fellow writer. What else could you be doing? Are there holes in your platform-creation plan? Are there things you have done in the past that helped or hindered your platform? Sometimes an outside opinion can expose missing items.

You can now evaluate the size of your platform. Big? Small? Medium?

Next, evaluate the engagement level of your platform. Do people comment on your blog posts, share your status updates, attend your webinars, and respond to your e-mails?

Last, how many of the items you included as you described your platform in list form are related to or have taken place in your target market? Are these activities directed at the audience you want to reach with your book? The answers to these questions give you an indication of the real size or efficacy of your platform—and if you are ready to publish now.

If you determine that you have a small but engaged platform comprised of people in your market, it could be fine to self-publish now or to approach a small publisher and continue growing your platform. If your platform is medium in size and engaged or large and engaged, you could try to publish with a larger publishing house or you could self-publish. If, however, your platform is nonexistent or small and unengaged, you might want to wait six months to a year—or more—until you have the kind of platform that results in book sales and fans who help promote your book. Waiting until you have created a healthy platform typically provides the path to successful authorship, even if it is not a popular one to take or one you prefer. It does make good business sense, though, which is why authors with small, nonexistent, or unengaged platforms do not land publishing deals or sell many self-published books.

The Platform section of a book proposal can make or break a traditional publishing deal. No platform, no deal in many cases—especially with nonfiction books and midsize to large publishing houses. Fiction authors and some memoirists don't have to worry quite as much about platform, but in the increasingly competitive world of publishing, platform has become even more important to these writers. So many celebrity memoirs exist because famous people have platforms—huge numbers of fans who will purchase anything that bears their name. For the same reason, cookbooks hardly ever get published these days without a celebrity chef as the author; publishers want a guarantee that the author has a built-in audience. The blog-to-book trend grew out of this same premise. To a publisher, a successful blog with thousands of readers a day represents a successfully test-marketed book idea, and the blog's readers or subscribers equate to potential book readers (i.e., platform).

If your platform doesn't quite make the grade, don't despair. You can fix it … over time. All the activities mentioned above will help build your platform. You don't have to do all of them. Pick the ones that resonate with you, and do them consistently. I personally find these some of my most fruitful platform-building activities:

- blogging
- choosing a few social networks on which to participate regularly
- guest-posting on blogs
- writing for online and traditional publications with large readerships
- radio interviews
- speaking

You may find something else appeals to you more and achieves better results, such as:

- YouTube videos

MANUAL

- podcasting
- moderating a group on a social network
- hosting an Internet radio show

While vital and necessary, remember that all of these things do take time away from writing. When it comes down to the wire, "enough platform" remains a subjective opinion, and each publisher will measure it with a different set of criteria. As Georgia Hughes, editorial director of New World Library, said, "If a proposal is really solid, even if the author has very little in the way of 'followers,' we might still be interested. And no matter the number of 'followers' or celebrity endorsers, if the proposal doesn't have something to say that we feel is fresh and useful for the reader, we aren't interested. There's no formula—[it's] still a very subjective process. Yes, certain types of things can make a big difference, but we need an overall sense of 1) is there a market, 2) does the author have something important to say, 3) does the author have a grasp of how to reach that market. It's a tricky business."

Do You Feel Compelled to Write and Publish Your Book?

Last, but not least, this part of Step #8 involves looking at how passionate you feel about writing and publishing your book. If you've gotten this far in the Author Training Process, it's time to check in on how you feel about your project now and see if you still feel inspired by your idea and the prospect of writing your book. Do you still feel passionate about it? Do you feel inspiration—creativity and the impulse to write—flowing through you? Do you feel you *must* write your book, or are you compelled to do so? Does writing and publishing your book feel like a personal mission or a soul purpose?

If so, that's a great thing. That type of passion will help you convince a publisher to take on your project, and it will help convince readers to buy your book.

Writing a Mission Statement is an optional part of a business plan, and it can be an important part of a book proposal. I encourage you to take the time to write a mission statement for four reasons.

1. Your mission statement clarifies why *you* need to write your book.
2. Your mission statement clarifies for your readers why you need to provide this information or tell this story to them.
3. Your mission statement becomes the foundation for your book; the book takes on your purpose, and you must make sure it fulfills or carries out that purpose by the time you have completed it.

4. Publishers will see your purpose and passion as a commitment to help the book succeed.

When you are done writing your Mission Statement, which need only be a paragraph or two long, read it to yourself and consider if it sounds like you have passion for your topic or story. Do the words sound like you are on a personal mission or have a sense of purpose you feel compelled to fulfill? Will readers or an agent or acquisitions editor read it and "get on board" with your cause or sense of urgency—your need to fulfill this mission? Will they understand why you are writing your book? Will they feel this statement shows your commitment to helping the book succeed through your promotional efforts? Does it make you feel confident that you will carry through on making your book a success?

Your sense of mission needs to come across the pages of your book. It needs to underlie everything—the benefits you listed, the TOC and all the content you write. It also needs to dovetail with the statement of purpose you wrote for the book itself. In other words, your purpose and the book's purpose need to be almost identical.

Go back and reread the purpose statement you wrote for your book in Step #2. Compare it with your own mission statement. Do the two align? If not, you may need to rethink your project or do a bit of editing and revising so they do. Possibly, you need to revamp your book's purpose or your mission statement.

Look at the work you did in Steps #5 and #6 to see if the TOC and Chapter Summaries or synopsis you produced carry out this mission. If not, something remains missing from your book—possibly your passion or purpose. If so, your book may not come across to readers as inspired. If you really feel "called" to write your book, make sure your passion and purpose comes through in every part of the business plan you have written as well as the manuscript you plan to produce.

If you feel it does, great! In fact, you should feel pretty inspired by now and ready to start writing! Passion, purpose, and inspiration tend to be contagious; they help you build excitement about your book. But if you don't feel passionate and inspired about your project anymore, ask yourself why you actually want to write this book—and if you still want to do so. It's possible that in the process of evaluating your idea, it changed too much or you lost interest. Or maybe you never had deep passion for the subject.

In his book *APE: How to Publish a Book*, Guy Kawasaki and Shawn Welch mention several reasons to write a book. These include:

1. to enrich readers' lives by providing knowledge (fiction or nonfiction), understanding (fiction or nonfiction), entertainment (fiction), or laughter (fiction)

MANUAL

2. to provide intellectual challenge

3. to further a cause

4. for catharsis

Why do you want to write your book?

I love writing my Mission Statement. I feel as if it's a chance for me to tell an agent or acquisitions editor a little bit more about me and why I feel so strongly that a book is necessary. It allows me to have a voice for a brief moment in the book proposal. Although written in the first person (and often the only first-person section), be sure you maintain a marketing focus; this part of your business plan must still argue for the salability of your book.

Answer this question before moving on: Could you just as easily *not* write your book as write it? If so, you better quit now! With all the work required to promote your book, you better have a large degree of passion and purpose for your topic and your message. When you combine these two elements, you feel inspired, and that inspiration comes across in your work. Plus, if you don't feel inspired, neither will your readers, potential book buyers, or potential publishing partners.

Not only that, your passion, purpose, and inspiration will keep you moving through the hard stuff—activities that feel like work or that you don't want to complete. It will help you do all those tasks that might feel tiresome or troublesome. It will remind you of why you are wearing all those different hats that leave your writer's hat hanging on the rack—to fulfill your purpose and the book's purpose.

Now you are ready to go on to the last step of your Author Training. *WOOT!*

Suggested Reading:

Create Your Writer Platform: The Key to Building an Audience, Selling More Books, and Finding Success as an Author by Chuck Sambuchino

Get Known Before the Book Deal: Use Your Personal Strengths to Grow an Author Platform by Christina Katz

Building Your Fanbase: A From-Scratch Guide for Indie Authors by Duolit and Shannon O'Neil

Platform: Get Noticed in a Noisy World by Michael Hyatt

The Author's Guide to Building an Online Platform: Leveraging the Internet to Sell More Books by Stephanie Chandler

MANUAL

STEP #9

Gauge If You Make a Good Publishing Partner or Indie Publisher

An integral part of your business plan involves considering *how* you will help your book succeed—what you will do to promote it once published. That's what a promotion plan details and what you must produce as you complete Step #9, *Gauge If You Make a Good Publishing Partner or Indie Publisher.* Your promotion plan is part of the overall business plan for your book. However, it's a plan in its own right.

This step is tied to the previous one, in which you determined if you have done anything to date to build author platform. Author platform serves as *prepublication promotion* for your book and for you as an author. The promotion plan you create serves as *post-publication promotion.* You need platform to successfully promote your book upon release. However, platform remains important during the book launch and post-launch periods and up until your next book has been published—and beyond. It's an ongoing process that requires an Author Attitude since you must be willing to build it continuously over time.

If you recall, in Step #1 you determined what success meant to you. You visualized success in a variety of ways—how it might affect your life, your ability to build a business around your book, and how many books you might sell per year. In the last chapter, you evaluated whether you have done anything to date to help you and your book succeed. Now it's time to put your platform to use with an action plan consisting of promotional ideas that target your market and sell books to readers.

Hold on to your business hat. Promotion equals business big time because it's all about selling books.

What Is a Promotion Plan … Really?

Your promotion plan represents the crux of your business plan for your book, and publishers take it very seriously. That's why approaching this step in your Author Training with an Author Attitude is crucial. Even if you hate salespeople, feel marketing is somehow dirty, or swore you would never sell or promote anything, if you want to succeed as an author, you *must* wear a promoter's hat. When you develop and evaluate your promotion plan, you want to clearly see what an agent or acquisitions editor sees and then evaluate in the same manner. They think "business" (and publishing business revolves around selling books), and so must you.

While the Platform section of a book proposal tells an agent or acquisitions editor if you have created an author platform from which you can sell your book, the Promotion section outlines specifically how you will sell that book once released to your desired market both from the author platform you have built and from beyond it in new places and in new ways. Remember, the Markets section relates how many potential buyers exist for your book; i.e., the audience for your book. Your business plan (if you are not trying to publish traditionally) does the same thing, but it's for your benefit as the self-publisher.

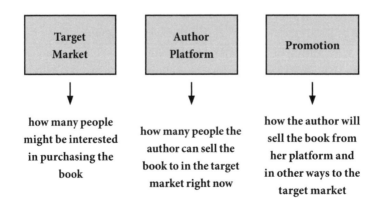

Target Market	Author Platform	Promotion
↓	↓	↓
how many people might be interested in purchasing the book	how many people the author can sell the book to in the target market right now	how the author will sell the book from her platform and in other ways to the target market

Thus, these three pieces work together to form an *almost* complete picture of your potential book sales. If you add the Competing Titles (the research and evaluation you completed in Step #4) into this formula, you form a more complete picture and the basis to make some fairly accurate conclusions about your book's potential to sell in a particular target market. Your Competing Titles section tells an agent or acquisitions editor—or just you—how well similar books have sold in your target market.

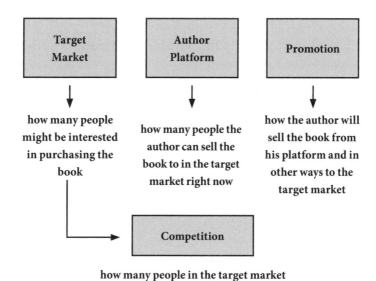

As you can see, the work you have done previously in your Author Training now comes into play as you put the final touch on your business plan—creating and evaluating how you will help promote your book. The way in which you plan to promote your book to potential readers is crucial to your book's success—more crucial even than the platform you built. Without a strong platform, however, you will find it very hard to succeed. Promotion turns into book sales, which is the name of the publishing game.

How to Create a Promotion Plan That Helps Your Book Succeed

Unlike some of the other steps in this training process, no difference exists between the Promotion section you will create for your business plan and the one you would include in a book proposal. In both cases, you tell a publisher—even when you are the publisher—what you will do to promote your book once it is released. The format is simple: At the top of the page, write "The author will:" (for traditional publishing) or "I will:" (for self-publishing), and follow this with a list of bulleted action items that describe how you will promote your book upon release.

Whether you plan to traditionally publish or self-publish, a promotion plan is essential. It is your to-do list once your book is published. It is how you will meet your goal of creating a successful book and serves as your roadmap beyond publication to your final destination—successful authorship. Without a promotion plan: You create a publishing business with no clear way of reaching customers—no way of letting readers know you and your book exist so they can purchase it. You wander around, book in hand, wondering how to get anyone to notice your book even if it has ended up in the online or brick-and-mortar bookstore.

Your promotion plan includes those things you will do online, such as:

- a blog tour
- a virtual book tour (blog tour plus podcast and online radio show tour)
- an e-mail blast to announce your book release
- a video book trailer
- online press releases
- blogging about your book
- free teleseminars based on the book

It also includes a list of those things you will do offline, such as:

- a speaking tour of the top three to five cities that target your market
- writing articles for top newspapers and magazines in your target market
- using a PR agent to seek out radio and television interviews and book reviews
- offering a series of workshops around the nation
- speaking at conferences in your target market

How to Target Your Market

Armed with your market research from Step #3, you can now think about how to target your market. Review the market description you produced. How can you reach that audience from your platform and use all you learned about building a platform? What do you know about the people in your target market? For instance, where do they hang out online and off? This type of information can lead you to ideas about where you could sell your book in bulk, such as a particular type of specialty store or online forum. It also might give you ideas about conferences at which you might speak or particular radio stations or podcasts you could pitch.

For example, if you are writing about dance, you might discover that your target audience—dance teachers—attends the Dance Teacher Summit each year. You could submit a speaking proposal to the summit organizers. Additionally, you could submit a proposal for a series of guest blog posts to danceadvantage.net, a highly trafficked website on the subject.

Let's return to the orchid example I mentioned earlier in this book. The research I completed makes it clear that a book on this topic might be sold in many places besides Amazon.com and brick-and-mortar bookstores. You could, for instance, sell it through small orchid shops as well as large garden-store chains, like Home Depot, and at orchid shows. Most people purchase their first orchid in a grocery store. Thinking like an authorpreneur, therefore, might lead to a way to target your book to grocery stores or to the orchid producers, who could market the book to grocery stores when they sell their flowers. Plus, publishers like books seen as gift items. Orchids make great gifts; if you can tie your book into the gift-giving aspect of orchids, all the better.

Remember Carla King and her self-published memoir about her escapades on her motorcycle? She sells her book not only in online bookstores and via Smashwords.com but also at motorcycling shows and adventure-travel shows. "At motorcycle shows, there is a big podium in the center of the convention hall and lots of noisy competition for attention, but usually when people walk by and see a woman talking and a slide show of motorcycling in China, Morocco, and Albania, for example, they slow down to take another look," King says. "I actually sell more books by hand at motorcycle shows than any other place. I walked away with $4,000 cash after my first one and was sold on doing conferences. I sell it for $20 flat, tax and autograph included, and people throw twenties at me all day."

If you know you have a niche market or a specific large market, consider creative ways to reach those readers. Often you can sell more books in places that are not bookstores. For instance, with my book *How to Blog a Book*, my publisher (Writer's Digest Books) explored putting the book in some Urban Outfitters stores with the thought that young, hip twenty- to thirty-year-olds might be interested in blogging. I have placed them in a local grocery store where some people know me. Whenever you're out and about, notice what types of books are being sold in untraditional places and think about where your readers shop or spend time. Could your book be sold in there?

If your book discusses coffee drinking, it could be sold in Starbucks or local coffee shops. If it's about business, it could be sold in FedEx/Kinkos or Office Depot. A novel about a lady with a dog-walking business in New York could be sold at dog shows and New York pet stores. The idea is to discover where your readers are and put your book in front of them.

Now take a look at your competitive analysis, which you created in Step #4. Did you discover anything about what your potential readers need and want that they *weren't* finding in other books? Apply this information to your promotion plan. You might write a short e-book related to your new book (like a spinoff) and give it to those on your mailing list for free if they purchase the book. You might offer those on your mailing list or those who subscribe to your blog a free excerpt from your book, then immediately follow up with a special offer. For instance, if they purchase the book, they get another free gift. Brainstorm ways to blog about your book in a manner that gives potential readers what you know they want and need and leads them ultimately to purchase your book. Provide a trail of bread crumbs, if you will, that leads to a "buy" button.

Before entering the marketplace, do some intelligence preparation—similar to what the military does before going into battle. "Spy" on other authors in your category. Find out where they speak, what organizations they belong to, and what activities they participate in online and off. How can you put that intel to use in your plan? Maybe you can arrange speaking gigs at the same places after your book is published, or you can join the same organizations. For example, many organizations will run newsletter articles about members who publish a book or have a success of some sort. Others will let you write an article or a blog post. By thinking ahead (as part of building platform), you can join the organization and make the impending announcement, article, or blog post a bullet point on your promotion plan.

Additionally, you can gather information from top websites in your category. Those of top bloggers and authors in your subject area may provide ideas for workshops, talks, teleseminars, courses, and more (or could provide a place to pitch a guest blog post). Notice how other authors promote their books. All of these items can be added to your promotion plan—especially if you can target an activity at a particular community or place that fits within your target market. Every time you can show that your promotional activities actually reach your audience, your promotion plan gets stronger in the eyes of an agent or editor. That means it should get stronger in your eyes as an indie publisher as well.

In addition, research specific publications that target your market and add writing for these magazines or newspapers to your plan. Figuring out how to approach specific organizations, online groups, or forums can prove fruitful. Of course, you want to use your social networks and mailing list. Be sure to take into consideration how you will promote via Facebook, Twitter, LinkedIn, Google Plus, and Pinterest, and include this in your plan.

Get creative as you build your promotion plan. Think outside the box. I love some of the things Patrick Schwerdtfeger, author of *Marketing Shortcuts for the Self-Employed*, did when his book was released. For example, he launched a Twitter tip campaign and a video tip campaign, providing one tip for every one of his eighty chapters. Take a look at his book for some out-of-the-box ideas.

Other great resources include:

- *Guerrilla Publicity for Writers* by Jay Conrad Levinson, Michael Larsen, and Rick Frishman
- *1001 Ways to Market Your Books* by John Kremer
- *Red Hot Internet Publicity* by Penny Sansevieri
- *The Frugal Book Promoter* by Carolyn Howard-Johnson
- *Plug Your Book* by Steve Weber

Don't forget to look at your platform-building activities for more ideas. You want to build on all you have been doing to promote your book. After all, that's what your platform is there for—to help you eventually sell books from it. Evaluate what has been achieving the best prepromotion results for you.

Then consider how to build on what's working. Could you:

- start a weekly Twitter chat?
- begin an online radio show using Blogtalkradio.com?
- create a contest via your blog or Facebook page?
- develop a thirty-day tip program (that includes a link to purchase your book) delivered by autoresponders to your e-mail list?
- host a series of Google hangouts?
- speak at conferences?
- teach or speak at colleges or in other classrooms?
- present your book as a supplemental text for a particular course in schools?

MANUAL

Last, as part of Step #7, you evaluated what resources you need to complete your book. It's time to revisit the issue of money. Promotion often takes money—money out of your pocket. Think about the funds you might need to carry out your promotion plan.

It's possible that you may need to stick to online promotion, which can be virtually (pun intended) free and a great option if you have a tight budget. Sometimes authors who receive a traditional publishing contract put their advance, even if it is only a few thousand dollars, toward promotion. They pay for the help of a public relations (PR) or a social-media expert, or they hire someone to help them organize a blog tour or give them media training. You might also need money to pay travel expenses to get yourself to your target-market cities for speaking engagements; often when you start out as an author, conferences and organizations won't pay for travel expenses or offer a stipend for speaking. Still, it's in your best interest to do these things.

Will Your Promotion Plan Make Your Book a Bestseller?

No one can look at your promotion plan and say, "This plan will create a bestseller." However, an agent can look at it and tell you if an acquisitions editor will believe you are willing and committed to promoting your book in ways that should prove effective. How do they know this?

First, they know what has worked in the past for other authors, such as speaking at notable conferences, doing interviews with magazines with large readerships or radio shows with large audiences, and producing blogs or newsletters with large readerships. That said, every author and book is different. No one can predict if doing the same things that made one book a bestseller will make yours a bestseller as well.

Second, they look at the size of your platform and the list of ways you say you will promote your book and determine if the plan has strength. They can tell if it builds on the pre-promotion you have done to date for yourself and your book.

Third, they also assess if your plan is realistic. If you have done nothing to create platform in the past, and you claim that you will do one hundred things that require you to be active online and offline every day to promote your book after it is published, they will not believe you. Such a plan will not instill trust. Venture capital partners need to trust potential partners before they invest in them; they need to know you will do what you say, hold up your end, and carry out the plans that have been made. That's why you need a track record, which in the publishing industry is called an author platform.

Be realistic. Don't say you will do things you won't or can't. That said, you can stretch … a little, but be prepared to do what you say you will do and base it on your previous accomplishments.

Fourth, agents and acquisitions editors must see consistency in your plan. It's important to put effort into your book's release. However, promotion has less to do with how to promote your book the first day it is available for sale and more to do with making sure your book has an extended stay on the Amazon bestseller list instead of simply making the Amazon Top 100 list for an hour. It's about longevity. It's been said that selling books, or creating a successful book, is a marathon, not a sprint. When reviewing a promotion plan, both an agent and an editor will look for the marathon aspects: How will you promote the book for the first month after it is released, the next three months, the next six months, and even the next year.

That's why your spinoffs, created in Step #7, may come into play during promotion. You can renew interest in your first book by putting out a second book. You might include the timing of the next book in a series in your plan: "I will write my second book twelve months after the release of my first book. Promotion of that book will begin that year and tie into promotion of book #1 in these ways …." Such a plan demonstrates long-range strategy as well as your determination to build a brand that will create a Long-Tail Effect.

Fifth, your promotion plan needs to show that you are willing to invest something more than just your time and energy writing the manuscript. An agent or editor will ask himself if your commitment comes through loud and clear in the list of things you say you will do to help promote your book.

Once written (you can do so in your journal by following the training exercises), evaluate your promotion plan by looking for the same five elements:

1. Does your plan contain tried-and-true promotion tactics used by best-selling or successful authors?
2. Is your plan based on what you have done to date to promote yourself and your book?
3. Is your plan realistic based on your prepromotion (platform building) activities?
4. Does your plan provide a long-term picture of how you will promote consistently over time?
5. Does your plan instill confidence that you are committed to making your book successful?

If you can answer yes to all five questions, you've got a strong plan that enhances and supports your overall business plan. It provides the map—and the directions—for the last leg of your journey.

MANUAL

Putting Promotion into Action

The first publisher who ever called me in response to a proposal I directly submitted without an agent asked me, "What are you willing to do every day to help promote your book?" I didn't have a definitive answer. I said, "I'll seek out speaking engagements so I can speak about once a month. I'll approach publications to write articles for them. I'll keep on blogging about the topic …." I had two young children at home and wasn't as willing to commit to as large a promotional effort as I might have indicated in my proposal. Although my proposal had a promotion plan, when it came down to seriously knowing what I would do each day, I didn't have a good answer to the question. I didn't land the deal.

You need to have an answer to the same question I was asked: "What are you willing to do every day to help promote your book?"

No matter how you plan to publish, your promotion plan provides that answer—or should. You shouldn't have to go much further than the plan itself to know what to do each day. Unless you are a successful author already (really, *really* successful), few publishers are going to help you with your promotion, so you have to be prepared to do this work yourself. If you self-publish, the work of promoting your book falls totally to you anyway. Plus, when it comes right down to it, no one can promote a book better than the author.

To answer the question above, include in your plan a list of things you can do every day to promote your book. Then, as one of your bulleted action items, say you will apply Jack Canfield's "Rule of Five" to your promotion activities. In *The Success Principles*, Canfield tells the story of how he sought the advice of a teacher who told him, "If you would go every day to a very large tree and take five swings at it with a very sharp ax, eventually, no matter how large the tree, it would have to come down." Jack and his partner, Mark Victor Hansen, took that lesson and began doing five specific things every day to move themselves closer to completing their goal of making *Chicken Soup for the Soul* a #1 *New York Times* Best Seller. For example, each day they would promote their book by:

- doing five radio interviews
- sending five copies to editors to review
- making five phone calls to network marketing companies
- giving five free copies to celebrities
- sending five press releases

They did this for two entire years and ended up selling over eight million copies of their book.

Put the Rule of Five in your plan (and be sure to put it to use daily). Then you'll have something to tell a publisher if asked what you will do each day to help promote your book upon release. You can say, "I will do one of these things every day …" and list such things as:

- respond to five reporter queries on Haro.com, reporterconnection.com, and pitch rate.com
- send out five guest blog posts queries
- contact five radio-show hosts
- write five e-zine articles
- send five press releases and books out for review
- comment on five blog posts
- contact five organizations or conferences where I might speak

Better Late Than Never

More often than not, aspiring authors send me book proposals for editing, and I turn to the promotion section and find it just as bare as the platform section. Yet they want to approach publishers the following week. You must evaluate if you are ready to become an author … *now.* Look at your promotion plan, and be willing to consider that it's highly likely that an agent or acquisitions editor will look at your lack of platform and decide it negatively affects your ability to promote your book—and that you seem to lack the commitment necessary to help yourself and your book succeed. Do you think they will consider you a publishing-business partner or sound investment? Probably not. What do you think that says about your ability to succeed as an indie publisher?

The time to fix this is now—better late than never—but you need to be able to show that you are willing to put in the time. As you look at your plan, ask yourself if your list of post-publication promotional activities makes it appear that you are willing to work five to fifteen hours per week on book and author promotion, as 47 percent of the respondents to Dana Lynn Smith's *Book Promotion Strategies Survey* indicate they do. Ten percent of the authors devote twenty-two or more hours a week to book promotion. And 32 percent spend less than five hours. Which authors do you think are succeeding? Will you give an agent or acquisitions editor reason enough to believe you will fall into the category with the higher success rate? Will you give yourself reason to believe?

What percent of your time will you put into promotion or business-related activities? It's been said that writing the book represents just a small percentage of the work that goes into making a book successful; the rest of the work involves promoting the book.

If Godin is right and all aspiring authors should start promoting three years before their books are released, you have a bit of time to play with. It could be two years or more from this moment until the time your book actually gets published by a traditional publisher. Let's say you want to traditionally publish a nonfiction book. Let's assume it takes you a month to write your book proposal and query, one to three months (or longer) to find an agent, one to three months (or longer) to find a publisher, one month to complete the deal, six months to finish your book, three months to complete editing of the book, and then six to twelve months until it is published. That means you have at least two years and a few months to build your platform. You have at least two to four months until you need to send out your proposal since it won't be put in the mail until after you've sent your query and received a request. In that amount of time, you can possibly create at least a small platform. You can put in enough effort to show a small, independent publisher you are committed and have begun platform-building activities. Your promotion plan can take off from there.

If you are writing a novel and want to traditionally publish, you won't approach agents until your manuscript is complete—which doesn't mean finishing the first draft. It means completing a polished manuscript and story. How long that takes is up to you—for some writers it takes many years. Once you finish, you might choose to have the manuscript professionally edited prior to submitting to agents. Let's say it takes you a year to complete your book; that's a year of platform-building you can do before you ever contact a publishing professional. You'll be a much more attractive publishing partner by then.

And if you self-publish, again, you will need to write your book and have it edited and designed. This could easily take you a year or longer. This gives you at least twelve months time to work on your platform so your promotion plan has a foundation.

Passion + Purpose in Your Promotion Gets Results

Remember to read over your promotion plan with an eye toward passion and purpose as well. As with everything you do, it's your passion that helps sell your book. In *How to Write a Book Proposal*, Mike Larsen claims many aspiring authors with whom he has worked felt compelled to place their mission statements at the top of their promotion plans rather than after their author bios. It's no wonder. If you feel a strong sense of purpose about writing your book—a true sense of mission—you will also feel a strong sense of commitment to making it succeed (sell).

Just as readers should feel your passion coming from the pages of your book, acquisitions editors should feel it in every part of a book proposal. Nowhere must it come through more clearly than in your promotion plan. As an indie publisher, you should feel excited about your promotion plan as well. If you feel excited about your idea, make sure that is clear in this simple list of activities. If you feel that your book carries out your "soul purpose," then create inspired ideas for promoting it to your target market so that agents and acquisitions editors get inspired to work with you on your project and make it as successful as possible.

It's difficult to judge passion from a list. Yet, your promotion plan must exude passion and purpose. It must be inspired. Don't approach it as a *must* or a *should*, however. It should not be a means to an end. If you feel you can fulfill your purpose with every promotional activity you complete, you will succeed. The question is, will your plan accomplish that for you and for your book? If so, you are ready to finish your business plan and your Author Training. *WOOT!*

Suggested Reading:

Guerilla Marketing for Writers by Jay Conrad Levinson, Michael Larsen, and Rick Frishman

1001 Ways to Market Your Books by John Kremer

Red Hot Internet Publicity by Penny Sanseveiri

The Frugal Book Promoter by Carolyn Howard-Johnson

Plug Your Book! by Steve Weber

Sell More Books! By J. Steve Miller and Cherie K. Miller

The Nonfiction Book Marketing Plan by Stephanie Chandler

THE FINAL STEPS:

From Aspiring to Published Author

Congratulations! You have finished the Author Training Process. You have gone through all nine steps, and along the way you have evaluated yourself and your idea from the perspective of a literary agent or an acquisitions editor. You also accumulated a lot of information and may even have begun your manuscript.

Now what?

It's time to put the finishing touches on your business plan and make some final decisions as you take the last steps from aspiring to published author.

Create a Timeline or Timetable for Your Plan

To complete your map, you need an estimated time of arrival (ETA) for each stop along the way. Review the information you compiled as you completed Step #1 through Step #9 and extract any action items you need so you can arrive at your goal. These are all of the things you know you need to do: start writing your book, build author platform, hire an editor, find a book designer, send your finished book to a printer, or write a query and book proposal to send to an agent. Create a timetable with these items on it. This helps you determine when you will arrive at each one of these stops on your map. It's like the timetable used by a train or bus. Passengers know which train or bus to take to get to their destinations. They know exactly when to get on the bus and when to get off.

Next, place these action items on a timeline. You can actually create a long line on a piece of paper with today's date at one end and the date when you want your book to be released or become a bestseller at the other end. On that line, place all of your action items. This type of tool works well for visual people.

Alternatively, you can create a to-do list organized by date. You can group actual activities under monthly headings so you know what you have to do each month and on what dates.

Last, place the items on your calendar. Use a handwritten calendar, Google calendar, the calendar on your phone, or some other type of calendar that allows you to easily see your tasks. One of those large dry-erase calendars can prove a good tool for this, too.

For those of you planning to self-publish, a timeline and timetable will prove invaluable to your business plan. To help you determine what you need to get done at each phase of your book's writing and publication process, break the process into five phases. By now you have begun or completed some of these. They are:

- Platform building (prepromotion)
- Evaluation of self and idea
- Writing and editing
- Production and publishing
- Promotion

Work backward from the final date, placing each action item on the list at the appropriate time necessary to meet your deadline and get to the next point on the timeline. If you want to have a self-published book in hand by December 31, for example, you will probably need to have it to the printer at least four weeks prior to that date (considerably longer depending on the type of printer you use). That means you need to have your full manuscript to the printer by December 1. It should be placed on your timeline on that date. Getting your edited manuscript to the book designer would be placed on the timeline at least four to eight weeks prior to that. Sue Collier and Marilyn Ross provide a detailed timetable for self-publishing in *The Complete Guide to Self-Publishing (5th Edition)*.

MANUAL

84599999999999999999999999999999999

For traditional publishing, if you want to find an agent by June 6, you might need to give yourself one to six months. You could plot out when to have your query written and submitted and when to have your proposal written and ready. You can work with your publisher to determine important dates to place on your timeline. Your contract will stipulate when you need to turn in your manuscript, but your editor can provide the editing schedule and the release date. You can create timelines, timetables, and to-do lists for building author platform, writing, editing, and promotion. Your evaluations of your idea and yourself (as an author) should have been handled long before you ever submitted your book proposal to the publisher.

It's essential to create a timeline and timetable for promotion, the fifth item on the list on the previous page. Remember all of those things you said you would do upon your book's release? Start putting them on the timeline or timetable. Put the items on your calendar—or use one system or the other. Find a way to ensure you implement the promotion plan you created in Step #9 of the Author Training Process.

Of course, if you didn't do the first two items on the list above, you'll need to create a timeline for those items as well. You can have a timetable, timeline, or to-do list specifically for creating platform and promotional opportunities. Or you can create a platform-building plan just like a promotion plan, and then implement it.

Write Your Business Plan

It's time to write your business plan, or your formal book proposal. If you plan to self-publish, I suggest you take the time to put all the information you have compiled thus far into an actual business plan. This is not difficult; gather all the documents you created as you went through each step of the Author Training Process, print them out, and place them in a binder or folder. Be sure to include the timelines and timetables you created; you can make one for each section. Go through your journal to find any areas you need to refine after you have completed the training exercises. These areas include:

- Overview (pitch, summary, list of benefits, purpose statement, special features)
- Markets
- Promotion
- Competing Titles
- Complementary Titles
- About the Author
- Mission Statement

- Author's Platform
- Spinoffs
- Resources Necessary to Complete Your Book
- Products and Services (Subsidiary Rights)
- List of Chapters
- Chapter Summaries

Voila! You have a business plan.

You might want to copy and paste your plan into one document on your computer. This way, you can save it there safely (and also save it in the "cloud" or on a backup drive).

Here are a few more items you might want to add to your business plan to round it out:

Operations and Management: Susan Spann, a publishing attorney and author, suggests you also include a section called "Operations and Management." List all the people responsible for each step of the writing, production, distribution, promotion, sales, and fulfillment process for your book. Include contact and payment information for each person. Such a list provides you with a superb resource as you produce your self-published book. It will also be a handy guide for the next time you publish a book.

Profit and Loss Statement: Publishing companies consider potential profits and losses as they evaluate a project. It's a good idea to take their lead and create a profit and loss statement for your business plan; calculate this before you self-publish and then regularly after you publish. You can use the information you compiled in Step #7 when you determined the Resources Needed to Complete Your Book. Now add in such things as production cost per book, ongoing costs for distribution, promotion, and platform-building. Include these items on your profit and loss statement:

- Sales (a total amount of money made from book sales) – Cost of Goods Sold (based on production costs) = Gross Profit
- Expenses (a list) and the Total Expenses (added up)
- Gross Profit – Total Expenses = Net Profit

A profit and loss statement might look something like this:

Profit and Loss Statement

Revenue		
Books	$9,990.00	Sold 1,000 books for $9.99 each
Other	$5,000.00	Provide Editorial and consulting services
Total	$14,990.00	
Cost of Sales		
Cost of Books	$2,990.00	Used a production house to produce books at $2.99 each
Cost of Other	$4,000.00	Used outside editor for these services
Total	$6,990.00	
Gross Margin		
Books	$7,000.00	Revenue from books minus cost of books sold
Other	$1,000.00	Revenues from other reveny sources minus cost of the revenue sources
Total Gross Margin	$8,000.00	
GM%	53.4%	
Operating Expenses		
Editoral	$1,500.00	Editorial service for book being sold
Design	$500.00	Cost of having book designed
Agency fees	$1,498.50	15% of sales price of books
Legal fees	$1,000.00	Contract and other legal fees
Consulting fees		
Website	$500.00	
Computer		
Other		
Rent		
Office Expenses		
Telephone		
Internet		
Employee		
Equipment		
Travel		
Airfare		
Lodging		
Meals		
Entertainment		
Other		
Other	$ -	
Total Operating Expenses	$4,998.50	
Operating Income	$3,001.50	Total Gross Margin minus Total Operating Expenses
Interest Income/Expense	$ -	
Tax	$1,200.60	Self-employment taxes at 40%
Net Income	$1,800.90	Operating Income minus Interest Expense or plus Interest minus Taxes

Then deduct any other withdrawals or expenses to come up with your retained profit.
Once you've done this, your business plan is complete!

If you plan to traditionally publish, it's time to polish all the material you accumulated into a formal book proposal. If you recall, these are the parts of a proposal:

- Overview
- Markets
- Promotion
- Competing Titles
- Complementary Titles
- About the Author
- Mission Statement
- Author's Platform
- Spinoffs
- Outline
    - ¤ List of Chapters
    - ¤ Chapter Summaries
    - ¤ Sample Chapters

You'll find information on what goes into each of the sections in this book. You can also find a short guide that I wrote, *Demystifying the Nonfictional Book Proposal,* and another reference titled "Easy Schmeasy Book Proposal Template," at writenonfictionnow.com. Carolyn Howard-Johnson also has a very short guide on writing a book proposal, *The Great First Impression Book Proposal: Everything You Need to Know About Selling Your Book to an Agent or Publisher in Twenty Minutes or Less.*

You've compiled all these pieces into a business plan; now you need to edit and make it conform to industry standards. A book proposal must be as perfect as possible, which explains why many aspiring authors hire a book-proposal consultant or editor, like me, to review their business plans prior to submitting it to agents and publishers. The average author does not know what belongs in a book proposal, how it should read, or how it should be formatted. Once edited, it also needs to be proofread.

Submitting a proposal to an agent or publisher represents one of those instances in which you want to remember the adage, "You only get one chance to make a first impression." In the publishing world, when you send a book proposal to an agent or acquisitions editor—especially one who doesn't know you—you really do get only one chance. So you better make a good impression.

That means your book proposal better:

MANUAL

- meet industry standards
- be polished and professional
- have no grammatical errors or typos
- catch their attention
- provide a convincing argument in each section for the marketability of your idea

Spending the money on a great proposal editor not only increases the likelihood that you make a good impression, it serves as your last chance to evaluate your readiness to become a published author. A proposal consultant has the ability to see you and your project objectively. If you have failed at doing this for yourself, he or she will catch your errors. Plus, some proposal consultants are agents and offer the advantage of seeing your work through the actual lens you've been trying to use during the Author Training Process.

It's possible that despite your best efforts you may not have:

- formatted your document well
- written clearly
- included all the necessary information or sections
- provided an enticing lead
- detailed the reader's benefits
- given all the details of the complementary or competing books
- offered a thorough enough promotion plan
- done enough to attract a publisher
- approached each section from a marketing perspective
- offered a convincing argument in each case for the salability of your idea
- provided information that supports your argument

A good proposal editor or consultant will not only edit your book proposal for grammar and punctuation but will catch the other "errors." He or she will make sure your proposal has everything an agent or acquisitions editor is looking for—and that you are everything a publisher wants in a business partner.

Working with a Writing Coach or Freelance Editor

Finding a good editor or consultant can seem difficult, and you might need one for your manuscript, query letter, and/or proposal. If you traditionally publish, you might choose to have your manuscript or sample chapters edited prior to submitting to agents or publishers. If you choose to self-publish, you won't need a query or proposal edited, but you will definitely need your manuscript edited if you want to hold yourself to the same standards as traditionally published books. (Your readers will expect you to do so.)

The move from aspiring to published author involves being mature enough to release your manuscript into the hands of a professional editor. Most writers treat their manuscript like a baby, and they are reticent to hand it over to someone else—especially if it comes back missing fingers, toes, or essential organs. Like every parent, you must let your baby go. For your book to have the ability to succeed in the real world, it has to be able to survive the tests and rigors of editing (a bit like going to school or falling down and getting up again when learning to walk).

You must be willing to have someone give you objective feedback on how to improve your manuscript, and you must receive that feedback objectively and willingly—and then put it to good use. Editing by an experienced professional *book* editor makes a manuscript better. It allows your idea to grow from a manuscript into a full-grown published book with the ability to succeed in the competitive publishing world.

Before you even begin looking for an editor for your book or your proposal (especially if the proposal editor will also read your sample chapters), prepare yourself for this experience. There are a few ways you can do so, such as:

1. Join a critique group where you can learn to get constructive criticism.
2. Ask your blog readers or other fans to serve as beta readers of your book and give you early feedback on your manuscript.
3. Go to a conference or workshop where you can get an editor's feedback on a small piece of your manuscript.
4. Hire a book doctor or coach to work with you.

I recommend reading *No Red Pen: Writers, Writing Groups & Critique* by Victoria A. Hudson and *The Writing & Critique Group Survival Guide: How to Make Revisions, Self-Edit, and Give and Receive Feedback* by Becky Levine if you plan to join a critique group.

While critique groups and beta readers leave you open to a wide array of untrained readers and editors, a book coach or book doctor can actually provide a great first experience with the world of editing. Most coaches work with you on an ongoing basis to help you mold and craft your book and offer feedback on your writing and on manuscript development. Many of my clients enjoy this process because they feel less alone as they write, they enjoy having a sounding board when they feel unsure, and the accountability of a coach helps them meet their writing goals.

I have spent many years working as a freelance nonfiction developmental and line editor. Although I have worked with many writers who have had their work professionally edited before, I probably have worked with more writers who have never encountered the editing process with anyone other than a writing buddy, someone in their writing group, a spouse, or a high school teacher or college professor. Thus, they have no idea what it means to work with a professional editor. For them, the process feels scary; they are often shocked by the "bleeding" copy returned to them.

Many types of editors exist, and they have different ways of working with writers and charging. You might need one or all of them for your manuscript. Your proposal, however, will only need a proposal editor or consultant and a line editor, who will check your grammar and sentence strength. After that, you will need a proofreader. For your manuscript, you might need a developmental editor, a line editor, a copy editor, or a substantive editor. After that, you will also need a proofreader, especially if you plan to self-publish.

You do not need to live close to your editor. Most editors work by phone or Skype, but all primarily rely on documents sent back and forth by e-mail. You can even live in another country than your editor and still develop a successful working relationship. The key lies in finding someone with whom you can work well.

Don't worry about theft of intellectual property. An editor has to treat the information you offer in the form of your book idea, proposal, or manuscript as "privileged." Despite what some people say, little idea stealing occurs in the publishing industry. If you are worried about this, you can always submit your manuscript for copyright (http://www.copy right.gov/) prior to having it edited, or you can speak with a literary lawyer or intellectual-property lawyer prior to having anyone read your work.

Choose an editor that suits your "style." Talk to editors before you begin working with one. Ask them if they like to "take off the white gloves" and dig in or if they like to coddle their writers. If you want a "warm and fuzzy" editor who prefaces every bit of constructive criticism with words of praise and encouragement, be sure that's who you hire. If you want someone who "tells it like it is" and is all business, make sure you find one who edits in that style.

Check out an editor's track record. Look for testimonials from past clients. And if possible, test them out. Often you can find editors who offer book-doctor sessions at a conference. Many give a free test edit of material before you hire them. This gives you an idea of their editing style.

Don't be surprised if an editor wants to do more than one round of work on your manuscript. Two or three rounds are typical, especially if she asks you to make considerable changes to the manuscript.

Charges vary from per word to per page to per hour. Most of the top editors I know charge by the hour. Depending on the length of your manuscript and the number of rounds of editing it needs, this could prove to be the most expensive aspect of producing your self-published book or preparing your manuscript for submission. The editing of a 50,000-word manuscript, for example, can range from hundreds of dollars to thousands of dollars, depending on the quality of the writing, the type of editing, the number of rounds of editing necessary, and the editor or editors you hire.

To find a good book editor, ask for recommendations from authors you know and trust. Get references. Find someone who has edited many books, preferably books in your genre. Make sure American English is the editor's first language. You can also look for an editor on these sites:

- The Editorial Freelance Association (http://www.the-efa.org)
- The National Association of Independent Writers and Editors (http://naiwe.com)

Know that everyone needs an editor—even editors and English majors and best-selling authors. Don't skip this step if you want to achieve successful authorship. As my agent says, "Behind every good writer is an even better editor!"

Also, there's a learning curve to improving your work. My student Rhonda has taken classes, gone to writing retreats, used critique groups, and hired a professional editor. "A writing group can become too friendly, in my opinion, and at a certain point I might not get the feedback necessary to improve my manuscript. A professional editor will tell it like it is. I had a professional editor review my current story," she said. "Her insight was invaluable. I was afraid of what she would say but found that feedback was an encouraging process, which helped me grow as a writer."

Your Publishing Options

If you haven't decided previously, you now need to determine how you will publish your book. Maybe you've known all along. You could be what I call a "traditional-publishing holdout." Or maybe you fancy yourself an indie publisher. It's important to know well what each of these options entails—and which one best suits you. Just as I advised you not to write a manuscript that you will later discover isn't marketable, I suggest you delay the decision to become a self-published or traditionally published author until you know everything you can about these particular publishing paths.

Why would you decide to self-publish your book project? You want to:

- be a "project manager" and manage editors, designers, accounts at printers, etc.
- invest your money in your project
- have more control of your work
- earn more money per book
- make your book available sooner—in months rather than years

Self-publishers manage a huge number of details as they take their project from idea to published book. They must have entrepreneurial spirits and a strong business sense. They must be authorpreneurs. Additionally, they must like having control of decisions and want to run a company since true self-publishing means starting a publishing company. Are you up to the job of being a publisher?

You can choose several ways to print your book, should you decide to go the self-publishing route. With offset printing you:

- hire all the subcontractors
- get an imprint of your own
- purchase large quantities of books
- arrange distribution

This is considered the "real deal." You end up with many boxes of books in your garage. It's the do-it-yourself (DIY) method. You will pay the least amount per book.

If this does not appeal to you, you can choose to publish with a subsidy press, also known as an "author services company" or "vanity press." This is not the best choice if you want to produce a commercial book, and you need to be extremely careful about the details of the contract and the quality of the services you purchase. These companies provide:

- a variety of services (editing, design, promotion)
- print and/or e-book conversion and distribution
- no imprint of your own (usually)
- distribution

You could also opt to DIY with a print-on-demand (POD) printer. This affords you the same level of control as offset printing, but you don't need to print as many books to get the price you desire. In fact, you don't have to order any books at all. You may pay more per book depending on the printer. The printer will print one book per order received. Most POD printers will offer distribution and your own imprint.

You could also opt to use a digital press. This provides a good option if you need books printed fast, want a short run for back-of-the-room sales, or want control of distribution for some reason. Such printers typically offer:

- fast, high-quality printing
- small quantities
- no distribution (or distribution at a cost)
- reasonable pricing

In a nutshell, this is the self-publishing process for a printed book:

- Evaluate your book.
- Create a business plan.
- Write your book.
- Have your manuscript professionally edited and proofed.
- Have a cover professionally designed.
- Have your interior professionally designed.
- Create an account with a printer.
- Purchase an ISBN.
- Upload your artwork to a printer.

Another option, assisted self-publishing, has cropped up in recent years. You may find literary agents and other publishing professionals, or simply some experts in the publishing industry, who can hold your hand through the self-publishing process—for a fee. Some of these are full done-for-you services, and others are not. Prices vary considerably.

Additionally, you can find hybrid models of self-publishing. These publishers partner with you to produce your book. They pick and choose the books they acquire, much like a legacy publishing house, but they ask you to help pay for the actual production of your book, as if you were self-publishing. This can be a nice option if you aren't sure which path to take or if you have had trouble finding a traditional publisher for your project but prefer the traditional publishing route.

Of course, you can also produce an e-book, the lowest-cost and fastest method of publishing a book. You will still need to hire all of your subcontractors—editor, proofreader, etc.—unless you choose to work with an e-book publishing company. Such companies are similar to subsidy publishers, offering services and packages of services for e-books. The largest free, reputable DIY e-book publishing and distribution platform is Smashwords, or if you prefer more handholding and don't mind paying a modest fee, try BookBaby.

In a nutshell, this is the self-publishing process for an e-book:

- Evaluate your book.
- Create a business plan.
- Write your book.
- Have your manuscript professionally edited and proofed.
- Have a cover professionally designed.
- Have your manuscript converted to e-book formats.
- Create an account with an e-book distributor.
- Purchase an ISBN.
- Upload cover and manuscript.

Remember, you are the publisher when you self-publish. You become the publishing professional. As such, you must hold yourself and your book to the same standards as a traditionally published book—it's the only way it will succeed. That means you must hire professionals every step of the way, including professional editors and designers. "Books from all publishers now compete on equal footing," says Joel Friedlander, author, book designer, and self-publishing expert at thebookdesigner.com. "Self-publishers need to realize that in exchange for this level playing field, they have to meet the standards set by traditional publishers. Otherwise, they face the possibility their books will suffer by comparison. Professional editing and design are essential to achieving this aim."

Friedlander shared these two stories to stress his point: "There was an interesting story about a woman who self-published a cookbook, which didn't sell very well. Puzzled, she started really looking at other best-selling cookbooks and realized her book didn't *look* like a cookbook, compared to the others. She pulled the book down, had it professionally designed, and put it back up for sale. It went on to sell over 250,000 copies. Cover redesigns can have a similar effect. A couple of years ago, a client brought me a book on self-empowerment, a deep work. The cover had a stock photo of a man jumping in a field of daisies and it couldn't have been more inappropriate for its category. We created a new cover that emphasized the psychodynamic aspects of the book and featured a male making direct and confident eye contact with the reader. The book is selling much better than it had before."

If all of these steps and the tasks and responsibilities of self-publishing sound appealing to you and fit into your life and schedule, and if you want to become a publisher and run a publishing business, super! You know what choice to make.

Let's look at traditional publishing next. Why would you decide to traditionally publish your book project?

- You don't want to be a "project manager."
- You don't want to invest your own money in your project.
- You want broader distribution for your book (for it to appear in physical bookstores).
- You want credibility or authority in your field.

A traditional publisher will handle most of the details of publishing for you—and even pay you to write your book in most cases. This payment is called an advance, and, as mentioned earlier in the book, an advance is calculated based on potential book sales. (It's an advance payment on those potential sales.) You don't get paid anything else until your book "earns back" the advance. Once your book has sold enough copies to cover the advance paid to you, you begin receiving royalty payments, which are also based on sales. These are calculated based on percentages—different percentages for print books, e-books, foreign sales, etc.—detailed in your publishing contract.

Plus, despite the growing acceptance of self-published books, the media and most of the general public continue to see authors of traditionally published books as more credible. Bookstores tend to carry only books produced by publishers.

Your agent will choose the appropriate publishing houses for you and your manuscript. But it's a good idea to understand the different types of publishing houses that exist and which ones you might approach on your own.

Large Publishing Houses

The publishing industry used to talk about the Big Six or the Six Sisters when referring to the number of large conglomerate publishing companies in the United States. These days, it's the Big Five or the Five Sisters since Penguin and Random House merged in early 2013. That made Penguin Random House the world's largest publisher, moving it ahead of the other four publishers: Hachette, HarperCollins, Macmillan, and Simon & Schuster. (At the time I wrote this, another merger was in the works.)

Each of these publishing houses, also known as the legacy publishing houses, operates many imprints. The large publishing houses have created smaller book lines that have broken off into small and midsize publishing houses that operate like separate profit centers. In some cases, the houses purchased independent publishers.

The conglomerates are actually bigger than they first appear when you look at who owns each of the Big Six companies. MacMillan is owned by German company Holtzbrinck; Ha-

chette is owned by French company Hachette Livre; and HarperCollins is owned by Aus-
tralian Media Corp owner Rupert Murdoch. Random House and Penguin were divisions
of German conglomerate Bertelsmann; Bertelsmann owns 53 percent of the new Penguin
Random House, while Pearson owns the remaining 47 percent.

To approach a large publishing company, you need a literary agent. Literary agents serve
as the gatekeepers to acquisitions editors. Acquisitions editors at large publishing companies do not accept "unagented" (also called "unsolicited") book proposals or query letters.
(Remember: Your agent will send a query letter first; if the editor is interested, he will request a proposal.)

Large publishing houses can feel impersonal to work with. You will be one among many
authors because these houses produce many books per year. You will be a small fish in a big
pond if you are a first-time author—or even a second-time author.

Small to Midsize Dependent Publishers

Small and midsize dependent publishers are those (mostly) not associated with or owned
by the Big Five. They might be owned by an organization, university, or some other midsize
publisher and thus not "independent" but "dependent" on an outside agency, association, or
company. A few examples include Andrews McMeel (associated with Universal Press Syndi-
cate), Chronicle Books (affiliated with the *San Francisco Chronicle*), Graywolf Press (a non-
profit publisher), AMACOM Books (affiliated with the American Management Association),
and Beacon Press (a division of the Unitarian Universalist Association).

Other such publishers include:

- Adams Media (owned by F+W Media)
- Globe Pequot Press
- Health Communications
- Quest Books
- That Patchwork Place

Sometimes you will find imprints of larger houses amongst the names of midsize publishers as well.

In most cases, midsize publishing houses only take agented submissions from aspiring
authors. Some acquisitions editors, however, will look at a query or book proposal from an
unagented author.

Working with a small or midsize dependent publisher can prove a more personal experience. You may still feel as if you are one among many authors since these houses do produce

a good number of books per year, but you won't be quite as small a fish in the pond. You also stand a better chance of becoming a big fish in that pond.

Independent Publishers

Independent publishers, also called small publishing houses, are independently owned. They are not part of the huge conglomerates, nor are they dependent on any other agency. These are different than "indie publishers"—individual self-publishers who have started their own imprints. Most of these publishing companies have been around a long time, such as:

- Career Press
- Chelsea Green Publishing
- New World Library
- Berrett-Koehler
- Chronicle Books
- Hampton Roads
- Jewish Lights
- The Other Press
- The Permanent Press
- Hay House
- Newmarket Press
- Prometheus Books

Almost all independent publishing companies accept unagented query letters and book proposals from aspiring authors. They have their own websites and submission guidelines. If you want a personal publishing experience with a traditional publisher, these are your best bets. These houses often produce a small number of books per year—but not always—and have a bit more time and energy to spend on their authors. You may be treated like a big fish in a small pond if your book does really well or if you show up with a big platform or a track record of previously published books. You are more likely to stay with one editor at an independent publishing house, too.

If you want to approach a literary agent, this is the process:

- You submit a query letter.
- The agent asks for a proposal, manuscript, or manuscript + proposal.
- You submit a proposal (or manuscript + proposal), if requested.
- The agent asks to represent you, and you sign a contract.
- The agent pitches to acquisitions editors at appropriate publishing houses.

MANUAL

- The agent submits a proposal to interested editors.
- You and your agent go through contract negotiations with editors who make offers.
- You sign a contract.
- You receive half (or possibly a third) of the advance (if there is an advance).
- You write the book on deadline.
- You receive the rest of your advance when the book is submitted in full or at agreed-upon intervals, such as when you turn in the full manuscript and upon publication.

Traditional publishers, with the exception of small independent publishing houses, require that your proposed book project or manuscript is seen and accepted by a literary agent first, then an acquisitions editor, and then by an editorial board or a pub board (including the marketing and sales team). Only then will you receive a contract.

To gain representation by a literary agent, you must send a query letter. If your query letter intrigues the agent, you will be asked to send along a book proposal or a manuscript (or even some sample pages), depending on your genre.

If the agent finds your proposal or manuscript acceptable, she will offer you representation. You then sign a contract agreeing to pay the agent a percentage of your advance and royalties, typically 15 to 20 percent.

Agents contact acquisitions editors by query letter. If interested, an editor requests a proposal or manuscript. She evaluates the material, and if interested, she takes the project to an editorial meeting or pub board meeting.

As mentioned early in this book, the decision by a publishing company to purchase a manuscript involves many people, all of whom are concerned with the creative aspect of the project as well as its marketability or salability. The editorial or pub board meetings at a publishing house typically involve a team of acquisitions editors and the publisher, but they often include marketing and sales personnel as well. If everyone agrees the project is viable from a business perspective, the acquisitions editor contacts the writer's agent and the publishing company's legal department draws up a contract. Some of the details in the contract can be negotiated and often are. The contract is sent to the agent, who sends it the writer. They consult on the terms. All negotiations are done via the agent, editor, and legal department.

Once all the concerned parties sign the contract, your traditional book deal is done. Of course, you still need to meet your deadlines and turn in a fabulous book.

If any of this process suits your personality, goals, or schedule, super! Get to work writing a query letter and polishing your business plan into a formal book proposal.

Write Your Book

The final step involves writing your book. Many writers never complete their books—even if they have a contract with a publishing house. This explains why publishers shy away from first-time authors. Many an advance is returned by writers who simply can't make good on the publishing deal after it has been made.

At this point, you are more prepared to write your book from start to finish than most writers. You also have put together the best writing guide possible: your Overview, TOC, and chapter-by-chapter synopses or a full synopsis. Let's explore this before you complete your training.

No matter how you plan to publish, each time you begin a writing period, I suggest you use this six-step process. It will help you remember everything you have learned in this training *as you write*. While you do want to get creative with the writing process at this point, you need to deliver on your promises—the benefits your book will offer readers—and you want to produce a marketable manuscript. You don't want to forget everything you've learned or lose your Author Attitude as you write. The following process offers you a reminder at the start of each writing session and a self-check at the end but allows you to be creative the rest of the time—as you write—so you produce a finished manuscript that sells to publishers and readers.

1. Take out your "[Book Title] Writing Guide." Remember, this is a document you created that contains the following:

    a. Your Overview (pitch, book summary, list of benefits)

    b. Your TOC

    c. Your Chapter Summaries or Synopsis

    d. Your book's purpose statement

2. Before you begin writing, read the Overview. This reminds you of the job you must do. Create a book that delivers on all your promises to your readers and fulfills the book's purpose.

3. Open a chapter document. In Step #6, you created a separate document for each chapter; each document contains the chapter synopsis you wrote for that particular chapter. If you are writing nonfiction, you may have broken the chapter summaries into bullet points or subheadings. (If you find it easier, you can determine what questions you need to answer, what benefits you need to provide, or what solutions you need

to provide to address the topics at hand in a particular chapter.) For fiction, you may have separated your chapter summary into scenes, vignettes, or flashbacks.

4. Write to the chapter synopsis. Now you can be creative! Review your complete summary, and then write! The planning has been done, and you can just flow. Write your chapter by moving from bullet point to bullet point, section to section, and scene to scene until you get to the end of your chapter. Of course, you can add, delete, or change anything as necessary.

5. Reread your synopsis. Then skim over your draft chapter, and determine if you achieved all the goals of the chapter. Did you cover everything you said you would cover and provide all the benefits you promised? If not, make notes on what you left out so you can add those points in your second draft.

6. Return to your "[Book Title] Writing Guide." Reread the Overview, and consider whether you delivered on your greater promises—the benefits and purpose—in this particular chapter.

Your timeline should have a deadline for the completion of your manuscript—self-imposed or imposed by a publisher. A deadline will help you finish your book. Too many writers start and never finish. Don't let this happen to you.

I always say, "Deadlines are my friend." I received a degree in magazine journalism and know deadlines well. I often create them so I have to meet them. The first draft of this book got written in eight weeks because I created a deadline as I taught a class on the topic. The first draft served as the class text. The participants also became my beta readers. I had to get them one or two chapters every week. I had to turn in the second draft to an agent (who served as a beta reader as well), which pushed me to revise three chapters per week for the next four weeks. I then had two months to complete the rest of my revisions, which included input from my beta readers, to meet my deadline at the publishing house.

I finished the first draft of *How to Blog a Book* in five months by writing just 300 to 500 words three or four times a week on my blog, howtoblogabook.com. Once I had readers tuning in to my blog, I felt I couldn't stop or miss a post. Those readers served as my accountability partners, and I had my self-imposed weekly blog publication schedule—a deadline.

Even if you have your manuscript completion date on your timeline, timetable, to-do list, and calendar, it's easy enough to skip the scheduled time for writing. You must make writing your book a priority. That means plotting out time daily or weekly for writing.

Maintaining your Author Attitude is inherent in the writing methodology I have described here. Finishing a book, much like evaluating your idea or becoming a successful author, requires tenacity and willingness to work hard despite challenges.

Final Evaluation

Now comes the final evaluation in your Author Training. Can you maintain your Author Attitude through the writing of your manuscript, through the editing of your manuscript, through rejection, through promotion, through the nitty-gritty details of production, and even through success? You have the manual that tells you how to become a successful author. Will you put the information to use? Or will you just read the book, try some of the training exercises, and then go back to your old ways? Will you remain an aspiring author rather than a published author?

Much depends on four things I mentioned early in your training: Beliefs, Decisions, Actions, and Results.

Beliefs determine what you accomplish. They affect your ability to achieve your goals. If you harbor a belief that you and your idea have what it takes to attract an agent or publisher and that your book will sell more than an average number of copies, achieving success becomes much more likely.

Remember that your decisions directly affect your ability to succeed as well. If you make the decision to complete the work, I suggest in this book that is *your* decision to make proactive affirmative choices. You move yourself closer to your goal when you make these kinds of decisions. Think about what other decisions you must make or have made that help you become a published author. Continue to make decisions that help, not hinder, your progress.

Like decisions, actions are simple to evaluate. Every day you act in ways that either get you closer or further away from your goal of becoming published. Taking no action at all is a decision that keeps you stuck where you are. If you worked through the process in this book, congratulations! You took action toward your goal.

Together these three things help you achieve *results*. Change your beliefs and begin making decisions and acting like a successful published author right now. (Fake it 'til you make it.) See if your results change as you do so.

If they don't, or if they do, remember why you wanted to become an author. You had an idea. You felt inspired.

MANUAL

Remain inspired. To do that, recall your passion for your idea. Combine that with your sense of purpose or personal mission. When you combine your passion and purpose, you will feel inspired every time. That inspiration will come through in your manuscript—and in your business plan or book proposal—and make you and your book successful. You will achieve inspired results.

And that will make it easier for you to maintain your Author Attitude, which will transform you from aspiring author to successful published author. And your training will, indeed, be complete. *WOOT! WOOT!*

SAMPLES

Note to the Reader: My students and clients submitted plans in two forms: business plans intended for self-publishing or book proposals intended for submission. You can tell the difference: The proposals are more polished while the business plans appear somewhat un¬finished or rough. The agents and acquisitions editors who reviewed them didn't always distinguish between a "plan" and a "proposal" in their feedback. After all, both documents are business plans and should contain the same information. Also, my students and clients were asked to submit only a portion of the material normally included in a proposal; some agents commented on missing elements, not realizing this was done purposely (as a courtesy due to their busy schedules).

Pay close attention to the agents' and editors' comments. Reading these documents and the agents and editors reviews trains you to see and evaluate your own business plan through the lens of a publishing professional.

1 State which one you're providing. "A marketing proposal for" should be sufficient. You don't want to appear wishy-washy before you even begin.

2 This inadvertently continues the wishy-washy feeling, like you have no real direction. If you're trying to guide folks, you need to present yourself as knowing where you're going.

3 Memoir is a unique animal that straddles genre requirements, but you must still write with conviction. I get what you're aiming for, but you don't appear to be certain. Pare it down more. Don't give me a Venn diagram. Give me the intersection. A common downfall of such proposed books is that they try to be everything and do everything for everyone forever. This is my impression, and I haven't even read the proposal yet.

4 I see these integrated more often than not, but they can be fine separate. As an agent, I'm looking for a robust offering here if the book is to have any chance in the commercial market. When I see these page numbers in a thirteen-page proposal, I'm all but certain that what follows will not convince anyone.

5 Not all agents and editors are quite so uptight about such things as consistency in phrasing and punctuation in your title, but enough of them are that you'll want to have your proposal proofread before you submit it.

SAMPLE

SAMPLE # 1:
WITH ANNOTATIONS BY AGENT GORDON WORNOCK

A Mini-Proposal & Business Plan for:[1]

From West to East and Part Way Back[2]: Seeking an Authentic Self

(Memoir: Spiritual, Religious, New Age)[3]

by

Meg Hill Fitz-Randolph

TABLE OF CONTENTS

OVERVIEW

Pitch:

From West to East and Part Way Back, Seeking the Authentic Self;[5] a spiritual road trip memoir that flies free of stale definitions of God. Moving from church to ashram to Benedictine abbey to Vedic fliers meditating for World Peace, Fitz-Randolph—poet, teacher, meditator—experiences holiness in each of these and returns with an understanding of the many faces of spirituality.

Description:

This is a memoir about disobedience. Not in the ordinary sense, bad behavior and the like, but about so-called spiritual disobedience, what from the Middles Ages to present time has been called heresy. Rather than being burned at the stake or fed to the lions, however, Fitz-Randolph has found a way to disagree with the mainstream voices of both her chosen spiritual vocations while maintaining **her**[6] practice and respect for each.

As a lifetime **disciple**[7] of a renowned Indian guru, late in mid-life she returns to her Christian roots, becoming a devotee of Christ, prayer, and liturgical communion. End of story. We'd assume her wandering soul had come home, right? Not quite. Making no claim or even choosing sides, Fitz-Randolph tells the story of one woman's journey to get beyond dogma and belief and settle into the uneasy paradox between two seemingly very different paths to faith. Is it the church or the guru or something else entirely?

Having grown up "churched," as it used to be called, and then followed the piper (in this case, think 'guru') beyond the familiar confines of Western religion into the deep waters of Eastern meditation, the author and her husband decide early in their marriage to make the move from the fast-paced suburbs to the cornfields of Iowa in order to join a well-known meditation community. Here they begin a new life, and for over twenty years, they peacefully abide, raising their daughter, building careers, and meditating for world peace in the Golden Domes.

Long story short, late in middle age comes the inevitable shift, which means for the author a slow, tortured melting away from the community followed by a solo return to the church of her childhood and a life of prayer. The real **kicker**[8] here is not so much Fitz-Randolph's return to the Christian fold but her resolve to bring her cherished Eastern meditation practice along with her.

Pulling from ancient Christian teachings as well as sacred texts of India, and simply following her poet's instincts for knitting unlikely worlds together, the author's story brings us to a wider place of spiritual inclusion and a more deeply felt relationship to a higher power.

As more and **more**[9] people sample Eastern practices such as yoga and meditation, they can become confused about how this fits into their own traditions. As someone who had to come to peace with these conflicts, the author of From West to East and Part Way Back understands the journey and how her story can benefit **others**.[10]

Benefits:[11]

Here is what a reader might learn from reading this book:

1. To recognize the key principles in one's own religious tradition are similar to those principles of other world religions.

2. To see maybe for the first time how two seemingly separate traditions dovetail in ways both illuminating and fulfilling.

3. To recognize the many faces of a higher, divine power as expressed in all the great world religions.

---

6 Phrasing is very important. You could be selling your audience a new and useful method, but one little pronoun makes this the simple telling of your story instead.

7 What is your relation? Are you one of many followers, or did you share a special connection that places you above the masses? Be specific.

8 If you have to say things like "long story short" and "the real kicker here is," I get the sense that what you're offering lacks focus and strength. Present the material so that it stands without the aid of a crutch.

9 Avoid unsupported blanket statements. Though this could be covered in your analysis of the target market, it wouldn't hurt to slip in a concrete figure or percentage.

10 Here's an example of how pitching a memoir in the third person can get awkward. It can be done well, but it's often more natural for you to tell your story as it happened to you. Also, making a point of something that is a given in the genre makes it seem like either you don't know your genre or you're trying to reassure yourself of your book's effectiveness.

11 Excellent. This type of book must have a specific purpose, something applicable that can be gained from reading. Not only having a separate section for this but having seven entries shows your familiarity with this requirement.

SAMPLE

12 This appears to be the culmination of the lessons learned into real-world action. I see how it can exist alongside the others, but I'm puzzled about why it isn't the final item on the list.

13 This is not a purpose. This type of statement, especially in this genre, can be dangerous because it tends to imply that you're relying on destiny to make your book a success.

14 This is another blanket statement to avoid. One minute on Amazon or at my mother's bookshelf can prove this false, even for a memoir.

15 My hopes were high when you presented a narrowed focus earlier on, and now they have been dashed in your attempts to make this a book for everyone. That only makes it a book for no one.

16 Instead of listing many, you'll usually want to explore a few in depth. Choose one primary target audience and a handful of secondary markets at the most. Provide figures and analyses that support your book's effectiveness in these markets.

SAMPLE

4. To recognize that at their heart all spiritual practices share the same root: a non-ending and eternal ground of being which is called by different names.

5. To understand how prayer and meditation, which arise from this same ground of being, are actually never in conflict with one another.

6. To translate this ever-growing sense of God's presence into right action and good works that help **humanity**.[12]

7. To naturally grow in deeper tolerance, understanding, and appreciation of all religions, even those seemingly most unlike our own.

Purpose of this Book:

This is a book whose time has **come**.[13] The market today is awash with books founded on both East and West spirituality: from new-age philosophies, meditation and yoga practices, practical tips from fitness and health gurus, all the way to treatises on ancient Christian doctrines and the rediscovery of centering and contemplative prayer. But there is no book out there, memoir or otherwise, that shows a life lived in the center of this **divide**.[14] This book answers the question of how one person gets to be both an Eastern meditator/mystic and a practicing Christ-centered Christian or Jewish or any other religion of one choosing or **tradition**.[15]

Markets:[16]

- Those people on a spiritual path already, whether Christian or from another tradition entirely but curious about other paths

- Those part way down their path, those just starting out

- Those who engage in serious yoga practice for exercise and health but feel some conflict with their Christian faith

- Those who want to know what this journey is all about, who have stuck to a more conservative path following the faith of their childhood or community

- Those just curious about what happened to all those old hippies who joined up with various spiritual movements and gurus first appearing in the late sixties

- Those curious about the nature of enlightenment. What it is and what am I missing?

- Those seeking to live an authentic life amidst a spiritual practice and discipline, traditional or non-traditional

- Those who see themselves as "spiritual but not religious," the largest group today

Competition:

Memoir: Biography; Spiritual or Religious

Memoirs which are most similar to author's memoir: From West to East and Part Way Back; Seeking the Authentic Self, provide the most competition. A few examples are included here (in order of ranking on the **Amazon.com**[17] list).

Eat, Pray, Love; One Woman's Search for Everything Across Italy by Elizabeth Berg. Harper Perennial (**2007**[18]). Popular memoir which satisfies worldly appetites for change, travel, romance; weak spiritual content with mostly derivative and superficial understanding of Eastern thought for beginners **only**[19]

Devotion: A Memoir by Dani Shapiro. Harper Collins (2010). A poignant search for her family's Jewish tradition in which she seeks a way back to that inheritance; resonates with those seeking that way back but does not approach in much depth the actual spiritual concerns or understanding of that tradition

The Adventures of a Bindi Girl; Deep Diving into the Heart of India by Erin Reese. Travel and Soul **Media**[20] (2012). More travel and adventure memoir along the lines of Eat, Pray, Love ; next to no spiritual curiosity of any depth and less understanding of world of the great religions whose temples she visits

Proof of Heaven: A Neurosurgeon's Journey into the Afterlife by Eben Alexander. Simon Schuster (2012). One person's near-death experience in which angels and higher realms are experienced; more new age excitement and fun but little in substance, either medically or spiritually.

Complementary Titles:[21]

American Veda: From Emerson and the Beetles to Yoga and Meditation: How Indian Spirituality Changed the West by Philip Goldberg. Crown Archetype (2010). Non-memoir but chock full of deep understanding on Eastern philosophy in terms Westerners understand easily.

---

17 Amazon rankings fluctuate so greatly and so frequently that they're almost guaranteed to not be the same when the proposal is written and when it is read. Do not rank them this way.

18 This is most often too old to be considered a comp title.

19 Instead of passing judgment, show how your book compares. This is especially important when you cite books that achieve the status of cultural phenomenon. You had better have a valid reason to choose that book. I'm not convinced that you do here.

20 Aim for books from major publishers first.

21 Though not necessarily a bad thing, I almost never see competing and complementary titles split up like this.

SAMPLE

22 Though less necessary for memoir and more so for prescriptive nonfiction, it wouldn't hurt to seek a foreword by a known author or thought leader in the genre. Having that in hand before you submit can greatly boost your platform.

23 Interesting. I didn't get this angle in your overview. Might be something worth mentioning earlier.

24 Unless this is your brand, which isn't evident in the rest of the proposal, you'll likely want to seek a title that isn't so close to one of your others.

25 Be aware of additional applications for your material. A wealth of this would make for good bonus content online.

26 You're citing a potential connection with someone who was fairly well known. If there's any applicable substance to this, you'll want to express it in your target markets and promotion plan.

27 Good. Cite specifics whenever possible. These not only vouch for your writing, but they imply what kind of feel your narration could have.

Roadsigns on the Spiritual Path: Living at the Heart of Paradox by Philip Goldberg. Sentient Publications (2006). Another non-memoir but filled with personal anecdote of one intelligent journalist's experience and appraisal of the spiritual cornucopia of teachers, practices, quandaries and pitfalls for earnest seeker.

Cloister Walk by Kathleen Norris. Riverhead Trade (1997). Included here as the model of what spiritual memoir might attain. Focus here on Benedictine spirituality and living a cloistered life. Norris spends time living and praying in the monastery with monks from whom she learns new ways to approach her own life as wife and author.

List of Chapters:[22]

Section One: Prayer
> Prologue: The Gypsy's Story: Portending the Path
> Chapter 1: Growing up Churched: Setting the Foundation
> Chapter 2: Motherloss: The First Emptying
> Chapter 3: Holding Patterns: Anger, Alienation, and Atheism

Section Two: Meditation
> Chapter 4: Finding the Guru: Is This for Real?
> Chapter 5: Magical Thinking: Transformation & Rebirth (sort of)
> Chapter 6: Fullness & Emptiness: Entering the Paradox

Section Three: **Poetry**[23]
> Chapter 7: Language Makes the World: A Poet's Complaint
> Chapter 8: Finding Form: Things I Thought I Knew Already
> Chapter 9: Emptying the Container: The Second Emptying

Section Four: Prayer **Plus**[24]
> Chapter 10: Return to Holiness, Return to Wholeness
> Chapter 11: Reclaiming Meditation & Prayer: Making It Real
> Chapter 12: Authentic Self: The Recalibration Continues

Appendices:[25] Exercises, Meditations, and Prayers for the journey to Authentic Selfhood

About the Author:

Meg Hill Fitz-Randolph is a poet, college professor, wife, mother, and card-carrying Episcopalian. She is also a thirty-year veteran of TM (Transcendental Meditation), having spent months at a time in deep meditation while alternately attending countless hours of lectures with her guru, the late Maharishi Mahesh **Yogi**.[26] With an MFA degree in poetry and another in world mythology, her poems and essays have appeared in a number of national literary journals, including *The Antioch Review, The Beloit Journal, Prairie Schooner, Cimarron Review, A Room of Her* **Own,**[27] and others. She has taught poetry workshops and college writing as well as courses in mythology and the creative process at various colleges and universities throughout the Midwest. Along with her poems, she has published in magazines, **both print and online,**[28] articles ranging from mythology to depth psychology (as informed by the work of Carl Jung), meditation, ritual, and prayer. Currently she is the only female living on a mountaintop in the hills of West Virginia with fifty to one hundred Purusha monks who are meditating for World **Peace.**[29] She and her husband, the project manager of this retreat facility, divide their time between West Virginia and another famous TM community in Fairfield, Iowa. Her blog, Transcendent Function Junction, addresses many of the questions that can arise pursuing prayer, myth, and meditation practice, issues more fully explored in the book.

Platform:

Author's Website: **Meg Hill Fitz-Randolph.com**[30]

- The author has created an author's webpage which introduces an overview of her book and lists publication credits and resume info.

Blogs include:

- The Transcendent Function Junction

- God Drifts: Western Prayer Meets Eastern Meditation

- Open Salon: The Talking Cure

Social Media **includes:**[31]

- Facebook

- Twitter

- LinkedIn

- The author will connect with **three**[32] more forums and communities in order to **post**[33] her ideas on prayer and meditation.

- The author will set up guest blogs with sites like The Huffington Post, Belief.net, etc to post under their religion and spirituality topics.

- The author will continue an active commentary on her **topic.**[34]

Promotion:

- The author has in place all necessary social media outlets such as author's website, Facebook, blogs, Twitter, and **LinkedIn.**[35]

- The author will arrange readings and book signings at popular **bookstores**[36] in Fairfield, Iowa City and surrounding urban **communities.**[37]

28 In contrast, this kind of general listing provides little of use.

29 This could be seen as beneficial if the retreat or attendees are well known and/or well connected. Otherwise, it makes you seem difficult to reach and a bit removed from society.

30 You get bonus points for proposals with functional hyperlinks, but don't rely on the agent to click through for the necessary info.

31 As with your website, blog, or any other type of media, specific traffic/follower/audience, figures help. The vast majority of people on these sites don't have a large enough following to adequately sell books.

32 Why three? And why only three? You don't want to imply that you'll give up, especially so soon.

33 It's best to at least imply purposeful interaction with the target audience, rather than just putting things up online.

34 This conveys no useful information. Be specific.

35 A plan for action is more effective than a state of being, especially when that state is already completely expressed elsewhere.

36 Listing them would show that you've done your homework and give a better idea of the potential.

SAMPLE

37 Agents and major publishers tend to want projects with national or international reach.

38 One old form of broadcast media to one city in Iowa seems rather limited, especially if you're trying to convince an agent or publisher in NY or CA, for example. At the very least, provide the appropriate audience figures.

39 Expressing your relation would give me a better idea of how feasible this is.

40 A promise alone is fairly weak. A promise with an appropriate connection is better. An expressed offer in hand is excellent. An expressed offer in hand with prior experience is ideal.

41 A well-organized plan will get you far. Try to group similar efforts and present them so that they build off of each other.

42 This is a missed opportunity to express focus, strategy, and brand. Show that you know how to utilize specific portions of your material. Show that you have a plan already in place.

43 This is a rather passive, general, and antiquated approach. Show me that you know your audience and how to reach them. Better yet, show me that you already have.

44 A list that begins with Deepak and Oprah could almost be detrimental if there's no expressed connection. Everyone in your genre would love to have their support. Show how you are able to get it. This appears to be best fit for self-publishing, which is perfectly valid.

- The author will arrange for radio interviews in **Fairfield, Iowa,**[38] home of transcendental meditation

- The author will arrange for radio interview with Christa Tibbets of **NPR**[39]

- The author will arrange to give a reading at a popular Writer's Circle in Brooklyn, New York (where she already has a **contact**[40]).

- The author will arrange to travel to Chicago, New York and other large hubs for more readings and book **signings**.[41]

- The author will arrange to give a webinars on her website to promote and elaborate on some of the ideas in her **book.**[42]

- The author will promote her book in each of these venues.

- The author will purchase a three-to-six month advertisement with **Radio-TV**[43] Interview Report or something comparable.

- The author will blast out information using social networking already set in place on Facebook, Twitter, and LinkedIn.

- The author will offer columns, essays, and articles to e-zines and print publications in exchange for a promotional bio.

- The author will contact the following opinion-makers for book **endorsements:**[44]
  - Deepak Chopra
  - Oprah Winfrey
  - John Gray
  - Richard Rohrer
  - Thomas Keating
  - Thomas Moore
  - Joan Chittester
  - Cynthia Bourgeault
  - John Hagelin

SAMPLE #2:
WITH ANNOTATIONS BY EDITOR MICHELLE HOWRY

A Proposal for:

Hope for Your Addicted Teen

A Step-by-Step Guide for Parents[1]

By

Deborah Cipolla

Address
Phone
Email

TABLE OF CONTENTS

INTRODUCTION

Overview

Hope for Your Addicted Teen
A Step-by-Step Guide for Parents

[1] A strong title and subtitle. The title offers a positive spin, and the subtitle clearly spells out what the book is and who it is written for.

2 I like to see statistics like this, identifying the scope of the problem/issue and showing the need for a book. I can use these stats in my own marketing materials for my publishing team, too.

3 This is pretty short—most books I'm looking at in this category are at least 50,000–60,000 words. Is there a reason this one is so short?

4 One important thing to address, either here or elsewhere (in Marketing section) is how you will find your audience at this critical time.

5 This is an interesting editorial addition, but a few things to keep in mind. Why all boys? There should be a mix of genders/geographical locations. And whenever including stories from real people on a sensitive topic like this, be sure that you get releases and/or that you change identifying characteristics if necessary.

About 2 million children aged 12 to 17 need treatment for a substance abuse problem. But only about 150,000 get the help they **need**.[2]

There are many reasons for this gap, but perhaps the biggest is that many parents don't know all of the options to help their children and are too emotionally wrought to do effective research in the midst of crisis.

Hope for Your Addicted Teen will provide parents of children suffering from substance abuse problems with a unique and comprehensive look at their options --- shared by a mother who discovered many of them through personal experience. This is the first book that gathers information about various treatment options for teenaged substance abusers in one place. The finished manuscript will contain approximately 35,000 words, or 140 **pages**,[3] as well as at least a two-page bibliography, an index and a table of contents.

At the point when parents realize their child has s substance abuse problem, the pain and panic can be almost paralyzing. Unfortunately, when parents must deal with this most daunting problem, they often have the fewest **resources**.[4] The parent in that situation will find *Hope for Your Addicted Teen* packed with vital information.

This book will help them:

- Learn how to discern whether their teens are abusing drugs or alcohol.
- Find out how ongoing abuse will affect their teens, long- and short-term.
- Get information about available options for help, and how to evaluate them.
- Gain an understanding of what to expect during the recovery process.
- Have a list of resources to begin their search for answers for their teens.
- Receive emotional and spiritual support in sidebars in each chapter.

Hope for Your Addicted Teen is written by a parent who has been through this experience with her own teenaged son. As someone who had to put aside her own confusion and emotions so she could educate herself quickly about the issue and help her child, her perspective and experience offers readers both empathy and no-nonsense information. This book will provide a parent with a comprehensive look at their options, found in one place -- avoiding the need for frantic parents to spin their wheels gathering information from a myriad of sources.

A special feature of the book will be the author's interviews with her son, other boys who have been in recovery programs, and their **parents**.[5] These will be written as brief vignettes and interspersed throughout the book.

Markets

The book will be aimed primarily at parents who suspect their teenaged child has a substance abuse issue, and secondarily at medical and therapeutic professionals the parents might consult with about their child's problem.

The Teen Drug Abuse Market

Who will read this **blog**[6] and this book?

The parents of the 2 million teens cited above who are abusing alcohol and drugs.

Grandparents and other concerned relatives and friends of the family who see the problem and are trying to help.

Members of Al-Anon and Nar-Anon who go to meetings because of their children; there are more than 13,000 Al-Anon groups in the U.S and more than 1,500 in Canada, according to a 2003 survey of Al-Anon members, and more than 25% of the members attend meetings because of their children's substance abuse.

Psychologists, therapists and other professionals specializing in children's substance abuse.

Publicity and Promotion[7]

Ninety percent of drug and alcohol addictions begin during the teenage years, according to The Partnership at Drugfree.org. A report issued by the group in 2012 showed "heavy" marijuana use among teenagers is up 80 percent from 10 years ago, with one in 10 teens reporting that they use the drug at least 20 times a month.

A National Institute on Drug Abuse survey last year found a rise in marijuana smoking in high school from its previous survey: 6.5 percent of high school seniors smoke daily, up from 5.1 percent five years earlier. The survey also found that nearly 30 percent of adolescents have consumed alcohol and 15.5 percent have smoked marijuana by the time they reach 8th grade.

With these rising numbers of children using drugs and alcohol at an earlier age, *Hope for Your Addicted Teen* offers valuable information at a critical time.

Promotion Plan

On publication, the author will travel to the following major markets to **speak:**[8]

1. San Francisco
2. Boston
3. Dallas
4. Seattle

6 Why the reference to the blog here? Confusing. Hopefully, you already have a blog and the book will be an outgrowth of that. If so, then one of the markets you can outline below would be: "The XXXXX readers of my blog, _____." Perhaps reference comp titles here, too? ("Readers of successful memoirs of substance abuse, like *Beautiful Boy* [which was on *The New York Times* bestseller list for XX weeks], want a more practical, action-oriented guide written from a parent's perspective.")

7 The stats below are interesting, but they don't inform the publicity discussion—this info belongs above, in the "Teen Drug Abuse Market" section. In the Publicity section, I'm most concerned with how you are going to promote your book.

8 I need more information on this—why these markets? Does author have a connection to one or more of the markets? Where will she be speaking—is she invited somewhere, or will she just seek out a speaking venue? It's very difficult to travel to a city where you don't have any family or professional connections and try to book an event "cold." I encourage authors to focus on events in places where they have friends/family/professional contacts, and where they can guarantee a good turnout. If you do have these connections here, say so. If not, omit.

9 I'm unsure of how useful this really is. Perhaps money will be better spent on a freelance publicist.

10 If you plan to hire a freelance publicist to help you, say so clearly—don't hedge.

11 For an author whose expertise lies in her personal connection to a topic (rather than in her professional credentials, like a doctor), social media is a hugely important factor. I'd expect this author to have a robust blog and social media presence ... and to talk about that earlier in the proposal. Any stats about the blog's traffic and exposure?

12 You need to elaborate.

13 Seems repetitive—isn't that the same as "The author will promote the book's release via her social networks ..." above?

14 Does the author have preexisting connections to any of these people? If not, it seems pretty unlikely that they will respond. Including these kinds of names in a proposal without a personal connection can seem inexperienced. I'd suggest that she dig deep and find other, more accessible authors and experts in this field—doctors, authors, and other parents who have written books on this topic. Contact them. Getting blurbs of praise from well-credentialed experts and authors can actually be *more* meaningful to an editor than chasing after A-list names that are unlikely to come through.

The author will use the services of ExpertClick.com during the first three months after the book's release.

The author will purchase a three- to six-month advertisement with Radio-TV Interview Report and/or Best Guest Digest to generate television and radio interviews to promote *Hope for Your Addicted **Teen**.*[9]

The author will send press kits to local media in cities where she is scheduled to speak, or will hire a publicity firm to **do so.**[10]

The author will promote the book's release via her blog with posts and **announcements.**[11]

The author will promote the book's release via her social networks with status updates, book giveaways, etc.

The author will seek out media opportunities such as:

Television news and talk shows (*Good Morning America, Today, CBS This Morning, Dr. Oz, Katie Couric, Dr. Drew*)

Feature articles in newspapers and magazines (print and online), specifically parenting publications

The author will arrange a virtual book **tour.**[12]

The author will send out information using social networking media already in **place.**[13]

The author will offer essays and articles to e-zines and print publications in exchange for a promotional bio.

The author will contact the following opinion-makers for book **endorsements:**[14]

1. Dr. Mehmet Oz
2. Dr. Drew Pinsky
3. David Sheff (author of *Beautiful Boy* and *Clean*)

The author's promotional and publicity efforts will be coordinated with those of the publisher.

Competing Books

Books on the topic of teen substance abuse fall into the following categories: anecdotal parent's perspective (*Beautiful Boy*), anecdotal teen's perspective (*Tweak, Go Ask Alice*), and various medical/social/psychological perspectives (*Healing the Addicted Brain*).

Beautiful Boy: A Father's Journey Through His Son's Addiction, by David Sheff (Mariner Books, 2009, 336 pages, paperback, $14.95). Very personal and wrenching account of how a parent dealt with his son's methamphetamine addiction; doesn't include resources for dealing with teenage substance abuse, other than those the author sought out.

Tweak, Growing Up on Methamphetamines, by Nic Sheff (Atheneum Books for Young Readers, 2009, 352 pages, paperback, $10.99). Powerfully written first-person account of methamphetamine addiction; doesn't include resources for parents or teens.

Adolescents, Alcohol, and Substance Abuse, Reaching Teens Through Brief Interventions, by Peter Monti, PhD; Susan Colby, PhD; Tracy O'Leary, PhD (The Guilford Press, 2004, 350 pages, paperback, $42). Covers a range of approaches to prevention and treatment; more suitable for clinicians than parents.

Hope for Your Addicted Teen will differ from these books by including aspects of both the first-person narrative and the clinical, subjective **approaches.** [15]

About the Author[16]

Deborah Cipolla is a journalist (Associated Press, Los Angeles Times and other publications), public relations and marketing professional (IBM, Siemens, Barnes&Noble.com) and mother. She has written extensively on a wide range of topics, and has been published in newspapers throughout the U.S.

She called upon her journalism experience as she conducted her research to find answers to her son's substance abuse problems, and interviewed therapists, school officials and consultants.

In an effort to give meaning to what she and her son went through, she wants to share her knowledge and experience with other parents, to help them through one of a parent's worst nightmares.

Author's Platform[17]

Social Media
1. Facebook (143 friends)
2. LinkedIn (38 connections)
3. Twitter (currently building)
4. Google+ (currently building)
5. Pinterest (25 followers)

Launched a blog where she has been blogging her book to promote it and gain potential readers. Has participated in groups and forums on those sites and will comment on related blogs and articles. She will publish her blog on Technorati.com and Blogcatalog.com and will participate in bloggers' networks for reciprocal linking and posting agreements.

The author participates in online parenting communities CafeMom and iVillage, which have discussion forums on parenting teens. She also will create a website for her blogged book, with articles, links, and additional resources.

---

15 This proposal needs more comp titles. As an editor, I'll need to provide at least 6–8 strong comp titles to my team, and I'd prefer if the author could help me out with those. Also, there are stronger comps to be found. *Beautiful Boy* is a wonderful book, and it should be here, but it's narrative, not prescriptive, so it's not really the best comp title. Think about books that would actually be shelved in the same section of the bookstore. (In fact, *go* to a bookstore and look in the parenting/self help/recovery sections.) Look for practical, prescriptive books offering advice for parents who want to keep their kids off drugs or that offer advice on how to help them once they've become addicted. And then tell why each book is different from the one you are proposing.

16 Author's previous work experience is impressive. Please flesh out this bio and really detail your writing and reporting experience. This is relevant experience, and it makes a difference to an editor reading your bio.

17 These social-media stats aren't impressive, so rather than calling them out in this separate section, I'd suggest that she delete the discussion of how many followers she has on these individual platforms. Instead I suggest folding the blog discussion into the previous section on publicity and promotion—that's what this is really all about.

SAMPLE

18 Rather than pulling this out into a separate section, I'd rework it and fold it into your author bio.

19 It's redundant to have an unannotated table of contents, followed immediately by an annotated table of contents—I'd delete this.

20 My advice is to be sure to filter all this information through the lens of a *parent*—that is what's unique here. Remember, there are other books on this topic written by well-credentialed physicians and experts, so you don't need to compete with them. The author needs to think about what she brings to this topic as a parent—what kind of information and perspective only she can offer.

Published Articles[18]

The author has published hundreds of articles in newspapers and magazines in her years as a journalist at the Associated Press and the Los Angeles Times. She has reported on a range of serious topics, including:

Presidential, gubernatorial, and other political campaigns
Mass suicide in Jonestown, Guyana
Immigration issues
Airline crashes
Business issues

She also has written many lighter feature articles and profiles, including pieces on:

Gloria Steinem
Hugh Hefner
Tournament of Roses Parade
Nude beaches in Los Angeles
International Flat Earth Society

THE OUTLINE

List of Chapters[19]

Introduction
Is It Addiction or Normal Experimentation?
What Other Factors Contribute To Addiction?
How Does Addiction Affect My Child?
Is My Child's Addiction My Fault?
What's the First Step to Recovery?
How Do I Choose a Rehab Program?
Can an Educational Consultant Help?
Can I Really Send My Child into the Wilderness?
How Do I Choose a Therapeutic Boarding School?
What Are Transitional Living Programs?
What Happens When My Child Returns Home From a Recovery Program?
Are 12-Step Programs the Answer?
Additional Resources

Chapter Summaries[20]

Introduction

The author will give a quick overview of her experience with her son's substance abuse, explaining her desire to save other parents from reinventing the wheel as they face similar **issues.** [21]

Is It Addiction or Normal Experimentation?

Too often, teen drinking and drug use is considered a rite of passage. Many kids will experiment with substances without becoming addicted, but there are far too many whose full-blown addiction is dismissed by their parents, especially if the parents experimented themselves as teens.

What Other Factors Contribute To Addiction?

The National Alliance for Mental Illness says as much as half of the mentally ill population also has a substance abuse problem. Children who have attention-deficit disorder or attention-deficit hyperactivity disorder, depression, anxiety or bipolar disorder are more susceptible to addiction than the rest of the population.

How Does Addiction Affect My Child?

MRI studies cited by the Science and Management of Addictions (SAMA) show that the development of the prefrontal cortex and outer mantle of the brain continues into the early twenties, and may not be complete until the mid-twenties. We'll address the neurological effects of early and prolonged substance use.

Is My Child's Addiction My Fault?

Addiction is truly a family problem. Addiction can be genetically handed down from a parent. Or a parent's style of child-rearing might be one that doesn't foster good decision-making or self-confidence. This chapter also will address how the parents most likely will change and grow as a result of their child's recovery process.

What's the First Step to Recovery?

Recognizing and accepting that your child has a problem that must be addressed is the parent's first step. Then they must determine what type of program or therapy is the best for their child.

How Do I Choose a Rehab Program?

Sometimes parents will make this decision alone, or they may consult with a physician, therapist, or other professional. This chapter discusses what a parent needs to know before choosing.

---

21 Overall, I think this author brings a lot of passion and firsthand experience to this material. But she needs to acknowledge what a competitive and highly published category she is entering—it's not going to be easy for someone without medical credentials and deep experience in the field to crack this category. If she feels strongly that this is a book that she is meant to write, I would advise the following:

• Play up her unique qualifications and perspective as a *parent*—this is what she has going for herself here, so really emphasize it.

• Demonstrate a deep knowledge of the category—really dig deep into her comp-title research, find out what else is out there, and work hard to make a strong case for why her book will be different/better. I think she still has some work to do make that case.

• Establish herself as a go-to parenting authority on this topic online. Blog, chat, give advice, and connect with others online. If you can show that you have a substantial online audience who cares about this topic and thinks of you as an authority, that makes you more marketable.

SAMPLE

Can an Educational Consultant Help?

It is an educational consultant's business to know and visit wilderness camps and therapeutic schools. They can tell you about various options and help you match one with your child's issues and temperament.

Can I Really Send My Child into the Wilderness?

What goes on at a wilderness camp? We'll discuss where they're located, how they're structured, and what your teen will learn there.

How Do I Choose a Therapeutic Boarding School?

There's a wide variety of approaches and techniques at various schools. We'll look at the focuses and priorities of schools.

What Are Transitional Living Programs?

After your child completes the program at a therapeutic boarding school, it may still seem too risky for his sobriety to bring him home. A transitional living program can bridge the gap between boarding school and home.

What Happens When My Child Returns Home From a Recovery Program?

It will be a whole new person returning home and yet the same person. This chapter addresses how to set boundaries and agree on terms of living together again.

Are 12-Step Programs the Answer?

12-step programs aren't for everyone, but they can provide a solid structure and support for the teen in recovery and for his/her parents.

Additional Resources

This will be an extensive listing of organizations, websites, books, blogs, and professionals who can help a parent with a teenaged substance abuser.

SAMPLE #3:
WITH ANNOTATIONS BY EDITOR VALERIE GRAY

A Business Proposal **for:**[1]

Wanting More:

Always Getting **Less**[2]

By La Donna **Robinson**[3]
Address
Phone
Email

TABLE OF CONTENTS

Introduction

THE OUTLINE

SAMPLE CHAPTERS

Introduction[4]

[1] As an acquisitions editor, the first thing I want to know is whether or not there is a good, solid story. No amount of promotion—however good—can replace such things as character development, plotting, structure, or good technical skills.

[2] The title here, and elsewhere, should appear in italics. Also, this title sounds like a nonfiction title to me. It does not convey romance or YA.

[3] Somewhere on this page you should indicate the approximate word count, along with the fact that this is a YA Novel.

[4] I was confused by this heading—there is nothing here. If you decide to use this heading, I would recommend centering it on its own page. Either that or enlarge the font to show that it is a heading and nothing more. Personally, I would remove this title as the following heading, "Overview," is really all that is required.

SAMPLE

5 Convention requires a word count rather than a page count.

6 First time writers are expected to submit a full, complete manuscript. This comment indicates the book is not written. With the quantity and quality of polished manuscripts available to most acquisitions editors, this comment would likely not generate further interest.

7 The "teen" market is commonly referred to as the YA market. It is rare that one book could appeal to YA readers and Adult Romance readers (Harry Potter being a notable exception). This sentence shows that the author has limited knowledge of the YA and Romance genres.

8 This comment has no facts to back it up. It is mere conjecture on the part of the author. This would be a good place for the author to speak a bit more broadly about the YA market, offer comparison between her book and current popular titles, and compare her work to well-known authors so that the acquisitions editor has an idea about the type of story being presented.

9 This term is not correct in this case. I believe the author is suggesting that she has a "series" in mind and that future books will focus on the heroine introduced in Book 1.

10 Writing contests are a great way to have your work read and critiqued, but they will rarely lead to book sales and/or author exposure. To

Overview

Wanting More:
Always Getting Less

Teenage girl who has both book and common sense, yet seems to make all the wrong decisions.

Wanting More: Always Getting Less is the story of a young girl name Ksenya who is 16 years old and thinks she knows everything. Deciding that she could no longer follow her parent's rules, she moves out on her own. She starts up an affair with her married boss, not realizing the full consequences of her actions. This book has an estimated 200 **pages.**[5] The author will deliver the manuscript 2 months after receipt of the **advance.**[6]

Markets[7]

Wanting More: Always Getting Less will be aimed at the Teen and Romance markets.

The Teen/Romance Market

In the Teen/Romance Market, *Wanting More: Always Getting Less* would be a good fit for any young adult to **find.**[8]

Spin-offs[9]

The author will follow this book with 2 more books. The books will continue the story from *Wanting More: Always Getting Less.*

- Finding Myself: Ksenya's Journey

- Around and Back: Welcome Home, Ksenya

Publicity and Promotion

Pre-Publication Promotion Plan

- This author will enter writing **contests.**[10]

- The author will join www.ExpertClick.com.

Post-Publication Promotion Plan

- This author will submit to online book and reading communities such as GoodReads, Amazon, and Barnes & **Noble**[11]

- The author will purchase a three-to-six month advertisement with Radio-TV Interview Report and/or Best Guest Digest to generate television and radio interviews related to *Wanting More: Always Getting Less.*[12]

- The author will employ the services of a publicist or PR agency, such as Annie Jennings PR or Planned Television Arts, to help her obtain television and radio **interviews.**[13]

- The author will use the services of PRWeb.com during the first three months after the book's release to blast out several press releases about *Wanting More: Always Getting Less.*

- On publication, the author will set up a publicity tour in the following major **markets:**[14]
  1. Los Angeles, CA
  2. New York, NY
  3. Chicago, IL
  4. Dallas, TX

- The author will send press kits to local media in the cities where she is scheduled to speak or hire a publicity firm to do so for **her.**[15]

- The author will give a minimum of 20 talks per year in locations around the country and 7 per year locally.

- The author will pursue speaking engagements by sending out letters and/or speaker's kits weekly.

- The author will sell a minimum of 250 books per year by offering them at all her lectures, talks, seminars, and workshops, as well as on her website.

- The author will arrange a virtual book tour.

- The author will blast out information using social networking already set in place on Facebook, Twitter, and **LinkedIn.**[16]

- The author will offer columns, essays, and articles to e-zines and print publications in exchange for a promotional bio.

- The author will contact the following opinion-makers for book endorsements:
  1. LJ Sellers
  2. Carl East
  3. I.M. Telling

me, entering writing contests does not fall under the category of "promotion".

[11] This is a good idea but it needs to be done before the book is published.

[12] This type of advertising is expensive and time-consuming. Additionally, this type of advertising is generally concentrated in the week or two before publication, and the week of publication.

[13] It is best to consult with the publicist about the best ways to reach an audience. Radio and TV are not always the most effective vehicles unless the author is already a well-known writer.

[14] This is a huge undertaking and would be best handled by a publicist. Bear in mind that, as an unknown author, there may be little or no interest in your book. Book tours today are generally reserved for authors who have a big following.

[15] These publicity ideas are good, but they will cost a great deal of money to execute. Also, the time commitment will be significant.

[16] Since this is a YA novel, using social media to get the word out is more important than any other item on this list.

SAMPLE

17 I would describe these books as Romance rather than YA. Also, Checketts writes a romance in the Christian vein, and Glines writes sexy romance. These are two very different genres. I recommend the author offer comparisons that are more similar to her own work.

18 These observations, while true, should have been made in the Overview section.

19 This topic has been covered already. I suggest the author include this material in the competitive title section. Furthermore, while it is good to support other authors, this idea is actually driving sales away from the author's title.

20 While possibly true, this comment is the author's own opinion. A published review—either in print or online—is a much better way to offer the same idea.

• The author's promotional and publicity efforts will be coordinated with those of the publisher.

Competing Books

The following two books are closest in subject matter and, therefore, represent the most direct competition to *Wanting More: Always Getting Less*:[17]

- *The Broken Path*, by Cami Checketts (Birch River Publishing, December 22, 2012, 252 Pages, E-book $.99, Paperback $11.69)

- *While It Last*, by Abbi Glines (Simon Pulse, October , 2012, 305 Pages, E-book $1.99, Paperback $8.59, Hardcover $13.08)

If your readers care about your characters, they will tell their friends and family to read your **book**.[18]

If your readers do not connect with your characters, they will more than likely take the time and leave a bad review.

Complementary Books[19]

Readers purchasing the following titles might also purchase *Wanting More: Always Getting Less*:

- *Silent Harmony: A Vivienne Taylor Horse Lover's Mystery* (Fairmont Riding Academy, by Michele Scott (Skyscape, 2013, 238 pages, $6.67 paperback).

- *Divergent, by Veronica Roth* (Katherine Tegen Books, 2011, 501 pages, $5.99 paperback, $14.79 hardcover).

- *The Last Boyfriend* (Forever Love) by J.S. Cooper (215 pages, $8.94 paperback).

- *Falling Into You*, by Jasinda Wilder (Jasinda Wilder, 2013, 368 pages, $11.92 paperback).

- *Until Tomorrow* (Christy and Todd: College Years Book #1), by Robin Jones Gunn (Bethany House Publishers, 2000, 288 pages, $4.99 paperback).

The above books are character driven stories that keeps the readers engaged and wanting to know **more**.[20] Each author including myself, developed characters that you are rooting for and can't wait to see how their story will turn out.

About the Author

La Donna Robinson is the author of *Wanting More: Always Getting Less*. She is a force to be on the **lookout for**.[21] When not glued to her computer, she enjoys taking weekend trips to Vegas and hanging out with her **family**.[22]

Mission Statement[23]

I love these characters and going on this journey with them. Sometimes you will want to laugh with them. Sometimes you will want to love and hate them. At times, you will think that you know someone just like them.

Author's Platform[24]

*Presentations Scheduled for 2013-**2014***[25]

- In discussions with Incredible Coach.com to speak December 2013

- In discussions with Transformational Author Experience to speak April 2014

- In discussions with Incredible Coach.com to speak March 2014

Additional Platform Elements[26]

- 150 friends on FB

- 1,945 friends on Twitter

- 20 connections on LinkedIn

THE OUTLINE[27]

List of Chapters

Introduction

CHAPTER SUMMARIES

Introduction

21 This is editorializing by the author. If this is a true statement, then it would be wise to include a quote or blurb from a legitimate source to support this statement.

22 It might be helpful to add info about the author's education, where she lives (i.e., Midwest or East Coast) and if she is working on her next novel. As written, this section does not say a lot about who the author is.

23 This should go in the beginning of the proposal. Also, this is not a mission statement, this is repetitive information about the author's opinion of the characters.

24 While not always essential in works of fiction, it can be helpful if an author does have a platform. In this particular case, the author does not have a platform that would bring attention to her or her book.

25 It would appear that none of these presentations is confirmed. While interesting, I'm not certain that participation in these events will drive sales of your book

26 There is nothing in this category that stands out to me. Based on the info here, I do not think the author has a viable platform.

27 As a reminder to the reader, it would be good to add two or three sentences here about the story synopsis.

SAMPLE

29 These comments are all about the characters. Info on the plot and structure should be included here.

In Chapter One, you are introduced to the main characters and how everyone is connected. You form an opinion immediately if you love or **hate them.**[29]

In Chapter Two, the story gets heavily involved with two characters whose lives become center stage. But then something happens to change everything.

In Chapter Three, having said goodbye to her best friend, determination takes over to find the killer. However, the killer may be closer than anyone thinks.

SAMPLE CHAPTERS

Chapter One

In life you are always told that if you work hard good things will come your way. That is not always the case. No matter how hard you work, there is still a good chance of never getting what you really want. There is always someone better than you, prettier than you and smarter than you. Sometimes you cut corners just to save face. It is everyone for themselves world. Sure I might sound a little bitter, but who hasn't. Sometimes that is the only way to survive.

My name is Ksenya James and here is my story. Please listen closely and you just may learn a few things. I thought I knew it all and no one could tell me shit. Not my teachers and damn sure not my parents. I constantly pushed my mother›s buttons to the breaking point. It got so bad one night, she nearly beat me to one inch of my life. That is when I knew it was time to go. Here I was a 16-year-old know-it-all and completely on my own. I talked my best friend, Pammie, into letting me crash a few days in her room without telling her mama. She agreed on one condition: I had to let me parents know that I was okay.

I had a job and few bucks saved in my bank account. All I needed was to find a place to stay that I could afford. That should be the easy part (yeah right). Every place I looked at wanted first and last month's rent. I had that but that was all I had. I moved into the cheapest place I could find. The roaches and rats came with the place for free.

(Sample continues with three full chapters.)

SAMPLE #4:
WITH ANNOTATIONS BY AGENT ANDY ROSS

A Proposal for:

A Slice of Faith:

Soothe Your Problems by Eating a Slice of Faith Each Day[1]

By Amanda M. Socci

Address
Phone Number
Email
http://asliceoffaith.wordpress.com

TABLE OF **CONTENTS**[2]

1 The title is OK. But the subtitle isn't. You shouldn't use the same words in the sub as you do in the title. The title should be catchy and poetic. The subtitle should be more explanatory. I find this subtitle to be confusing.

2 I should note that after reading this entire proposal, I feel this book is not likely to find a traditional publisher. You should probably be thinking of self-publishing. It's going to be hard to interest a publisher in a book that is really no more than personal reflections and observations. This proposal hasn't really made a strong case that the book contains material that would have a wide readership. And the author's platform is too modest to drive sales.

3 (Next Page) First impressions are important, and first paragraphs are extremely important. I recommend that you either have a catchy hook or a very clear statement of what the book is. This first paragraph contains neither. After reading it, I don't have a sense of what this book is about. Additionally, it's confusing because it's unclear what the genre is: business, memoir, or religion.

SAMPLE

4 This is just my personal preference, but I usually advise my clients to write in the first person. It sounds more natural.

5 By paragraph 3, I still don't know what the book is about.

6 Book proposals need to be tight. Every paragraph needs to convey a message and needs to answer the questions that the acquisition editor will be asking. This paragraph says that the reader will cringe and rejoice, and be shocked. But there is nothing that I have read so far that will do any of those things. Its better to show the things that are shocking, than simply to assert that it is shocking.

7 You probably want to give some more descriptive detail about the photographs and the designs to let the editor better visualize the book's design.

8 You should estimate the delivery date from the date of contract execution. To base it on the receipt of the advance gives me a sense that the author is perhaps too suspicious. This section should also include an estimated word count.

9 This overview doesn't really work. After reading it, I don't have any sense of what the subject matter is or how it is organized.

INTRODUCTION

Overview

A Slice of Faith: Soothe Your Problems by Eating a Slice of Faith Each Day

Leadership is a learning activity that is good for resume-building, if done properly. If not done properly, leadership can lead to disaster, and possibly a huge meltdown. The huge meltdown is what happened to **Amanda M. Socci**.[3]

Amanda was a Girl Scout leader of her daughter's troop. She was creative, dedicated, and hard working. She studied the Girl Scout guide, learning the ins and outs of proper leadership. She thought she was doing so well. Amanda poured hours into developing interesting lesson plans, writing detailed charts of every badge the girls earned, and collecting art supplies for the next **project**.[4]

That next project never came. Right as cookie sales began, Amanda quit the Girl Scouts at the height of her leadership. Every single plan was left on permanent hold with a bunch of parents who were confused and angry. She had reached a boiling point and decided she had been unappreciated long enough. It was time for a change. Her change. It was time she started focusing on a larger leadership, in charge of her own **faith**.[5]

Now is a good time for Amanda to help you take charge of your faith as well.

Get ready to cringe, cry, and rejoice with *A Slice of Faith: Soothe Your Problems by Eating a Slice of Faith Each Day*. First-person stories of one woman's worst life moments will shock. Faith lessons soften the blow. Renew your faith by "eating a slice" **each day**.[6]

Amanda estimates this book will contain 75 personal essays and faith reflections in a 150-page book. Amanda plans to include one photo per essay, for a total of 75 photographs, along with subdued graphic design for each page of the faith reflection. There are no plans to include a glossary. She does plan, however, to add a short introduction to the front of the **book**.[7]

The reader will benefit from reading *A Slice of Faith: Soothe Your Problems by Eating a Slice of Faith Each Day* by being entertained and encouraged with faith reflections to help them practice faith more frequently in their lives. *A Slice of Faith: Soothe Your Problems by Eating a Slice of Faith Each Day* features faith reflections in the form of faith lessons that are interesting and easy to digest, without being preachy.

Author Amanda M. Socci will deliver the manuscript one month after receipt of advance **payment**.[8 and 9]

Markets

A Slice of Faith: Soothe Your Problems by Eating a Slice of Faith Each Day is written for men and women over the age of 30 who have had a chance to live and experience their own trials and tribulations of life. They would most likely appreciate renewing their faith. Because this is a nondenominational book, no effort will be made to tie into any specific religion. (The Christian market is likely not applicable because Christian books are mostly tied to scripture.)

A Slice of Faith: Soothe Your Problems by Eating a Slice of Faith Each Day will be aimed at the nonfiction book market in the following categories: inspirational, motivational, and new thought.

Inspirational Market[10]

Inspirational market books entertain with true stories of people overcoming great odds, often with inspiration for readers to see the world through new eyes.

Motivational Market

Motivational market books suggest positive ways to help readers look at the world differently and transform their lives.

New Thought Market[11]

New thought market books offer optimistic views of life with elements of practical and speculative qualities.

Spinoffs[12]

Author Amanda M. Socci will follow this book with four more in the A Slice of … series, with *A Slice of Faith: Soothe Your Problems by Eating a Slice of Faith Each Day* as the first book to be published.

Additional books in the works are as follows:

- *A Slice of Writing Prompts for Nonfiction Writers: 150 Theme-Based Nonfiction Scenarios to Encourage Nonfiction Writing*

- *A Slice of Gratitude: Giving People, Places, and Things Flowers in Life with Thoughtful, Living Tributes*

- *A Slice of Creative Ideas: 1000 Ideas Executed in 100 Creative Projects*

- *A Slice of Artistic Recycling: A Focus on Waste Materials and Creative Reusage in Salvage Art*

Publicity and Promotion

The author will:

- contact the following Christian radio stations to arrange author **interviews:**[13]

10 I like the way you have broken down the potential audience and tried to define specific characteristics of that audience.

11 This category is not commonly used in the book business. It's pretty vague and, I think, confusing. You need to familiarize yourself with terms of art that are commonly used.

12 Its good to mention these spinoffs. You might want to do it in the Overview. Remember that publishers are not likely to commit to a spinoff until they see the sales of the original title.

13 In the market section above, you mentioned that it would not be appropriate for the Christian market. But here you are saying that you will target the Christian market. That's confusing.

14 The editor doesn't really know anything about these blogs. What are they? How will they promote your book? Do they have a wide readership? If they have modest audiences, it's not likely to impress an editor.

15 The promotion section of the book proposal tells the editor exactly what you will do to promote the book. You need to be convincing. I tell my clients not to use the word *might* in this section. To a publisher, that usually means "might not". Saying that you will contact a periodical is weak. You want to say that you have commitments from periodicals.

16 Same as above. Talking about the "possibility" of an author signing sends the message that there is also a possibility that there won't be an author signing.

17 Saying that you will contact celebrities for endorsements is similarly weak. You want to tell the publisher what celebrities have committed to endorsing or blurbing the book.

18 This is a weak marketing plan. The bullet points are vague. And the voice seems to send the message that the author isn't really savvy about how to engage in marketing. It's vitally important for the author to aggressively market his book after publication since the publisher's efforts will be modest.

¤ WGTS 91.9, which serves the Washington, D.C. metropolitan area

¤ WAVA 105.1, which serves the Baltimore, Maryland area

- contact the following bloggers to arrange online author interviews on their blogs and discuss the possibility of doing a virtual **book tour:**[14]

    ¤ Michelle Miles http://michellemiles.net

    ¤ Penny Lockwood Ehrenkranz http://pennylockwoodehrenkranz.blogspot.com

    ¤ Lee-Ann Graff-Vinson http://www.leeanngraffvinson.com

- contact the following Christian bloggers to arrange online author interviews on their blogs and discuss the possibility of doing a virtual book tour:

    ¤ Jennifer Thorson http://www.thepurposefulmom.com

    ¤ Anna Christensen http://feminineadventures.com

- query Guideposts magazine to write a freelance article as a means of book **promotion**[15]

- discuss the possibility of a book author signing with Family Christian Stores retail store in Alexandria, **Virginia**[16]

- join Christian-based "street team" marketing groups through the World Literary Cafe

- promote *A Slice of Faith: Soothe Your Problems by Eating a Slice of Faith Each Day* through active participation in Goodreads online

- blast out information using social networking already in place on Triberr, Facebook, Twitter, Google+, and LinkedIn

- contact the following relevant opinion-makers for book **endorsements:**[17]

    ¤ Susan M. Heim

    ¤ Jeff Goins

- Author Amanda M. Socci's promotional and publicity efforts will be coordinated with those of the **publisher.**[18]

Competing Books

The following two books are closest in subject matter and, therefore, represent the most direct competition to *A Slice of Faith: Soothe Your Problems by Eating a Slice of Faith Each Day*:

- *Your Choice: Fear or Faith* by Dr. Joe Vitale (**Burman Books,**[19] 2013, 201 pages, hardcover, $22): Good for helping readers handle uncertainties of life by choosing to live in faith instead of fear, bad for not supporting the concept of **blind faith**.[20] Other titles by Dr. Joe Vitale: *Instant Manifestation: The Real Secret to Attracting What You Want Right Now* (2011). *The Law of Attraction* (2012).

- *Thank God I: Series of Inspiration for Every Situation* by John Castagnini. (Inspired Authors Press, LLC, 2008, 304 pages, paperback, $19.99) Good for its true stories of gratitude for adverse situations such as rape, death, divorce, cancer and alcoholism; bad because it's an anthology and does not **discuss faith**.[21] Other titles by John Castagnini: *Think and Grow with a Friend* (2000), *Making Love with Poetry* (2003), *Thank God I...Was Cheated On* (2009), *The 4 Steps to Loving or Leaving a Cheater* (4 Step Products) (2013), *The 4 Steps to Turning Abuse to Empowerment* (4 Step Products) (2013).

My book, *A Slice of Faith: Soothe Your Problems by Eating a Slice of Faith Each Day* differs from *Your Choice: Fear or Faith* by Dr. Joe Vitale by focusing on an undying blind faith in God that is tested but not weakened. It also differs from *Thank God I: Series of Inspiration for Every Situation* by John Castagnini by featuring true stories that are personal to the author and featuring faith as the solution to soothing problems.

Complementary Books

Readers purchasing the following titles might also purchase *A Slice of Faith: Soothe Your Problems by Eating a Slice of Faith Each Day*:

- *Faith: Trusting Your Own Deepest Experience*, by Sharon Salzberg (Riverhead Trade, 2003, 192 pages, paperback, $14)

- *Fresh Faith: What Happens When Real Faith Ignites God's People*, by Pastor Jim Cymbala. (Zondervan, 2003, 256 pages, paperback, $14.99.)

- *Faith (From Apostolic Into True Hope)*, by Keith Shephard. (Xulon Press, 2013, 58 pages, paperback, $19.99)

- *Inspired Faith: 365 Days a Year: Daily Motivation in God's Word*, by Thomas Nelson. (Thomas Nelson, 2012, 384 pages, hardcover, $16.99.)

- *From Faith to Faith: A Daily Guide to Victory*, by Gloria Copeland and Kenneth Copeland. (Harrison House Publishers, 2013, 438 pages, e-book, $7.99.)

19 It's important to use major publishers. This is not one.

20 It's important to describe clearly what the competing title is about and to distinguish it from your book. I think you need to go further than saying what's good and what's bad.

21 First, this is a self-published book so it's not the best example. And you are going to have to use more than two examples. Five or six is probably better. The comp analysis section is extremely important. This is how editors judge whether there is a strong audience for the book based on sales of the competitive titles. The worst thing you can say is "There is no other book like this on the market." That says to the publisher that there probably isn't an audience large enough to justify a book like this. You want to use comps from major publishers that have had strong sales. This shows a strong potential audience. At the same time, you need to show that you have something different to offer.

SAMPLE

All of these complementary books discuss some sort of conflict or challenge and offer similar solutions in God's Word as a series of songs, scripture readings, or devotionals. *A Slice of Faith: Soothe Your Problems by Eating a Slice of Faith Each Day* is complementary but unique in its approach. It distinguishes itself as a series of personal introspective essays by one person (no anthology) that contains humor and pop culture references capped with thoughtful faith reflections.

About the Author

(Note: The author chose to insert a photo here.)

Amanda M. Socci is a diehard creative person who has dabbled in many forms of art, including writing. Amanda has written professionally for the National Catholic Educational Association's *Momentum* magazine, the Business Center of Washington, D.C., Washington Independent Writers, and DCSportsFan.com (TheSportsFanNetwork.com). Amanda self-published *Consumers Everywhere* magazine and *National School Fundraising Guide for K-12 Schools*. Amanda currently blogs in a thoughtful and analytical style at CreativeIdeaGal.com and provides prompts to nonfiction writers at WriteNonFictioninNovember.com. Amanda is also blogging her book, *A Slice of Faith: Soothe Your Problems by Eating a Slice of Faith Each Day*, on an online news service.

Despite her many writing credits, Amanda has never considered herself a full-time, full-fledged writer until fairly recently. In 2011, a series of negative life experiences motivated Amanda. She began coming up with definitions of faith in her heart, but did not capture them in formal writing. In early 2012, a life-changing incident with the Girl Scouts inspired Amanda to change the course of her life. Suddenly, Amanda immersed herself in all things writing, began to slowly develop an author platform online and started blogging a book, *A Slice of Faith: Soothe Your Problems by Eating a Slice of Faith Each Day*. Amanda's new confidence in her writing abilities has motivated her to write a lot and develop ideas for future books.

Author's Platform

Author Amanda M. Socci has created a Facebook community fan page for *A Slice of Faith: Soothe Your Problems by Eating a Slice of Faith Each Day*. It is here: http://www.facebook.com/ASliceofFaith. As of April 21, 2013, A Slice of Faith has a reach of 41 "likes" or fans.

Author Amanda M. Socci has created a blog to describe the author's journey to publication. That blog is here: http://asliceoffaith.wordpress.com

SAMPLE

Presentations Scheduled for 2013:

- None to date. It will take some time and effort to research appropriate venues and opportunities for speaking engagements.

- Open-minded to teleseminar, podcast, television, radio, and Internet radio opportunities.

Additional Platform Elements:

The following statistics are current as of April 21, 2013.

- Unique visitors to the Mount Vernon Patch website http://mountvernon.patch.com (the online news service where Amanda M. Socci is blogging *A Slice of Faith: Soothe Your Problems by Eating a Slice of Faith Each Day*): unknown (this information is not provided to bloggers)

- Unique visitors to A Slice of Faith blog (http://asliceoffaith.wordpress.com): roughly 20 per month (blog created in May 2012, but not used until March 2013)

- Number of **Facebook friends**[22] (personal profile): 141

- Number of Facebook likes (A Slice of Faith profile): 41

- Number of Facebook likes (freelance writer profile): 109

- Number of followers on Twitter: 824

- Number of connections on **LinkedIn**:[23] 193

THE OUTLINE

List of Chapters

A page count of 150 pages is estimated.
    Introduction – Why am I writing this book?
    Chapter 1 – Religion Versus Faith
    Chapter 2 – Parenting Pains
    Chapter 3 – Marriage Conflicts
    Chapter 4 – Husband's Prickly Career Choices
    Chapter 5 – Dead-end Businesswoman
    Chapter 6 – Broken House
    Chapter 7 – Rocky Finances
    Chapter 8 – Hodgepodge
    Chapter 9 – Lighthearted Moments

[22] You are going to need to show hundreds of thousands of Facebook friends/followers to impress publishers.

[23] Platform is important to publishers. And their idea of an impressive platform is different than ours. It's important to provide numbers to publishers if those numbers can establish a strong platform. These numbers don't. A blog with 50,000 unique views per month is worth mentioning, although it is unlikely to influence a publishing decision.

SAMPLE

24 I'm concerned that the subjects in this book are just too personal and won't resonate with a wide audience. Everyone's life is interesting to himself. Everyone's life is a hero's journey. But the challenge is to get other people to connect.

Chapter Summaries[24]

In Introduction – Why am I writing this book?, the introduction will discuss Amanda M. Socci's reasons for writing *A Slice of Faith*. The author will discuss the major incident that prompted her to write about faith.

Please note that Socci plans to organize *A Slice of Faith* nontraditionally as loosely based chapters that contain personal essays along with faith-based reflections.

In Chapter 1 – Religion Versus Faith, Socci will distinguish the concepts of religion and faith by rejecting them as synonyms for each other and highlighting important differences.

In Chapter 2 – Parenting Pains, Socci will discuss select conflicts with her daughters, Margarita and Leoanna, and reveal how faith got her through each one.

In Chapter 3 – Marriage Conflicts, Socci discusses the different degrees of conflict that occurred in her marriage and the creative ways she dealt with them.

In Chapter 4 – Husband's Prickly Career Choices, Socci will discuss the thorns in her side when her husband's career choices added stress to the marriage. Among the topics to be discussed are: the decision to provide lobbying services for free, the decision to create an anti Hillary Clinton political organization, and political conversations.

In Chapter 5 – Dead-end Businesswoman, Socci will discuss how ideas can be diabolically creative and still fail in the marketplace.

In Chapter 6 – Broken House, Socci will discuss the $20,000 in repairs needed to her home which is valued at $29,000. The author will poke fun at the types of materials used to build her home and the humorous ways in which things have fallen apart.

In Chapter 7 – Rocky Finances, Socci gears into over-drive, revealing personal moments of financial hardship that border on too-much-information (TMI). Among the topics to be discussed are: living without a financial safety net and losing temporary funds.

In Chapter 8 – Hodgepodge, Socci incorporates discrete conflicts that don't fit into a unified theme. Among the topics to be discussed are: women's reproductive rights,

In Chapter 9 – Lighthearted Moments, Socci wraps up *A Slice of Faith* by focusing on lighthearted pains and struggles. Among the topics to be discussed are: a prayer chain in Spanish and a fierce need to recycle.

TRAINING EXERCISES

HOW TO USE THESE EXERCISES

Each training exercises section has one or more goals associated with an Author Training Process step. All exercises, evaluations, and questions are meant to help you reach that goal. I suggest you use them all until you reach your goal or refine the information you have that helps you evaluate your book idea and yourself. This becomes an extremely detailed road map for successful authorship.

Once your plan is complete, train yourself to follow the map each day, moving from signpost to signpost, landmark to landmark. Determine how far you want to travel daily, weekly, monthly, and yearly by creating a timetable, timeline, to-do list, or calendar with all your deadlines (dates to arrive at each destination). Place your action items on the calendar as well.

The exercises, evaluations, and questions in this book are grouped under subheadings that can be found in the chapter that describes a particular step. If you need to review the text related to a particular training step, you need only find that subheading in the chapter.

The book you have read tells you everything you need to know to complete your Author Training, but your real Author Training takes place by doing these exercises.

Use a special notebook or journal for your notes and answers to the following questions and exercises.

STEP #1: DEVELOP AN "AUTHOR ATTITUDE" AND PLAN YOUR SUCCESS

Goal: Create a plan for success by evaluating your definition of success, making plans, and sticking to them.

Author Attitude

1. **Evaluation:** Do you really want to become a successful author? In three sentences, what makes you think so?

2. **Exercise:** What do you believe being an author will be like? Write a description that includes the positive and negative things you believe.

3. **Exercise:** What are your three most negative beliefs about your ability to succeed as an author? Turn these into three positive statements or affirmations.

4. **Exercise:** What past decisions, actions, and results lead you to believe you really want to become a successful author? List them like so:
   - Decisions:
   - Actions:
   - Results:

5. **Exercise:** Can you think of any decisions, actions, or results that lead you to believe you might not really want to become an author or a successful author? List them like so:
   - Decisions:
   - Actions:
   - Results

6. **Exercise:** Find an author you know, and interview her for your own purposes, not for publication. If you don't know one personally, behave like a journalist: Contact one you admire, and interview her. What did it take her to get published and become successful? How has she handled failure, rejection, and other challenges? How many books does she sell per year? How many books does she write per year? What kind of attitude does she have? How does she maintain that attitude? How did that attitude affect her ability to achieve success and maintain it? What is her life like? How does she spend her time? What does she like about being an author? What was her publishing experience like? What tasks take up most of her time?

7. **Evaluation:** How do you approach challenges? Rejection? Problems? Are you optimistic or pessimistic?
   - Are you willing? On a scale of 1 to 10, with 10 being the highest, how willing are you to make changes, take on new roles, and wear a variety of business-related hats (promotion, social media, PR, media darling, etc.)?
   - Are you optimistic? On a scale of 1 to 10, with 10 being the highest, how optimistic are you about accomplishing difficult goals?
   - Are you objective? On a scale of 1 to 10, with 10 being the highest, how objective will you be about stepping away from your work and looking at it with new eyes?

TRAINING

- Are you tenacious? On a scale of 1 to 10, with 10 being the highest, how tenacious are you about taking on new challenges?

8. **Evaluation:** What characteristics of an Author Attitude do you need to work on most? Choose one, and write a paragraph about why you feel you need to work on this characteristic.

9. **Evaluation:** Why do you think you have the right Author Attitude?

Define Your Success, and Set Your Goals

10. **Question:** What's your definition of success? Write out as many or as few specific, quantifiable definitions (goals) for yourself as you wish.

Create a Plan for Your Goals

11. **Exercise:** Now that you have defined success, solidify your primary goal by describing it in one concise sentence, and include a deadline: a month, day, and year by which you want to achieve it. Do the same with your other goals as well.

12. **Exercise:** Break down your primary goal into smaller goals, or signposts and landmarks, for your road map to success. Consider all the different tasks you might have to do to achieve your goal; each one might be another individual, small goal. Define each goal specifically below. Also, create a deadline for each one, and remember that you can also use your 3" × 5" index cards to make them "real."

13. **Exercise:** Determine what price you are willing to pay to achieve your goal. What are you willing to give up? List at least three to five things per goal, signpost, and landmark. (Example: half of my TV-watching time; thirty minutes of morning sleep; thirty minutes of newspaper reading in the morning.)

14. **Exercise:** List three to five things you are willing to do every day or every week to help you move toward each goal or landmark. (Example: work on my manuscript for an hour every day; publish three blog posts per week; spend fifteen minutes per day

on social networks; research at least one literary agent; learn one new skill to help me self-publish.)

15. **Exercise:** Write down one to three ways you will you remind yourself of your goals every day. (Example: write my goals on 3" × 5" cards and read them in the morning when I wake up and at night before I go to bed; write them on sticky notes and put them around my house, for instance on the refrigerator, bathroom mirror, computer, and in my calendar.)

16. **Exercise:** Put a program like RescueTime or Time Doctor on your computer. Track how you spend your time during the day so you can determine how you might spend more of your workday on tasks that move you closer to becoming a successful author. Also, create a time chart of how much time you spend watching television and doing other activities that you could cut out to make more time to pursue successful authorship.

Create a Vision of Success

17. **Exercise:** Create a visual picture of success for your book and yourself. Visualize all aspects of successful authorship, including how your book's sales will affect you and all parts of your personal and professional life or business, and write down what you envision. Simply answer the following questions to help you visualize:
    - Will success allow you to build a business around your book or blog, travel more, become a speaker, or teach at a university? How so?
    - How will successful authorship change your personal life and affect those around you and with whom you are in relationship?
    - Will success make it possible for you to spend more time with your spouse or children, pursue your hobbies, or write more books? How so?
    - Will success make you feel as if you have fulfilled your purpose or potential? How so?
    - How will success affect your income? How much money would you like to make from book sales?

18. **Exercise:** Consider the number of books you'd like to sell per year and include that number in this vision of success. Write your vision similarly to what follows, and include figures on book sales and a deadline.

TRAINING

For me, book publishing success looks like ...

It also includes my book, [Book Title], selling _____ books per year.
I'd like my book, [Book Title], to sell _____in its lifetime.

My book, [Book Title], will be published by _____, and I will
achieve this level of successful authorship by [Date]_____."

Try your hand at writing your vision in the past tense. Imagine it is a year or a year and a half after reaching your goal of successful authorship. You can even attempt to write a vision that is five years into the future looking backward. What would you be like? What would your life be like? What has the experience of reaching your goal been like? Don't forget to include the same figures as above (books sold, money earned, changes in your personal and professional life, and the dates when you achieved success).

19. **Exercise:** See if you can find sales figures for books similar to the book you want to write. These can be difficult to find. Look for articles written about these authors. Or use KDPCalculator.com. Find a book's sales rank, and input that number to come up with copies sold per day. You can multiply this by seven days/week or thirty-one days/month to arrive at some estimated sales figures for most books listed on Amazon.

20. **Exercise:** Calculate your potential book income. Assume that if you self-publish you will earn 70 percent on your book—if you don't discount in some way or offer it for free. Take the time to check comparative titles in your category. Discover how they are priced. You can now figure out what you will make per book. This figure does not include the cost of producing the book. Nor does it include the cost of giving away free books as promotions or to reviewers. If you really want to know what you will make, take the time to price:

- editing the book (estimate your word count to get an accurate price; ask for developmental editing and line editing) and proofreading
- cover and interior book design (for printed books—and possibly also for conversion if you plan to produce an e-book)
- cover design and manuscript conversion (for e-books)
- printing (maybe nothing if you go with an e-book or POD, but some companies have a setup fee, shipping costs, or a cost for a preview copy)

You now need to figure:

Price – 30 percent – cost of production = net per book

If you traditionally publish, you can figure you will earn whatever percentage you have agreed upon in your contract for an e-book or print book, typically 7.5 to 20 percent for a print book or 25 to 50 percent for an e-book. You will then typically give 15 percent of your earnings to your agent. Your publisher will determine the price of your book.

21. **Exercise:** Find another author that you know and interview him for your own purposes, not for publication. If you don't know one personally, behave like a journalist and contact one you admire. Interview him or her. Find out what this author's life is like. How does he promote his books? How many hours does he write, promote, speak, travel, etc.? How many books does he sell per year? How many books does he write per year? How does he define success? Is this definition different than yours? What has he sacrificed? Do you need to do something different to achieve the same or a different level of success?

Are You Willing to Sacrifice to Become an Author?

22. **Evaluation:** Are you committed to making your book and yourself as the author of that book successful? What does that commitment look like? Take some time to consider and then create a visualization of a successful author's typical day. How many hours will you wear a writer's hat, and how many hours will you wear other hats? What will you do, and what won't you do? How many hours must you commit to other things in your life, such as a normal job, children, elder care, housework, charity work, and other responsibilities? Visualize a normal day from morning to evening. Put these details down on paper, and then determine the level of commitment you can make right now. Does this level of commitment allow you to pursue your goal at this time, or do you need to wait (and for how long)?

How to Develop Willingness

23. **Question:** On a scale of 1 to 10, with 10 indicating "very badly," how badly do you want to write and publish a successful book? Why?

24. **Question:** On a scale of 1 to 10, with 10 indicating "very reluctant," how reluctant are you of making the necessary sacrifices? Why?

25. **Question:** What will I gain if I ignore the task of building a big enough platform to land a publisher? What do I lose?

26. **Question:** How do I profit if I choose to ignore social networking? What do I lose?

27. **Question:** How do I improve my chances of successfully selling my book by not bothering to show up in front of audiences? What do I lose?

28. **Question:** What do I gain by leaving my business hat hanging on the wall? What do I lose?

29. **Question:** If your book sells only an average amount or fails to sell, what will you lose or gain?

30. **Exercise:** If you have difficulty finding your payoffs—negative or positive—go back to your vision and mine it for rewards. What did success "look like" in terms of:
    - income
    - authority
    - awards
    - fulfillment
    - helping others
    - time
    - relationships

31. **Evaluation:** If my book fails to sell, this means I lose:

32. **Evaluation:** If my book sells an average amount, I lose:

33. **Evaluation:** If my book becomes a bestseller, I gain:

34. **Exercise:** Begin training. Start with small sessions and tasks that you know will help you become a successful author, and repeat them daily or weekly. Build up your strength and tolerance. Here are some ideas:
    - Spend ten minutes per day on Twitter or Facebook.

- Read and comment on three blog posts daily.
- Visit an online forum related to the topic of your book daily, and leave a comment.
- Start a blog, and write one short post three times per week.
- Create an Excel sheet to track your daily, weekly, or monthly readership and subscribers on an existing blog.
- Send one letter a week to a radio show in an effort to land a media appearance.
- Send a query letter per week to a magazine in an effort to get an assignment related to your book idea.
- Spend fifteen minutes a week watching videos online to learn how to blog, load files to Kindle, or write a press release.
- Work on your book business plan for thirty minutes per day.
- Research one literary agent per day.
- Research competing books on Amazon.com.
- Enter a fiction contest.
- Send a short story to a magazine.

35. **Exercise:** If you are considering spending more time doing business-related activities, consider these ways to train:
    - Get an egg timer and set it for the amount of time you have agreed to take on business-related tasks.
    - Use a free program like Cool Timer to either keep track of how much time you spend on business-related tasks or to tell you when you have completed the time you agreed to spend with your business hat on.

36. **Exercise:** What are the top five reasons you don't spend more time on the business end of becoming published? This includes every activity that helps promote you and your writing and that traditionally is called author platform-building or marketing. Be honest. Are these really problems you can't get around, or are they excuses? (Example: Could you delegate a task, hire an intern or college student, or ask your spouse, partner, or retired parent to help you so you can work toward getting published?) If excuses, why are you making them?

37. **Exercise:** Take the time now to turn those five reasons for not seeing your project from a business perspective into challenges—daily or weekly. Make them opportunities to move closer to your goal of becoming published.

TRAINING

38. **Evaluation:** Your willingness, determination, and perseverance make a huge differ-
    ence when it comes to becoming an author. You need to determine if you have what
    it takes to become an author. Published authors found a solution. They didn't let any-
    thing get in their way. Write honestly in the space below or in your journal, and ask
    yourself: How badly do I want to become a published author? Am I willing to find
    solutions to the problems or issues that stand between remaining an aspiring author
    and becoming a published author? Do I have what it takes—willingness, objectivity,
    optimism, and tenacity—to become an author?

STEP #2: KNOW WHAT YOUR BOOK IS ABOUT AND WHY SOMEONE WOULD WANT TO READ (BUY) IT

Goal: Learn what your book is about by developing and writing your Overview.

Note: If you are in the early conception stages of your book and you don't have a loose idea of what content is going in your book, you might have difficulty with some of the exercises in this section. That's okay. Just keep working through this chapter's exercises to the best of your ability. Then move on to complete the steps that follow. You will be asked several times to return to this step to review and revise.

What Is Your Book About?

1. **Exercise:** Write a short description of your book—a "book summary." Describe your nonfiction book, or summarize your novel to the best of your ability. For a novel, this summary is shorter than the typical synopsis. Keep this description at one to three paragraphs in length. If you can summarize your book in one or two paragraphs quickly and easily, you probably know what you are writing about. If not, you have some work to do, but the following exercises will help.

Your Book Idea and Angle

2. **Question:** What is your broad idea? Write it in one sentence. Now write it in one word.

3. **Question:** What is the unique angle of your idea? Write it here in one sentence.

Your Book's Theme

4. **Question:** What is the theme you will stress in your book?

5. **Exercise:** Write three more themes you *could* use in your book, even if you won't. Most books have one major theme, but some have minor themes as well.

6. **Exercise:** Pick three novels, memoirs, or nonfiction books—preferably bestsellers—in your preferred category. Study their back-of-the-book copy, inside-cover copy, and introductions to discern their primary idea, angle, and theme. Write them down.

How Will Your Book Benefit Readers?

7. **Exercise:** Study the back cover of books in your category. What nonfiction books make promises or offer benefits or some sort of added value to readers' lives? What are those benefits? Write about at least three books. If you write fiction, what do the covers and flaps of fiction books promise?

8. **Question:** Are you giving readers a solution to a problem? If so, what is the problem? What is the solution?

9. **Question:** Are you offering readers a way to fulfill a desire? If so, what is the desire? What is the process by which you will help them fulfill that desire?

10. **Question:** Are you offering readers an answer to a question? If so, what question? What is the answer?

11. **Question:** In what way are you providing a service to readers or adding value to their lives with your book?

12. **Exercise:** Read the back of a variety of books in your category or niche (fiction or nonfiction). Which ones hit you emotionally? Which ones can you relate to? Do they make you feel you must read the story or gain the information—or else? Or else what? Can you see how your book could make readers feel the same way?

13. **Question:** How will your book benefit others? List as many ways as possible, no matter how minute.

14. **Exercise:** Consider your favorite books. How did reading them benefit you? How did they add value to your life? At the time in your life that you bought them, did they "speak to you" in some way or for some reason?

15. **Exercise:** Go to the bookstore, or look at the books on your bookshelf. Determine the "What's in it for me?" (WIIFM?) factor in the books you would like to purchase or have purchased. Do this with books in the same category as the book you want to write. How does your book compare? Will the benefit in your book, or the degree to which it addresses readers' interests, be higher or lower than these other books you chose?

16. **Question:** What knowledge do you possess that your readers need? Will your book idea provide this knowledge or information?

Does Your Book Have a Purpose?

17. **Question:** What is your purpose or mission in writing this book? Write it down, and keep it with you so you can read it often.

18. **Question:** What outcome do you want your readers to achieve?

19. **Question:** What commitments is your book making to readers?

20. **Exercise:** If you only had thirty seconds to tell someone the reason you feel compelled to write this book, to complete this project, what would you tell them if you only had thirty seconds to do so? Practice saying this aloud until you feel comfortable enough to write it here.

21. **Question:** If readers choose not to purchase your book, what will they miss out on? What do they stand to lose? In other words, can they live without your book, or is it essential in some way? Will not having read it hinder them or cause them to feel held back?

22. **Exercise:** Look at the books on your shelf. Read the back covers or flaps. What made you purchase them? How does the promise the author made relate to the value you received? Choose three books, and answer those two questions for each.

23. **Question:** What do you want readers to remember after they put your book down or when they first pick it up?

24. **Exercise:** What are the one or two lines of copy you would place on the back cover that would make someone feel they couldn't leave the store without your book (the one or two benefits they can't live without)? Write them in your journal. Write as many as you want, but make sure they are just one or two sentences each.

Create a Title for Your Book

25. **Exercise:** Write a marketable title and subtitle. Come up with three working titles and subtitles for your book. (*Tip: Go back through your notes in search of key words and phrases that will help you. Underline the words or phrases that stand out as important. See if they work with your title.*)

26. **Exercise:** If you are writing a nonfiction book, its title will be different from a fiction title. Write three titles for fiction as if it were nonfiction and three titles for nonfiction as if it were fiction. How would you get your book's purpose across if it were in another genre?

27. **Exercise:** Do an Amazon search for titles of books in your category. Compare your title to the top five titles used by other authors, especially bestsellers in your genre. How does yours compare? How is yours different? Similar? Which titles seem to sell best? Jot down your notes.

Writing a Pitch or Elevator Speech for Your Book

28. **Exercise:** Complete the "business-card test." Get a business card, or a piece of paper the same size (3.5" × 2"), and write the subject of your book or your storyline in this amount of space. Don't make the type microscopic. It must be legible. Can you do it?

29. **Exercise:** Using all the information you now possess about your book idea— angle, theme, benefits, and purpose—write a new book summary (or rewrite or revise the one you wrote at the beginning of this step). Do not write more than 150 to 300 words. Include your title in this description. Answer this question: "What is my book about, and why would someone want to read (buy) it?" You can also answer these three questions: Why this book, why now, why me?

30. **Exercise:** Make a copy of the book summary you just created, and save it as a new document. Edit it down to 100 words. Save that version. Then edit it down to 75 words—maybe two sentences. Next, edit it down to a 50-word book pitch, or elevator speech, hopefully one sentence that includes your title. Last, try to edit it down a bit more to a shorter one-sentence log line. (*Tip: Go back and underline key words and phrases that you've used repeatedly or that stand out. In particular, think about your book's benefits and how it is unique. You can compare your book to best-selling books.*)

31. **Question:** Will you include any special features in your book? If so, list them.

32. **Exercise:** If you want feedback on your idea, use your pitch to conduct test marketing. Contact people in your target market and say, "I'm writing a book called *(use your title and subtitle here)*, and it's about *(say your pitch here)*. Would you purchase that book?" Take notes on why or why not.

Create an Overview of Your Book

33. **Exercise:** Compile your Overview. Take the 150- to 300-word book summary or description you wrote, your book pitch, and list of benefits (and special features), and combine them into one document. Follow the order of: hook, pitch, summary or synopsis, benefits, and features. When you are done, you should have a two-page document that accurately describes your book. Read it carefully. Ask yourself if this is the book you plan to write—and want to write. Ask yourself if you think readers want this book—or, better yet, need to read this book. (*Tip: To create a document that can later serve as sales copy, start with an intriguing or enticing paragraph. Sell your book. Grab the reader. This is just like the first paragraph in a query letter—in fact, it is often the same exact paragraph. Then use your pitch to say exactly what your book is about and how it will benefit readers. Use "benefit" words to continue describing your book. How will readers benefit from reading your book? What will they gain? What will they learn? You might include these as bullet points. Also include any special features your book may offer.*)

34. **Exercise:** If you balked at the idea of writing a promotional document in the exercise above, be aware that you aren't developing an Author Attitude! And you've hardly started the process. Can you find the willingness inside to embrace this task? It in-

TRAINING

volves writing, after all. Think of it as a writing prompt: How would you describe your book to a potential reader? Or as a game: What creative way can you find to describe your book so readers will feel they can't live without your book? In fact, at some point, you may need to write promotional copy for your book even if you choose to prepare a business plan, and not a formal book proposal, during your Author Training.

Note: Rewrite your overview and pitch after Steps #3 to #6.

STEP #3: ANALYZE HOW MANY PEOPLE *REALLY* MIGHT BUY YOUR BOOK

Goal: Create a market description and analysis to evaluate if your book has selling potential.

Can You Describe Your Market?

1. **Exercise**: Describe the audience, or large, general target market for your book, such as dog owners, people with cancer, romance readers, memoir readers, people interested in stories about Italy, entrepreneurs, technical or business people, etc. Describe as many broad audiences as you can.

You Need Actual Figures to Determine the Size of Your Market

2. **Exercise**: Describe your market specifically using statics or numbers to indicate its size. Find figures for your specific market and add them here. (Wrong: People like me. People who like cats. Right: The 1.3 million cat owners in the United States. The 80,000 veterinarians licensed in the United States today; 20 million people with cancer; half of the U.S. population; 4.5 million dog owners.) To find the information you need to describe your markets, try researching in the following places:
   - U.S. Census Bureau
   - Associations and organizations related to your topic
   - Newspapers and magazines
   - Blogs
   - Manufacturers
   - Wikipedia (with accompanying source)
   - Search engines (Google, Yahoo, Bing, etc.)

3. **Evaluation:** Does the idea for your book have a market or a market big enough to justify writing your book? Does it appear that you can sell enough books to your audience to earn back the costs of producing your book? Consider what type of publisher you would like to approach; each publisher will have a different requirement for market size—large publishers, larger markets. If you self-publish, you determine this.

TRAINING

Re-Angle Your Market for Success

4. Exercise: Think about how you planned to angle your book. Rewrite those angles here as a reminder. Does your current angle and theme hit your target market? How so?

5. Evaluation: Could you angle your book differently to include a different theme in an effort to increase the size of the markets you plan to target, thereby increasing the sales potential for the book and, therefore, its marketability? If so, how? Would it be better to aim for a niche market? If so, why? Could you write your book in such a way that it hits the best market, the one that makes your book the most viable—that makes it possible to sell the most books? Describe that in your journal.

Write for Your Market

6. Exercise: Create a profile of your ideal reader. Describe your reader in detail—as if you were creating a character in a novel. Determine your reader's demographics. Figure out where your reader lives, what she buys, what she does in her free time, how much she earns, etc. (Here is a post by Darren Rowse of Problogger about profiling readers: www.problogger.net/archives/2009/09/26/how-to-create-reader-profilespersonas-to-inspire-and-inform-your-blogging/)

7. Exercise: Discover where your ideal reader actually hangs out. Where can you find these people—online and offline? Google social-networking sites. Hang out in the places your readers hang out. Listen in on conversations. Ask questions. Get to know them. Go to meetings and events. Here are some examples of sites you might find:
- sermo.com (for doctors)
- therapynetworking.com (for therapists)
- catster.com (for cats)
- Goodreads.com (for readers)
- Redroom.com (for writers)
- Meetup.com (for anything)

8. Exercise: Listen in on conversations held on the blogs or social-networking sites of authors of similar or competing books. "Cyber-spy" on those authors' fans to find out who they are. Go to their Face-book pages and Twitter accounts. See if you can find them in other forums. Read their blogs. Discover who they are and what they like. Add this information to your ideal reader profile. See if authors of similar books talk about their readers and describe them. Add this information to your ideal-reader description.

9. **Evaluation**: Does what you discovered in the last few steps make you think of any other markets for your book? What additional information does it give you about your readers? Does this change your idea, angle, or theme? If so, how? If not, why?

10. **Exercise**: Make a list of ten things you now know about your readers that you didn't know before. How will you use this information to improve your book's content or story?

11. **Exercise**: With all the information you have on your reader, write a target-market paragraph below, as you might if you were submitting a formal book proposal. Use all of the research and insights you gained in this section to write a clear, direct assessment of your target audience. Include figures to outline your large and niche markets. If you have more than one market, do this for each market.

TRAINING

STEP #4: COMPARE THE COMPETITION AND DISCOVER IF YOUR IDEA IS UNIQUE AND NECESSARY

Goal: Create a competitive and competing titles analysis to evaluate if your book is unique and necessary (or how to make it so).

1. **Exercise:** Determine the book's category. Where in a bookstore will you find it? On what shelf? (Example: Religion, History, Business, Self-help, Fantasy, Romance, Chicklit, etc.) If you don't know, ask a bookstore clerk; tell them about your book (use your pitch), and ask where it would be located in the store.

2. **Exercise:** Begin compiling a list of competing and complementary books for your book's business plan by searching such books on sites like:
   - Amazon.com
   - BarnesandNoble.com
   - Google.com
   - LibraryThing.com
   - Goodreads.com
   - Redroom.com
   - BookDepository.com
   - NetGalley.com

   You can also do this kind of research in a bookstore. Come up with a list of ten to fifteen books you consider direct competition to yours—books that cover the same type of information or that tell the same type of story. Then narrow the competition down to five you feel are closest in subject matter or storyline. List these by bestseller status or by date of publication. Include this information: title, subtitle, author, publisher, copyright year, number of pages, paperback or hardcover, and price. Then for each book, describe the ways in which it is similar to your idea (or how it helps readers) and the ways in which it is different or unique; Finally, write a brief paragraph about how your book is unique in comparison.

3. **Exercise:** Do the same type of research you did above, but this time do it for complementary books (those that are not direct competition or that readers would buy in addition to yours).

4. **Exercise:** If you have trouble discerning complementary books, consider this: If a reader buys your book instead of another book, that other book is your competition. If a reader is interested in buying your book, what other books might he buy to gain different information? These are complementary titles. You can also go to Amazon and look at the section on a particular book's page that says: "Customers Who Bought This Item Also Bought." These may be complementary books (or competing books).

How to Gather Detailed Data for Your Competitive or Complementary Analysis

5. **Exercise:** Begin searching for sales data on the top competing books in your category. If you don't have a BookScan subscription (which most aspiring authors do not), use Google or another search engine to find sales figures on popular books in your category.
   - Look for articles that mention sales.
   - Use the free version of *Publishers Weekly.*
   - Use the Amazon.com bestseller list as a way to discover which books are selling better than others. This list is updated hourly and is based on BookScan data. You can find the list by inputting "Amazon Best Seller List" into the book search engine on the site. Then begin clicking through the category list on the left until you find the category for your book. Or find a bestseller in your category. Go to its page. Scroll down until you see its bestseller ranking. Then click on the link to the list. Then peruse the appropriate bestseller list in your category.
   - Use KDPCalculator.com to make some educated guesses about competitive book sales in your category. Input the current Amazon Best Seller Rank of any book on Amazon (it does not have to be a Kindle version). You can find the Amazon Best Seller Rank under the book's product details. This site tells you how many copies per day a book sells on any given day. You can then estimate how many it sells per week, month, or year.
   - Find historical statistics for particular books in *A Guide to Book Publishers' Archives*, which identifies archival collections from actual publishers—a reliable source of sales data.

6. **Exercise:** Do a competitive book tour. Take a trip to both online and physical book stores. Look for books similar to your book project. Do this online using search terms that are the same or similar to your book topic in the Amazon.com, BarnesandNoble.

com, WriterDigestShop.com, LibraryThing.com, or Google.com search engines. In a physical bookstore, look in the appropriate category, or ask a salesclerk, "Where can I find books like _____," and describe your book. Once directed to the correct section and shelf, begin exploring the books there. (You can also do this in a library by asking a librarian for the correct shelf and category after describing your book.) Look for ones that earlier searches did not discover, and examine the ones you already have identified. Bring a pad and pencil, and take copious notes. Include information about:

- their tables of contents
- the promises they make on their back covers
- their introductions
- their forewords
- the author's bio
- special features, such as quotations, a workbook element, case studies, tips, or tools
- the style, tone, character archetypes, endings, beginnings, story arcs, illustrations, etc.

If working online, do this research using the "Look Inside" program offered by Amazon.com and BarnesandNoble.com.

7. **Evaluation:** Once you finish your research, consider these factors about the competing books you have identified:
   - How it is different from the book you want to write?
   - How it is similar to the book you want to write?
   - Is the scope of the book different? How so?
   - Does it have different benefits? What are they?
   - What are its pros and cons?
   - How would you improve it?
   - What do you like about it? Dislike?
   - What promises does the author make to readers? What promises does the author fail to make that he could or should (or that you can)?
   - What are the author's credentials (or lack of credentials)?
   - How do your credentials compare to the author's?
   - What other similar people could have written the foreword?

8. **Exercise:** Study reviews of best-selling books in your category and the competing books you have identified. You can learn a lot about a book by what others say about

it—and about what readers think is good, bad, or missing from these books. This is gold! Include in your book the things that are missing in these other books. Study the positive and negative things readers and reviewers have identified. Make special note of the negative comments. Look at your project, and ask yourself how you can make sure your book improves on these issues—or addresses the issues in a positive manner.

9. **Exercise:** Visit the websites or blogs of the authors of the competing books you have identified. See if you can find any additional information on book sales, market, readership, etc.

How to Use Your Competitive Research to Improve Your Book Idea

10. **Exercise:** Create a spreadsheet for all the information you are gathering on your top five competitive and top five comparative books. This will help you put the research into perspective visually.

11. **Exercise:** Is there a hole on the shelf in your category? If yes, describe it. In other words, what type of book is missing from your niche? Do not describe your book project but the "perfect" book to fill that hole. Write down a description of that "perfect" book based on your research. Now, how does your book idea compare to the book you just described? Are you offering readers of these other books something the other authors have not delivered previously? Or not?

12. **Question:** How might you affiliate with the authors of the complementary books you have identified? How can you become venture partners with them?

13. **Evaluation:** Spend time comparing your credentials to that of the authors of the competing books you have identified. Then answer these questions:
    - How do you differ from them, or how are you similar to them?
    - Will it help you or hurt you to have different qualifications or similar ones?
    - Do you have the experience to join the ranks of these other authors?
    - What do you need to do or be to compete with them?
    - What would you have to do to make yourself stand out from the other authors?
    - Do you need a larger platform? In what way?

- Do you need to be scholarly? Or would it be better if you wrote from your life experience? Why?
- Do you need to write a series? Why or why not?
- Do you need to have a degree in literature? Why or why not?
- Do you need to specialize in an age group? Why?

14. **Exercise:** Make a list of things you need to do to stand out in your category or niche.

15. **Evaluation:** Based on your research and your evaluation, decide if you need to make changes to your concept. Explain how your book:
   - tells a fresh story
   - offers a different perspective
   - provides a compelling argument that other authors have not made
   - provides a different set of data or more current information
   - has a totally new angle on a tried-and-true topic
   - takes readers on a singular journey

If you need to make adjustments, jot down some ideas here. Then go back to the previous steps, and adjust your plan.

STEP #5: EXAMINE THE STRUCTURE OF YOUR BOOK

Goal: Create a table of contents (TOC) for your business plan, and evaluate it.

Delineating Chapters

1. **Exercise:** Create a TOC to include in your business plan. Break down your book idea into the steps you want to take to ensure you fulfill your promise to the reader. Aim for ten to fifteen (or as many as necessary). If you need help, try one of these methods:

   - Create a list of ten to fifteen topics you know you want to cover and put them in the order you want to cover them. Write a compelling title for each topic; you can refine it later, but this will eventually become the chapter title.
   - Think of ten to fifteen common questions you want to answer for your readers. Then write creative chapter titles for each one of those questions; you could leave the titles as questions.
   - Think of ten to fifteen most pressing problems you want to solve for your readers. Then write creative chapter titles for each one of those questions; these could be "how-to" titles.
   - List ten to fifteen benefits you want to offer readers. Write titles that entice readers into those chapters by telling them the WIIFM? factor—the added value that speaks to their interests.
   - Create a timeline. Draw a line with the start date and end date of the period about which you plan to write; begin placing dates on the line that indicate major events you want to include in your story. Then organize these into chapters.
   - Plot vignettes you plan to write on a storyboard. Once you have organized them in chronological order, identified themes, and considered the narrative arc, write your TOC.
   - Create an outline. List the events you plan to include, and organize them logically with lesser events "under" more important events. (Add in flashbacks in appropriate places.)
   - Profile your characters. Give them backstories and motivations so you get to know them before you set them within the dramatic or comedic arc of your creation. Then outline your storyline. Write down the scenes you plan to include in that

storyline (like a timeline) with your characters. Consider how the themes of your novel play out on that storyline and where the dramatic arcs occur. Then break this down into chapters, and create a TOC.

- Create a storyboard. Break this down into chapters and then a TOC.
- Number the lines on a sheet of notebook paper, and put a word by each one that best represents what you want to happen in each chapter. That becomes the chapter title. Then make notes about specific events that will occur in that chapter.
- Use a spreadsheet to block out chapters and the scenes within them. Move events around as necessary. (You can also write biographies of characters as part of this exercise.) Then create a TOC.

2. **Exercise:** Organize your research, if you have any, into potential chapters. Explore programs such as Scrivener, Evernote, Excel, Dropbox, Box.net, and Google Drive. Options to using these sites include creating folders on your favorite browser or on your computer, or using index card boxes, filing cabinet files, boxes, or piles. It's important to get organized in some way.

How to Mind Map Your Book to Create a TOC

3. **Exercise:** Mind map your nonfiction or fiction book using posterboard and Post-it Notes.
   - Put a larger Post-it Note in the middle of the board, and write your topic, book title, or storyline on it.
   - Start writing related topics, events, memories, scenes, or characters on the smaller sticky notes. If you are writing fiction, brainstorm all the things that might happen in your story, elements of your character development or story development.
   - When done, organize the notes into related topics, time periods, or storylines on the board.
   - Pick up the sticky notes, and move them around. The new groupings become chapters.
   - Use a different-colored note at the top of each grouping to indicate the chapter name or topic.
   - Type each chapter name, category, or subject into a TOC.

- Each of the sticky notes in the groupings below the chapter becomes a topic, event, or issue to write about in the chapter. You might also use them as subheadings if you are writing nonfiction.

4. **Exercise:** Here are mind-mapping instructions for using a posterboard and colored pens or pencils for a nonfiction book. You can also do this using a white board.

   - Get a large, blank piece of paper. In the center of the paper, print your book's topic.
   - Draw a circle around the keyword or phrase. (For example, if you are writing a book on the topic of training dogs, you might use the key phrase "dog training.")
   - Draw a line from your keyword and write down the first word or phrase that pops into your mind. (For example, *stay.*) Circle the word or phrase. This is a subtopic that may become a chapter in your book.
   - Now draw a line from that word and jot down the next word that comes to mind (For example, *tips.*) This represents a sub-subtopic, or a subhead in your chapter.
   - Repeat until you've run out of word associations.
   - Now, return to your keyword or key phrase, and repeat the exercise. Come up with another subtopic and as many word associations (sub-subtopics) for that subtopic as possible, and then move on to another. Continue until you have created ten to fifteen subtopics, each with several sub-subtopics.
   - Arrange the related subtopics and sub-subtopics into a table of contents for your book. It will look like this:

Book Subject (or title and subtitle)
Chapter 1 Topic
> Subtopic
> Subtopic
> Subtopic
> Subtopic

Chapter 2 Topic
> Subtopic
> Subtopic
> Subtopic
> Subtopic

TRAINING

Evaluate Your Book's Structure

5. **Evaluation:** Go back to what you wrote in Step #2: book pitch, summary, and list of benefits, and read what you wrote. Imagine this is the back-cover copy. This is what you see when you click on the "Look Inside" feature on Amazon.com and click to read the back cover. This is what the author promises will be inside the covers. Now, imagine you open the book to the TOC or you click on the "Look Inside" feature and ask to read this page or pages. Read this "list of chapters," and answer these questions:

- How would the reader you profiled in Step #3 respond to the question, "Is there anything in this book that interests you?"
- Why would an agent or acquisitions editor feel your TOC has followed through on what you described in your Overview in a compelling manner?
- How does your TOC reflect the information you have accumulated so far about your markets and competition?
- What does your TOC provide that is different and unique compared to competing titles?
- How does your TOC show what your book is about, why it is unique, and why it is necessary?
- How does your TOC provide an order that reflects a beginning, middle, and end of your topic or story?

6. **Exercise:** Do market research. Give your TOC to someone who doesn't know about you book but is in your target market. Let them read it, and have them explain what the book is about. If their description sounds exactly like the one you plan to give to an agent or editor, you are on the right path. Now ask them if there is something in the book that addresses their interests. What else would they have to see in order to take it to the register? (For novelists, you will need to have descriptive chapter titles for this to work.)

7. **Exercise:** Compare your TOC to the competition's. How is yours unique?

STEP #6: DECIDE IF YOUR BOOK'S CONTENT MATCHES YOUR INITIAL VISION

Goal: Create a chapter-by-chapter synopsis (fiction, nonfiction and/or memoir) based on your TOC—and/or write a full synopsis (fiction)—and compile your writing guide before beginning to write.

Giving Your Book Form and Life

1. **Exercise:** Create a chapter-by-chapter synopsis based on your TOC. Write a brief (no longer than one page) description of each chapter you named in your TOC in Step #5. This will give you the detailed directions you need to follow the map you created with your TOC so you know exactly what content you must produce when the time comes to write your book. By using your TOC (plus any subheading or subtopics) you can build a comprehensive chapter-by-chapter synopsis. (Fiction and nonfiction writers should do this exercise.)

2. **Exercise:** If you write fiction, craft a full synopsis for inclusion in your business plan. This is a short (usually a page or two at most) description of your novel that provides the key information about your story, such as plot, theme, characterization, and setting. This allows an agent or acquisitions editor to get an overview of how these elements coalesce to create a compelling story without making them read the entire novel. It also gives you a clear picture of the book you plan to write.

Final Content Evaluation

3. **Exercise:** Once your summaries and synopsis are complete, evaluate these documents by answering these questions:

   - Does your content match your TOC? What is missing, if anything?
   - Does you content match your pitch? What else might you add?
   - List your benefits again. Does your content live up to the benefits you said your book would offer readers?
   - Do you have enough to say to fill a whole book? What else might you add?
   - Is the content unique and necessary? How so?

TRAINING

- Is there anything that feels unnecessary? Why?
- Does your content target your market? How?
- Does your content interest your ideal reader? How?
- Does your book fill a hole on the shelf in its category?
- Have you told a compelling story? How so?
- Is your book marketable? How so?

Based on your answers, determine if you need to edit your angle, theme, purpose, pitch, summary, or benefits. Make sure the chapter summaries target your market—that the market is still the best one based on your content—and that your book still falls into the same category you chose. This way, your competition remains the same, and your book rises above it.

4. **Exercise:** Add another 100 to 300 words to the general description—the summary—of your book, which you created in Step #2, bringing the final version of your Overview to 300 to 500 words.

Knowing How Large Your Book Will Grow

5. **Exercise:** Find similar books to the one you want to write, and determine their word count. You can model your manuscript after that book. If you want to write a memoir, for example, look at four or five similar memoirs and determine their length. If you plan to traditionally publish, check out the length of the books published by the publishers you plan to approach. Having a model is always a good idea. Place the number of proposed words for your manuscript in your Overview. (You can complete this exercise using any of the following activities as well.)

6. **Exercise:** To make an educated guess at the length of your published book, use agent Michael Larsen's tool. Equate each line of copy in your chapter-by-chapter synopsis with a page in your finished book. Add up the number of lines you wrote for each chapter synopsis. You can obtain a figure for word count as well. A typical double-spaced one-page summary might have eighteen to twenty-four lines of copy on it. That's 3,750–4,500 words per chapter. A nonfiction book with twelve chapters would be approximately 50,000 words in length.

7. **Exercise:** Determine your final page count in your published book based on your manuscript length. The average Word document has about 275 words per page, making a 50,000-word document 180 pages long. Publishers take a word count and reduce it to a page count. You can try this method used by Kristen Eckstein: If you format your Word document using 12-point Arial (or Helvetica), and 1.5 spacing with 1" margins, you can arrive at almost the exact final page count for a 5½" × 8½" or 6" × 9" standard book.

8. **Exercise:** Determine page count and word count based upon the number of chapters you plan on including and their estimated length. Write a sample chapter or two. If your first two chapters are about 3,000 words long, you can assume the others will be about that length as well. Multiply the number of chapters by the average chapter length, and then take the total and divide by 275 to get the number of manuscript pages. For book pages, repeat the calculation above.

Write Some Content!

9. **Exercise:** Create your writing guide. Combine the items in Step #2—your Overview (pitch, summary, list of benefits, and purpose statement), Step #5—your TOC, and Step #6—your chapter-by-chapter synopsis and/or synopsis, and you now have a phenomenal writing guide. Label this document "[Book Title] Writing Guide." Next, if you are working in Word, copy and paste each chapter summary individually into a new file and save it as "Chapter X." Also copy and paste your pitch into that document; place it above the chapter synopsis. This creates a document for each chapter you need to write. If you are writing nonfiction, take each chapter synopsis and break your sentences or paragraphs down into smaller segments—maybe subheads or bulleted points. Think of these as little chunks of content you need to write. If you are writing fiction and wrote chapter synopses, break these down into scenes. You can simply leave space between the paragraphs or sentences or use bullets. (You can find material from your mind-mapping exercise.) Then use this process each time you write:
   a. Take out the first document, "[Book Title] Writing Guide."
   b. Read the first page or two: pitch, book description, list of benefits, and purpose statement; this reminds you of the job you must do—the book you must create—and your promises to your readers (benefits you must provide).

  c. Open the chapter document you are working on today, and begin writing. Go from bullet point to bullet point, scene to scene, or section to section until you get to the end of your chapter.

  d. Reread the complete summary of "Chapter 1" (or whatever chapter you worked on); determine if you achieved all of your goals.

  e. Reread the first page or two of the guide (pitch, book description, and list of benefits); ensure you delivered on your promises in this particular chapter.

If breaking down your chapter synopses into smaller chunks does not work well for you, simply leave the full summary at the top of the first page of your chapter and refer back to it as you write. It still serves as an effective writing guide.

10. **Exercise:** If you plan to write a nonfiction book proposal for submission to traditional publishers, write twenty-five pages, or one to two chapters of content. Memoir writers and creative-nonfiction writers are still nonfiction writers; you don't necessarily need a full manuscript. That said, because your books read more like fiction, you may be asked for one if you approach a publisher.

11. **Exercise:** Fiction writers who want to seek traditional publication can now produce a complete manuscript; you will also need a proposal with a synopsis instead of chapter synopses, although more and more publishers like to see chapter synopses for novels.

12. **Exercise:** If you plan to self-publish your book, begin writing your manuscript! You can take the same approach as nonfiction writers and produce twenty-five to thirty pages initially and submit these to a freelance book editor (or a critique group) for feedback. Or you can simply write your whole book.

13. **Exercise:** Compare your sample chapter to one or two books you named as competition. How does it compare? Be objective, and list the pros and cons. Ask someone else to read both and offer feedback.

14. **Exercise:** Hire a freelance developmental or line editor (or both) to read your whole manuscript or sample chapters. Based on her evaluation, should you proceed with your book as is? If not, how should you change it or your writing?

STEP #7: DISCOVER WAYS TO BRAND YOURSELF AND EARN MORE MONEY

Goal: Complete the following sections for your business plan—Spinoffs, Products and Services (a.k.a. Subsidiary Rights), and Resources Necessary to Complete Your Book (and/or Build a Business Around Your Book).

How to Spin Your Book into Multiple Titles and a Brand

1. **Exercise:** Brainstorm ideas for books related to the book you've already described during the Author Training Process. You can mind map additional related book ideas—spinoffs or series. Put the title of your current book project in the middle of the mind map and see how many book topics you might think of that could "spin off" from that one. Try to create two or three new ideas. For each spinoff, write a short pitch of about 50 words and place this list in your business plan. These spinoffs should support each other and possibly create a brand or series. If planning out two or three books seems too difficult, keep your current book in mind and think about just one book that could logically follow it. Write a pitch for this spinoff, and include it in your business plan.

2. **Exercise:** Think of other subject areas that interest you or about which you might want to write. List five subjects, and write a sentence about how they may tie in to your original book idea. Is there a central theme running through them all? Could you find an "umbrella" theme to tie them together or help brand you as an author?

3. **Exercise:** Come up with a brand for yourself as an author, and let the spinoff books you've thought of support your brand. Put yourself in the middle of a mind map. Think of all the different topics you'd like to write about and all the different things you do now (like teaching classes, coaching clients, offering webinars, or even writing fiction and nonfiction or writing young adult fiction and writing creative nonfiction) and products and services you could offer. Group them by subject matter, and then find a theme that would serve as the umbrella for how people could perceive you or how you would want them to find you on the Internet. To create a brand for yourself, answer these questions:
   - What do you do in a broader sense?
   - Who are you as a writer and a person?

TRAINING

- How do you want to be known?
- How can the books you write help you become who you want to be?
- How can they help you fulfill your purpose as a person as well as a writer?
- How can you build a business around your book?
- Does your name, title, or personality translate well into a word or title that could serve as a public nom de plume to brand yourself? Jot down a few possibilities and see if any sound professional, creative, and tactful.

4. **Exercise:** Ask others to describe how they see you. When they read your work or blog posts, when you work with them, when you speak with them … what do they remember most? Write down the words they use to help you describe yourself or come up with a brand.

5. **Exercise:** Look for authors you know who have written more than one book or who have also built a business around their books. Interview them, or study them to see what they have done to brand themselves beyond just writing more than one book.

6. **Exercise:** Write a one-page proposal for each new spinoff idea you plan to pursue in the near future. Include details on the market, the competition, and the way in which you will promote the book. Note, too, how you can promote the book in a way that helps sell your originally published title. How can you build your career around these books?

Become an Authorpreneur

7. **Exercise:** Create a Products and Services page in your business plan that details what products and services you might offer to help build a business around your book. For each of the following suggestions, how might you transform the book into one of these products or services? How would your idea fit this product? How would your audience use this new service? Write a few sentences for each of the following:

- audiobook
- courses, teleseminars, and webinars
- movies
- a television show
- action figures, clothing, jewelry, etc.

- membership sites
- keynote speeches
- online streaming videos
- apps and games

Ready and Able to Write and Publish?

8. **Exercise:** Create a "Resources Necessary to Complete the Book" or "Resources Necessary to Build a Business Around the Book" section for your business plan. For each of the following, determine the costs associated with self-publishing your book, promoting your book (for both self-publishing and traditional publishing), and creating products and services that will monetize your book (for both self-publishing and traditional publishing).

- a website or blog
- editors and designers
- business cards
- a professional headshot
- help with social networking
- help with video or audio production
- a webinar or teleseminars line

Then determine if you have the funds now to move forward with your book-project or associated-products monetization plans. Consider how to raise necessary funds, and come up with an action plan and a time frame or deadline for when you will be ready to move forward, if you are not ready now.

STEP #8: WEIGH WHETHER YOU ARE THE BEST PERSON TO WRITE THIS BOOK ... *NOW*

Goal: Write an author bio, mission statement, and platform description, and evaluate if you are ready and qualified to write your book or if you need more qualifications or expert status or platform.

Who Are You?

1. **Question:** Why are you the best person to write this book?

2. **Question:** What makes you the expert on your topic? Your answer can be used to help craft your author bio.

3. **Exercise:** Write a third-person bio about yourself. Include all the pertinent information that highlights your qualifications and expertise. Include your most important or relevant credentials first and all other details in descending order of importance. Be sure to include your:

   - education
   - personal background
   - life experience
   - business (if relevant)
   - interests
   - passions
   - books you have published (along with the publishers and sales figures, if impressive)
   - awards
   - special skills
   - conferences you've attended or participated in
   - contests you've won
   - professional memberships

   At the end of the bio, include a list of quotes or reviews about your work from publications or opinion makers and letters or publicity that others would find impressive. Do this exercise in six parts:

- Write a one-page bio.
- Write a 150-word bio.
- Write a 100-word bio.
- Write a 75-word bio.
- Write a 50-word bio.
- Write a 140-character bio for Twitter.

Note: A first-person bio works well on a blog if you want to be more personal. Some agents and editors prefer first-person bios for memoir; keep this in mind should you want to turn your business plan into a proposal later.

4. **Exercise:** Craft an elevator pitch or branding statement about yourself. You can do this by answering these questions: Who are you? How do you want to be known? How might your spinoffs help brand you? Will people recognize you by your name, a brand name, or something else?

5. **Evaluation:** Evaluate your bio to determine if it makes you look like someone qualified to write the book you have outlined and described in previous steps. Find three bios for authors of the competing and comparative book list you have already researched. Write your bio to the same general length as theirs. Then remove the names from all four bios. Have an objective individual who may or may not know you well read the bios and rank them in order of:

- credibility
- uniqueness
- overall personality
- which author's book they would most likely purchase

This will help you evaluate your bio and make adjustments based on objective feedback.

6. **Evaluation:** Ask yourself if you need to take time to get more experience, hone your craft, or obtain extra credentials to gain some authority. If so, list five things that will help you do so. Make sure they are realistic, obtainable goals that will truly help make you more credible.

What Is Author Platform, and Why Do You Need It?

7. **Question:** If you wrote your book today with your current platform, how many people could you immediately contact? Does anyone know who you are? How many copies would you sell today? This week? This month?

8. **Exercise:** Evaluate if you have the type of platform that will attract a publisher or make your book successful right away. To do this, list all the things you've done up until now and that you plan to do in the next six to twelve months that will help promote you and your book and give you visibility, such as:

- speaking engagements
- teaching
- teleseminars
- radio appearances
- television appearances
- blogging
- social networking
- podcasting
- hosting a radio show
- starting a forum or membership site
- writing for publications
- joining or participating in professional organizations

Also, write down the number of people in each of your social networks, on your mailing list, on your blog subscriber lists, etc. When you are done, you should have a list of pertinent information with dates, places, names of organizations, titles of talks or articles, and numbers associated with your different activities.

Now evaluate:

- What is the size of your platform? Big? Small? Medium? How do you know this?
- What is the engagement level of your platform? Do people comment on your blog posts, share your status updates, attend your webinars, and respond to e-mails?
- How many of the items are related to or have taken place in your target market?
- How many of the activities are directed at the audience you want to reach with your book?

The answers to these questions indicate the real size or efficacy of your platform—and if you are ready to publish now.

9. **Evaluation:** Take another moment to carefully evaluate your visibility, authority, reach, and target audience using these definitions and questions written by Jane Friedman. Answer each of her questions. Then explain how you could improve each one over the next six to twelve months.

   - **Visibility:** Who is aware of your work? Where does your work regularly appear? How many people see it? How does it spread? Where does it spread? What communities are you a part of? Who do you influence? Where do you make waves?

   - **Authority:** What's your credibility? What are your credentials? (This is particularly important for nonfiction writers; it is less important for fiction writers, though it can play a role. Just take a look at any graduate of the Iowa MFA program.)

   - **Proven reach:** It's not enough to *say* you have visibility. You have to show where you make an impact and give proof of engagement. How are you doing this? This could be quantitative evidence (e.g., size of your e-mail newsletter list, website traffic, blog comments) or qualitative evidence (high-profile reviews, testimonials from A-listers in your genre).

   - **Target audience:** You should be visible to the most receptive or appropriate audience for the work you're trying to sell. For instance, if you have visibility, authority, and proven reach to orthodontists, that probably won't be helpful if you're marketing vampire fiction (unless perhaps you're writing about a vampire orthodontist who repairs crooked vampire fangs).

10. **Question:** Do you have a small platform adequate for a small, independent publishing house or maybe even a midsize publishing house?

11. **Question:** Do you have a large enough platform to approach an agent and a large publishing house or to self-publish successfully?

12. **Question:** Is your platform small or nonexistent or small and unengaged? Do you need to wait six months to a year—or more—until you have the kind of platform that will result in book sales and fans who will help promote your book?

TRAINING

13. **Question:** In what ways can you or are you willing to build your platform now? (Example: start blogging, build a mailing list, start a blog tour, get more media gigs, go out and speak, etc.)

14. **Question:** How much time are you willing to devote to platform-building knowing that this is one of the most important things you can do to change your status from aspiring to published author?

15. **Question:** How long will it take you to build a strong platform—one that guarantees success?

16. **Question:** Based on your last answer, when is the best time to write or publish your book? Now? In three months? In six months? In a year? (It's best to publish when you have a strong platform.)

Do You Feel Compelled to Write and Publish Your Book?

17. **Question:** At this point in the Author Training Process, do you still feel passionate about your idea? Do have the impulse to write? Do you have a sense of mission or purpose? Do you feel you must write your book?

18. **Question:** What's your goal with this book? What do you want to achieve by writing and publishing it?

19. **Question:** What outcome do you want your readers to achieve from reading your book? Why is it important for them to read your book?

20. **Question:** If you don't feel passionate and inspired, why not? Could you just as easily not write your book as write it?

21. **Exercise:** Write a one- to two-paragraph mission statement that:
    - clarifies why you feel the need to write your book
    - tells your readers why you feel the need to provide this information for them
    - gives your book a purpose to fulfill
    - makes a publisher feel your commitment to help the book succeed

Evaluate if your mission statement is strong enough to get readers, an agent, or an acquisitions editor "on board" with your cause or your sense of urgency—your need to fulfill this mission. Do you feel confident that you will carry through on making your book a success?

STEP #9: GAUGE IF YOU MAKE A GOOD PUBLISHING PARTNER OR INDIE PUBLISHER

Goal: Create a promotion plan, and evaluate it.

How to Create a Promotion Plan That Helps Your Book Succeed

1. **Exercise:** Create your promotion plan. At the top of the page write, "The author will:" and follow with a list of bulleted action items that describe how you will promote your book upon release and in what time frame you plan to do so. You can break the list into the following categories: three months prior to publication (these should not be platform-building activities but actual book promotion activities); the day of publication; three months after publication, six months after publication, etc. Be creative. Think outside the box. Consider all the ways best-selling authors promote their books and themselves. This is a to-do list to be completed once your book is published. Include things you will do online, such as:

   - a blog tour
   - a virtual book tour (blog tour plus podcast and online radio show tour)
   - an e-mail blast to announce your book release
   - a video book trailer
   - online press releases
   - blogging about your book
   - free teleseminars based on the book

   Include things you will do offline, such as:

   - conduct a speaking tour of the top three to five cities that target your market
   - write articles for top newspapers and magazines in your target market
   - use a PR agent to seek out radio and television interviews and book reviews
   - offer a series of workshops around the nation
   - speak at conferences in your target market

2. **Question:** How many books are you able/willing to sell each year? You can include this number in your promotion plan.

3. **Question:** How many places will you go—travel—to help sell your book? Be specific. You can include this in your promotion plan.

4. **Question:** How much time will you spend each day promoting your book before and after its release? Be realistic.

5. **Question:** What will you do to promote yourself and your book one year, six months, and three months prior to publication?

6. **Question:** What will you do to promote your book for the first three, six, and twelve months after it is released?

How to Target Your Market

7. **Exercise:** Add ways to target your market to your promotion plan. Use the information you accumulate in Step #3. Review the market description you produced. Consider how you can target that market from your platform and by using all you now know about building a platform. Return to the profile you wrote about your ideal readers. How can you reach them in the places they frequent online and offline? Are there places where you could sell your book in bulk, such as a particular type of specialty store or online forums? Are there conferences at which you might speak or particular radio stations or podcasts you could pitch? Brainstorm. Add another five to ten items to your promotion plan.

8. **Exercise:** Use the competitive analysis you created in Step #4 to add another five to ten items to your promotion plan. What did you discover about what your potential readers need and want that they weren't finding in other books? How can you apply this to your promotion plan? Add another five items to your promotion plan.

9. **Exercise:** Evaluate your platform to determine how to put it to use in your promotional efforts. Where are fans and followers most engaged with you online? What social networks have built the largest following for you the fastest? Is your mailing list serving you better than other forms of communication, and are your speaking engagements bringing in the most people to your mailing list as well as to your social networks? Are you really good at radio appearances, and does this send a lot of traffic

to your blog? Or is your blog your best tool for engagement? How can you use these tools once your book is released? Translate your answers into promotional activities.

10. **Exercise:** Do a little cyber-spying on the authors you discovered during your competitive analysis. Find out where they speak, what organizations they belong to, and what activities they participate in online and offline. How can you put that intel to use in your plan? Can you speak at the same conferences or do readings at the same bookstores? Can you get involved in the same activities so you can promote via those organizations?

11. **Exercise:** Visit LinkedIn.com and see if you can view anything in the profiles of authors who have written complementary or competitive books. Or connect with them there. Maybe they belong to the same LinkedIn groups you do … or just send them a message saying you are writing a similar book and would love to share notes about promotion.

12. **Exercise:** Check out these same authors on Facebook. Do they have an author page or just a profile? What do they do with it? How do they promote their books on this social network? How can you apply what you learn?

13. **Exercise:** Find these authors' websites and blogs. Do they have a special page for the media or a list of places they've spoken, etc.? How do they blog to promote their books? Use the information and ideas you gather for your promotion plan.

14. **Exercise:** If your book is a specialty book or targets a niche, research if it could appear in any specialty stores.

15. **Exercise:** Brainstorm workshops, teleseminars, talks, readings, webinars, etc., that could help you promote your book.

16. **Exercise:** Research specific publications that target your market, and add writing for specific magazines or newspapers to your plan.

17. **Question:** How much money will you spend to promote your book and in what ways? (Example: advertising, PR agent, travel, radio campaign, virtual book tour, etc.)

TRAINING

18. **Question:** Do you need an advance of a certain size to carry out your promotion plan?

Will Your Promotion Plan Make Your Book a Bestseller?

19. **Evaluation:** Does the plan you have created show that you are willing and committed to promoting your book in ways that will prove effective? How do you (objectively) know this?

20. **Question:** Does your promotion plan build on the prepromotion you have done to date for yourself and your book?

21. **Evaluation:** Based on the size of your platform and your past efforts to prepromote yourself and your work, is your plan realistic?

22. **Evaluation:** Does your promotion plan instill trust—will publishers believe that you will carry it out? How so?

23. **Evaluation:** Does your plan have longevity and consistency over time? Or is it a one-month or three-month sprint? Does it look like a promotion marathon?

24. **Question:** Can you put your spinoffs to use in your promotion plan?

25. **Evaluation:** Does your commitment to making your book successful come through in your promotion plan?

26. **Evaluation:** In addition to considering the answers to the previous questions, evaluate your promotion plan by looking for these five elements:

- Does your plan contain tried-and-true promotional tactics used by best-selling or successful authors?
- Is your plan based on what you have done to date to promote yourself and your book?
- Is your plan realistic based upon your prepromotion (author platform-building) activities?
- Does your plan provide a long-term picture of how you will promote consistently over time?

- Does your plan instill confidence that you are committed to making your book successful?

If you can answer yes to all five questions, you've created a strong plan that will enhance and support your overall business plan.

Putting Promotion into Action

27. **Question:** What are you willing to do every day to promote your book? Include in your plan at least five things you can do every day to promote your book. Include these in your promotion activities as bulleted action items you can apply as Jack Canfield did with his "Rule of Five."

Better Late Than Never

28. **Evaluation:** Do you have a strong promotion plan? If you don't know, show it to a published author. Ask their opinion. Or ask a proposal consultant to look it over.

Passion + Purpose in Your Promotion Gets Results

29. **Question:** Does your promotion plan exude passion? How?

30. **Question:** Does your promotion plan show your purpose? How?

31. **Question:** At this point in the Author Training Process, do you feel you will struggle with book promoting?

32. **Question:** Did the exercise of creating a promotion plan and considering once again the amount of time and effort involved in promoting make you feel resistance?

33. **Evaluation:** Successful published authors are good book promoters. Right now, given how you are feeling about this exercise, do you think you are ready to become a successful author? Do you have an Author Attitude? At this point you are ready to compile your business plan. Refer back to the final chapter for instruction on how to do so.

INDEX

WRITER'S DIGEST

Is Your Manuscript Ready?

Trust 2nd Draft Critique Service to prepare your writing to catch the eye of agents and editors. You can expect:

- Expert evaluation from a hand-selected, professional critiquer
- Know-how on reaching your target audience
- Red flags for consistency, mechanics, and grammar
- Tips on revising your manuscript and query to increase your odds of publication

Visit WritersDigestShop.com/2nd-draft for more information.

A PERFECT COMPANION TO *THE AUTHOR TRAINING MANUAL*

The Writer's Market Guide to Getting Published

Learn exactly what it takes to get your work into the marketplace, get it published, and get paid for it!

Available from WritersDigestShop.com and your favorite book retailers.

To get started, join our mailing list: WritersDigest.com/enews

FOLLOW US ON:

Find more great tips, networking and advice by following @writersdigest

And become a fan of our Facebook page: facebook.com/writersdigest